FIGHTING FOR
AMERICA

FIGHTING
FOR
AMERICA

BLACK SOLDIERS—
THE UNSUNG HEROES OF WORLD WAR II

Christopher Paul Moore

One World
Ballantine Books ★ New York

A One World Book
Published by The Random House Publishing Group

Copyright © 2005 by Christopher Moore

All rights reserved under International and Pan-American Copyright Conventions.
Published in the United States by Ballantine Books, an imprint of
The Random House Publishing Group, a division of Random House, Inc., New York,
and simultaneously in Canada by Random House of Canada Limited, Toronto.

One World and Ballantine are registered trademarks and the One World colophon
is a trademark of Random House, Inc.

www.oneworldbooks.net

Library of Congress Cataloging-in-Publication Data is
available from the publisher upon request.

ISBN 0-345-45960-1

Manufactured in the United States of America

2   4   6   8   9   7   5   3   1

First Edition: January 2005

Text design by Mercedes Everett and Mary Wirth

To

Pfc. Norma Katherine DeFreese Moore

and Sgt. WIllard Morris Moore:

Thank you for teaching me

to love God, my family, and my neighbors.

And to fight for my country.

ACKNOWLEDGMENTS

In the making of this book, my first thanks goes to the angelic Catherine McKinley, who happened upon my 150-word letter to *American Legacy* magazine in 2001, about my father's connection to the subject of David Colley's fine article about the Red Ball Express. She thoughtfully clipped it and sent it to superagent Charlotte Sheedy, who contacted me with a suggestion and the kind of advice that can change a writer's life for the next few years: Why don't you write a book about WWII?

In committing to the idea, I learned quickly that there was a lot to be told about black soldiers in the war. *Army Air Forces in World War II,* edited by Wesley Frank Craven and James Lea Cate, shaped this book immeasurably. Researched over a ten-year span, from 1948 to 1958, the seven-volume set is remarkable for several reasons, including its inclusion of the contributions of black soldiers. It's also incredible that those published contributions are almost never cited in the other "great books" about WWII. No one source better encompasses the range of carnage, heroism, labor, and suffering of World War II, as experienced by all Americans. My profound thanks to Craven and Cate for making my job relatively easy. My appreciation, too, to those historians who followed in the path of telling a fuller story of the war: Ulysses Lee, Stephen Ambrose, Mary Penick Motley, and Phillip McGuire.

The U.S. National Archives and Records Administration was my first serious starting point and the source of the bulk of archival information relating to military documents and troop deployments contained within this book. My deep appreciation to former regional director Robert C. Morris for his friendship and kindness in helping me to navigate the wealth of resources at the NARA. For aiding me in finding some of the most wonderful photos taken during the war, my thanks to several archivists, including Tim Rives of the NARA; Janea M. Milburn of the Naval Historical Foundation; Joseph D. Caver of the Air Force Historical Research Agency; and Lena Koljot of the U.S. Marine Corp archives. I am grateful, too, to Renee Klish, Army Art Curator of the U.S. Army Center of Military History, for providing the striking paintings that document the work of black soldiers; and to Mary B. Dennis, Deputy Clerk of Court, U.S. Army Judiciary, for providing Freedom of Information Act documents for this project.

The New York Public Library, and its Schomburg Center for Research in Black Culture, was the single most important venue for this project. My deepest thanks to librarians Genette McLaurin, Sharon Howard, Betty Odabashian, Michael Roudette, and Koreen Duncan. I am indebted, too, to Diana Lachatanere, the consummate archivist. My thanks also to Mary Yearwood, for her extraordinary expertise in locating photographs, and to Antony Toussaint and Michael Mery. My gratitude especially to Roberta Yancy and to Howard Dodson, chief of the Schomburg Center, whose exuberant leadership in recording, restoring, and reporting the history of the African diaspora is a constant inspiration.

Many other institutions and organizations, large and small, were also important to this project, including the Library of Congress, the U.S. Military Research Center, National D-Day Museum, British War Museum, U.S. Holocaust Museum, FDR Presidential Library, Truman Presidential Library, Kentucky National Guard, Patton Museum at Fort Knox, Maywood Bataan Day Organization, Proviso Bataan Project, The Hermetic Society, Port Moresby (New Guinea) War Cemetery, Manila (Philippines) American Cemetery, Port Vila (Vanuatu) War Memorial, Allied War Memorial Burma (Myanmar), and Northern Mariana College Archives.

Special thanks to individuals whose advice or materials I have used including: Buffalo soldiers experts Anthony Powell and Kareem Abdul Jabbar; Col. Janice Hudley of the U.S. Military Academy; Calvin Bass of the 92nd Division Association; Marvin Platz (liaison pilots), Dr. Joe Clark, and Brian Vincent Davis (Australian baseball); Lt. Col. Philip C. Grinton (U.S. Army Ret.); and Jim Opolony (Robert Brookes). My appreciation, too, to those who provided me with new scholarship about

Valaida Snow and other WWII music insights; my thanks to Dan Morgenstern of Rutgers University, Dr. Jayna Brown of the University of Oregon, and Candace Allen, and to Prof. William Seraille of Lehman College for steering me to more evidence of the brilliance of the forgotten Robert T. Browne.

My thanks as well to those who lived through the war and wrote about it: Tullio Bertini, author of *Trapped in Tuscany, Liberated by the Buffalo Soldiers;* Nelson Peery, *Black Fire: The Making of an American Revolutionary;* Hyman Samuelson, *Love, War, and the 96th Engineers (Colored);* Roy Weaver, *I'm in the Army Now: Memoirs of WWII;* Roger T. Erickson, *A Pilot's Story by Paul Schifferli;* and Walter A. Luszki, *A Rape of Justice: MacArthur and the New Guinea Hangings.* And to the many men and women, who are named and unnamed within this book, who took the time to speak with me about their lives, thank you.

I am indebted, too, to my family for digging into attics, closets, and memories for information about our past, including the contributions of Dowell Moore, Marcus Moore, Vernon Lee Defreese, Adrienne Coleman, Ed Wynn, Kenyatta Rivers, Gregory Moore, Robert Fields, Sr., Christine Saunders Fields, Jasper Watts, Jr., Marsha DeFreese Vinson, Ann Marie Milligan, Nancy Lipscomb, Daria Holcomb, and Willard Moore, Jr.

For the publication of my book, my special thanks to Charlotte, and to Anita Diggs for accepting my proposal. My deepest appreciation and thanks to my editor, Elisabeth Dyssegaard, for her enormous generosity and skill, frequent patience, and constant care. Thanks, too, to Signe Pike for her editorial assistance, and to the designers, Mercedes Everett and Mary Wirth, for their extraordinary talent.

Finally to my wife, Kim Yancey, and to my sons, Terence and Matthew, who sacrificed too many evenings, weekends, vacations, and holidays for my simple thanks to ever be sufficient, I give as much thanks as I can muster, and my love. And to make it all worthwhile, I pray that this book may be somehow beneficial to someone.

Christopher Paul Moore

CONTENTS

The death rate of our World War II veterans presented the greatest personal urgency for me in the writing of this book. At publication, more than 1,100 World War II veterans are dying every day—at a higher rate than during the war. Since black men live, on average, shorter lives than white men, the population of black veterans is even more perilously close to its end. About 70,000 of the 1.1 million African Americans who served in World War II are still alive.

I learned an unfortunate but valuable lesson about death early in this project. I learned never to delay an interview. I had reached an eighty-year-old former sergeant by telephone one Friday evening to ask him about his experience with an artillery battalion at Guadalcanal. My call had come late and unexpectedly, but he was eager to talk. Satisfied that I had established the contact, and thinking myself courteous, I said I would call back after the weekend, on Monday morning. I did call back, but when I did, a family member told me he had died that Saturday afternoon. I never again postponed an opportunity to talk to a veteran.

I received my father's World War II military war service record on the afternoon of September 11, 2001, and so my thoughts about black patriotism and World War II got pushed aside that day.

"Today we feel what Franklin Roosevelt called the 'warm courage of national unity,' " said President George W. Bush a few days later at a memorial in Washington, D.C., for the people who had lost their lives.

For the first time since the Civil War, two American cities had been devastatingly struck. Almost sixty years after Pearl Harbor, a surprise attack again tested America.

"In every generation, the world has produced enemies of human freedom," Mr. Bush continued. "They have attacked America because

My son Terence and I at Fort Greene Park in Brooklyn. After the September 11, 2001, attack, he asked me for an American flag.

we are freedom's home and defender. And the commitment of our fathers is now the calling of our time." The *New York Times* reported that Mr. Bush then "glanced at his own father, a World War II pilot."

All races and religions were among the victims and heroes of the attack. Working on the ninety-second floor of Tower One was Michael Richards, an African-American sculptor who was crafting a memorial to the Tuskegee Airmen, a segregated unit of black World War II fighter pilots. Richards died in the tower's collapse, and lost forever with him is his unfinished sculpture depicting an airman riding a burning meteor.

Though there are still great gaps between the races and ethnic groups, in those days and weeks we acted as neighbors and patriots—as if war unified us and we were fighting against a common enemy and there was an unspoken truce. Our differences were suspended and we were all Americans.

Like millions of our countrymen, my own family did its best through the national tragedy. Through our church, we provided food, clothing, and support for the National Guard, the fire department, other emergency workers, and the families of people lost in the attack. My son's elementary school conducted a drive to donate flashlights and boots for relief workers at Ground Zero. A few days after the attack, my son asked for an American flag.

From our veterans of the Greatest Generation, we have learned about bravery, dedication, and patriotism. For my family, as for millions of Americans, there is an unmistakable connection between the events of the past, present, and future. From every generation we have learned about the hope and responsibility our nation gives to us all.

I think the only man ever to call me an American, and say it like I was as good as any American he was likely to find, was a little Jewish man. We took our trucks to get them out of the concentration camps (Buchenwald, Dora-Mittelbau, Mauthausen and Birkenau). My eyes never saw a worse sight in my life than these people, dead and dying, and I may never understand how God could let any man do that kind of evil and ugliness to his fellow man. I had just got out of the truck and a Jewish man, who looked like a dead man walking, came right up to me. He called me "American" and he fell into my arms. I am ashamed to say I was afraid to touch him but he hugged me like nobody ever hugged me in my life. I looked at him and I wanted to cry because he looked so bad, and he looked at me like I was a big piece of candy. I would like to think this man liked me for being a good Christian, but I think he loved me for being an American.

S. SGT. WILLARD MOORE,
3,438TH QUARTERMASTER CORPS,
1943–45

My four brothers already were serving and scattered abroad in the war—Charley was in the Philippines, Rick in Europe where he got a Purple Heart from injuries he suffered, Harry was in the States, and Erskine was helping to build the Burma Road where he got malaria which he suffered from later in life from time to time. This was probably as much a reason as any that prompted me to think about going into the Service myself. There was patriotism in my decision too, because we were a patriotic people.

PFC. NORMA K. DEFREESE MOORE,
6,888TH POSTAL BATTALION,
1943–45

WHY ARE AFRICAN AMERICANS PATRIOTIC?

What makes any person patriotic, particularly an African American? White folks built this country, didn't they? That slaves contributed to building America is a foreign thought to many Americans. Black folks were victims, not contributors, right? How could any black child grow up to be a patriot? Do many black (or white) Americans really buy the original ideal of America as a people chosen by God, first to conquer the continent and then to lead the world?

More than ten million Africans were enslaved and transported against their will to North America, South America, and the Caribbean. It is conservatively estimated that between three and five million more perished in the Middle Passage—the sea voyage from Africa to the Americas. Why, then, would African Americans ever be patriotic? If one experience by any group in American history should elicit an unpatriotic feeling, slavery would surely be it—but it does not. It may come as a surprise to some folks, but black Americans are among the nation's most patriotic citizens.

I once asked my father why he had gone to war for America. He told me he went because he was drafted. Still, I, who had learned to read as a five-year-old kid in the 1950s by observing FOR WHITE ONLY at public water fountains and FOR COLORED at motels where my family stayed on trips to the South, wanted to know why any black man or woman would risk his life for America. He said defending his country was his duty as an American citizen. And, he said, who knows the importance of protecting and preserving the promise of freedom better than African Americans? If asked to fight for his country again, he would do it.

My father's answer did not make a whole lot of sense to me. If our country was so miserable to its black citizens, why would any African American choose to defend it? Or why would any African-American family give its children to our nation's defense?

MY FATHER, S. Sgt. Willard Moore, is one of the two WWII veterans to whom I have dedicated this book. The other is my mother, Pfc. Norma

K. DeFreese Moore. They told me the stories that inspired me to learn about the history of my family, and therefore the history of my country.

MY FATHER WAS a great storyteller. Bill Moore was from the South, and like many southerners he could tell a story far better than the rest of us. His animated voice ranged from the serious bass of James Earl Jones to the tickled tenor of a hilarious Bill Cosby routine. With sheer enthusiasm and detailed memory, he spoke about growing up during the Depression, with his parents and fourteen brothers and sisters, in the rural South. Born in Warrior Stand, once a Native American settlement near Tuskegee in Macon County, Alabama, he would go on and on about his slave ancestors and their many skills and talents, and of how he learned to barber when he was sixteen to earn money to go to college. He told me often about the most famous customer who ever graced his barber chair, George Washington Carver. And he talked forever about the value of education, and his love for his family.

But the subject of World War II he treated differently. He talked about the war only when asked. He would usually pause first, as if to adjust or edit his memory of those experiences for his children. We always enjoyed our favorite story about how, on Easter Sunday in April 1944, he met our mother, Pfc. Norma DeFreese. We laughed at the tale of his cross-country jaunt in a "borrowed" jeep, truck, and motorcycle to rendezvous with his new bride in Rouen, France, on their first anniversary in 1945.

He talked proudly about the role the 3,438th Quartermasters Corps played in the famous Red Ball Express, which transported fuel and supplies across France to help defeat Germany. He spoke less easily about digging graves to bury American soldiers, or about trucking American POWs out of German stalags, and less easily still about transporting liberated Jews from the Holocaust camps. Never were his stories filled with bravado. He seemed to me, from his telling, an average American soldier who undertook a difficult job as best he could.

I often wondered if my father's stories were true. To me, the most dubious was his account of Lena Horne visiting the 99th Pursuit

Squadron at a Tuskegee training air base in 1943 and selecting him—a lowly student mechanic—over the dashing pilots for her first dance partner. I did not know of any photographs of him as a nineteen-year-old, but his middle-age paunch did not strike me at all as starlet bait. Even as a child I wondered why on God's earth Lena Horne would choose to dance with my father? He must have looked pitiful, I thought. In researching this book, I discovered that my father was remarkably accurate in his accounts of the war and his experiences in it.

My mother told me many stories, too. My earliest memories are of her describing her experiences in Europe, just a decade earlier, during World War II, and about how she left home to join the army and see the world.

The stories that my parents told me piqued my interest to study further the history of my family and my country. My conversations with my mother and father regularly linked our present with our past. Our American ancestors were both free and slave. Among them, one is known to have served in the Revolutionary War, twelve in the Civil War, four in the Spanish-American War, and six in World War I. In World War II, my mother was the first woman in the DeFreese family to serve, along with four of her brothers, all honorably. Among the Moores, six brothers served with honor and one sister was employed as a nurse in the Veterans Hospital in Tuskegee, Alabama. In their respective families, four other siblings worked at defense-industry jobs.

AN AMERICAN FAMILY

My Mother's Family

> Sure, I loved my country, and that is why I was proud to enlist. I had heard from the old folks that we had fought in every war since the Revolutionary War, so me enlisting was not anything really special for us, and two or three cousins who were girls were already in, so that wasn't really very special either. But I was the first woman in my immediate family to go. So, yes, I signed on to serve my country, and to see the world, and to send home money to Mama, who really needed it badly.
>
> Norma K. DeFreese Moore

I never knew or met my grandmother, Mary Adelia DeFreese, who died six years before I was born. A decade before WWII, she was dealt two consecutive blows: the death of her husband, which nearly devastated her family, and the Great Depression, which affected the entire nation.

Unable to find steady employment because of polio in one arm, she was left with eleven children to support. She received a widow's pension of $48 a month—"And she had to account for every penny spent," said my mother. "She would give me fifty cents to buy a big bag of old bread. Sometimes the bread was mildewy, but she knew how to transform stale bread and cakes, muffins, and broken cookies, into meals and desserts. She would give me another half-dollar and send me to the butcher to buy meat bones, which were bones left over from people who had the money to buy meat. He kept aside the bones for poor folks like us."

If coming from a very old American family is a measure of patriotism, then my mother's family, though poor, was second to none. In her heritage are Native Americans, Europeans, and Africans. Her European forebears were Dutch, who came as ship captains, merchants, and fur traders. Her African ancestors came to America as slaves.

As a little boy, I grew up in my mother's hometown of Hillburn, New York, a small, racially segregated town about twenty miles northwest of New York City, where my family had lived for many generations. "Triracial" or "Negroes, Indians, and whites" is how my mother's family was described in anthropology and sociology journals, and by historians who had written about the DeFreese family for more than a century. "Colored" is what we called ourselves. A variety of racial types could be observed in our immediate family, and among my cousins there were those who were undoubtedly white, unmistakably Indian, and certainly Negro. My mother had many relatives, and most lived in Hillburn.

My great-great-grandfather, Samuel DeFreese, Sr., was patriarch of our large extended family, comprising more than 500 people, or about half the town. Carrying a fishing pole or a hunting rifle, he walked almost daily along the dirt road that became the Route 17 highway—the same route along which Gen. George Washington had led the Continental troops through the Ramapo Pass at the New York–New Jersey border in the Revolutionary War. Centuries later, the route became the

Samuel A. DeFreese was a carpenter who built wagons for the U.S. Army during the Civil War.

racial divide of Hillburn. Separated geographically, the colored lived by the river and in the mountains, the whites on the flats in "White Town."

Known to many local people as "the Indian," and as "Uncle Sam" to his family, my great-great-grandfather lived near the top of the Ramapo Mountains. From the porch of his modest wood-frame house, he could see the Manhattan skyline, such as it was at the turn of the last century—an island of tall buildings, factory smokestacks, and church steeples. My great-great-grandfather loved to watch the sun rising over Manhattan. He called the view *helape chen kwaelas*—the place where the sun is born. Outsiders, mostly white hunters or fishermen from the city, sought his opinion only for a good place to fish, hunt, or trap beaver or muskrat.

As a boy I learned from my mother that my great-great-grandfather did not care how outsiders described us—unless it was with the N-word. He wanted people to know our family only as "hard-workers" and law abiding. "We were first here, no matter what they want to call us," he told his family. Every Fourth of July, the family would picnic at a spot by the Ramapo River. At night the men and children would light fireworks and Uncle Sam would shoot off his shotgun to celebrate the nation's birthday.

To anyone who inquired about his heritage, Uncle Sam, whose English was seasoned with Indian and Dutch words, said that his "first blood" was Indian but that he was "proud to have some of the blood of the rest of you" who came later. He didn't know it, but by archaeological estimates, his ancestors had been in the region for more than 12,000 years—since the New York Metropolitan area was known as Lenapehoking, or Land of the Lenape.

To my Dutch ancestors the natives were terrorists, and vice versa. But some did find friendship and live peaceably together. Intermarriage with immigrant adventurers, sailors, and traders named DeVries (DeFreese), Van der Donck (Van Dunk), DeGroot (DeGroat), and Van Salee gave our natives new family names. "We lived on Manhattan Island with the white families, until we were made to feel unwelcome" was an observation repeated in our family for several generations.

SLAVES IN THE FAMILY

To be called a descendant of a slave was uncomfortable for Uncle Sam's family, as it was for many African Americans, whose factual knowledge of slavery and Africa was practically nil. That African empires like Songhai and Benin were smelting iron at a time when Europeans were making do with stone tools; or that Ghana, Mali, Dahomey, and Kongo were flourishing when the European nation-states were just taking shape was unknown to us—thus had the devastation of the African slave trade rendered even the heirs of one of America's first families ignorant of our own history, and deprived us of the pride and joy in our African ancestry. No one would dare boast of a connection to Africa, and certainly not to slaves. But the African blood in the family did come from slaves, one enslaved man and one enslaved woman, who are documented as among the earliest residents and pioneers of New York City—and, indeed, of America. Around the 1620s, Emmanuel and Christina Van Angola (meaning "from Angola") came to North America as part of a slave workforce that helped to build the early colony on Manhattan.

According to the city's archival records, the work tasks for slave men like Emmanuel included: widening a narrow Indian path that ran the length of the island (Broadway); building a wall that extended the island's width from the Hudson to the East River (Wall Street); and clearing a forest in northern Manhattan for a new settlement (Harlem).

Christina, like the other enslaved women of New Amsterdam (later New York), likely worked in the tanneries, treating furs and leathers, and on farms and in gardens, growing and preparing food, and in the grist- and windmills, grinding wheat into flour.

Emmanuel and Christina were among the first wave of Africans who were transported to the Americas during slavery. Of the first 6.5 million people to cross the Atlantic to the New World, 5.5 million were Africans. Rarely commented upon by historians, but common in the first three centuries of the slavery era (1500–1800) was the use of slaves as colony builders—clearing shorelines for shipping, draining swamps, removing trees for farms, and building roads and fortifications for new colonies, which is precisely how slave labor was used in early New York City and all along the eastern seacoast cities and towns of North America.

Typically, slaves built fortifications and fought the Indians. In 1643 the Dutch declared all-out war against the Indians, and slaves were en-listed to fight for the Dutch cause. In return for battling the Indians, Em-manuel and ten other black men received their freedom. Given wilderness land to farm in the territory north of Wall Street—in the vicinity of what would become Greenwich Village—the frontier black farmsteads served as a buffer between the Indians to the north and the white settlement. Fighting in the first colonial army, they helped make permanent the settlement of Europeans.

The emancipation act of February 25, 1644, that freed the men also freed their wives, but their children were still enslaved. In 1649 Christina and Emmanuel brought their son to the Dutch church in lower Man-hattan for Christian baptism. Using Dutch patronymics, or naming pat-terns, he was presented as a free child and named Nicholas Manuel, meaning Nicholas, son of Manuel. His freedom was probably purchased before his baptism. He is my first known African-American ancestor who was born in America.

In 1673 Nicholas, also called Claus, married Louise Lowis at the Bowery Church on the property of Peter Stuyvesant. Standing as god-parent and witness at the baptism of their first child, Christine, was a fu-

FEBRUARY 24, 1644 Dutch colony on Manhattan Island recruits free and enslaved Africans to fight Indian wars. From 1600 to 1776, European settlements, including English, French, Swedish, and Spanish colonies in North America, enlist free and enslaved blacks to fight Indian wars.

ture relative, Jan DeVries II (son of a Dutch sea captain and an Afro-Brazilian woman named Swartine, meaning "lovely dark woman"). My mother's recipe for delicious Dutch ollycakes (doughnuts) likely dates back to that generation.

In the early American neighborhood on Manhattan Island were about one hundred families. Among them was ours—and others that would become far more wealthy, famous, and powerful. Like my ancestors from Africa, they attended the Church in the Fort, also known as the St. Nicholas Church, where the American Christmas tradition of Santa Claus was born.

Fellow citizens like Van Cortlandt and Rutgers lived in modest homes for a generation or two before their hard work and investments took root. A fur trapper, Claus Van Roosevelt, lived near the Land of the Blacks, where a community of free Africans owned farms. The patriarch Roosevelt's humble status was probably much like their own, yet his descendants prospered enormously and included two American presidents.

By the eighteenth century, our family had moved—been pushed, really—out of Manhattan. Settlement by new European immigrants to the region, rising real estate values, and racism contributed to their flight to the New York and New Jersey frontier. A New York law of 1712 prohibiting free blacks, Indians, and "mulattoes" from inheriting or transferring land to their heirs was the final straw. In 1716 property owned by my distant great-uncle Francisco Bastian, the last black landowner in colonial Manhattan, was sold in compliance with the law. By then most of the family surnames were gone from the city. Still, there is ample evidence that my family believed themselves loyal to their emerging country.

In 1760 grandcestors John DeFreese and Nicholas Manuel were members of the Colonial Militia, fighting for the colonists and the English in the French and Indian War. Both were probably unaware that two of their commanders, Col. Henry Bouquet and Gen. Jeffrey Amherst, were conspiring to distribute smallpox-laden blankets and shirts to freezing natives, mostly Lenape, who were huddled outside Fort Pitt in Pennsylvania. Eventually most surviving Lenape were driven off, either southwest or north, to Canada; only those who stayed totally to themselves or intermarried with the foreigners survived.

IN 1776 DEFREESE, and possibly Manuel and other family members, continued to bear arms and fight alongside their colonial countrymen, this time for the fully "American cause" in the War for Independence. Yet even as free men, their new nation did not offer them the full fruits of liberty. In 1798 a New Jersey law restricted the rights of free blacks from other states—including Revolutionary War veterans—to travel across county or state boundaries. "And be it enacted, That no free negro or mulatto, of or belonging to any other State in the union, shall be permitted to travel or reside in this State, without a certificate from two justices of the peace of such other State," the law read. Within a few years many of our family who were property owners sold their homes in New Jersey and moved across the border to New York.

More than a dozen of my mother's ancestors served in the Civil War, including Philip DeFreese, who served in Company H, 33rd Regiment; James DeGroat and Obadiah DeGroat, of the 26th New York Colored Troops; and Private William Van Dunk, who signed on as a substitute and died at the U.S. Army General Hospital in New Orleans in 1865.

A century later the descendants of the colonial American pioneers in my family still lived modestly. In the 1940s some in the family continued to earn a living trapping beaver and muskrat for trade. In a nation where four of its first five presidents (and ten of its first sixteen) owned slaves, slavery and the lingering issue of race had long ago sullied the American dream for many Americans. Yet from their small hometown, my mother and her four brothers, Erskine (Sgt.), Charles (Sgt.), Rick (Sgt.), and Harry (Sgt.) served in the U.S. Army, and thirty-four known cousins signed on to serve in the army, navy, and Marines in World War II.

"American homes with a son or husband in the war displayed a white star in the window. My mother had five stars in her window," said my mother. "And she was very proud."

My Father's Family

On the Moore side, the earliest known ancestor is Sukie, a West African–born woman who as a young girl was captured and shipped to an American port around 1840. Sold into slavery in cotton-rich Alabama, Sukie was about thirteen when she first became pregnant. A family Bible entry notes that she had nine children, five who were mulattoes "by a man named Moore." Mama Sukie, as she was called, liked to wear bonnets and enjoyed gifts of fresh fruit. She, like other slaves, worked from "can to can't see" on a cotton plantation.

Mama Sukie's great-grandchild, Harvey Moore, was my grandfather. In 1901 he married Nancy Whitlow, the eighth of fourteen children, daughter of Mary Kennebrew and Jim Whitlow. That my grandmother Nancy's father was a mixed-race child who was once left intentionally outdoors to die as an infant—by the order of a plantation owner's wife— was a family story passed on to her new family, the Moores.

Even months before Jim Whitlow's birth on a cotton and lumber plantation in Bibb County, Alabama, rumors circulated among the farm's slave community that Anna, a young slave girl, was pregnant with a child fathered by the plantation owner, John "Jack" Thrasher. Told by the older slave women to stay away from the owner's wife and never let anyone know the truth about her baby once it was born, Anna kept to herself, as best she could, throughout her pregnancy.

In November 1853 Anna gave birth to the child, a tiny but robust baby boy who looked nearly white. She tried to keep him from being seen closely by anyone, black or white, but she was not able to hide him.

About a month passed before the plantation owner's wife, Mary, went to Anna's cabin on word from someone that the baby "looked just like Jack Thrasher." When she entered Anna's room, her "tiny pink lips" were clenched tight in a taut smile. The family story tells of her eyes raging in anger upon seeing the light-complexioned infant lying close to Anna's dark-brown face.

"He is yellow like a pig, and I am going to see to it that he lives with

Jim Whitlow was twelve years old when he was freed from slavery by the Union Army, for whom he fed and watered livestock in Macon County, Alabama.

the pigs" was the memory of the event Anna passed on to her only child. "Those words," said my great-grandfather, "were etched in her mind like stone."

Mary Thrasher left Anna that afternoon without saying another word, but about an hour later a male slave came and snatched the child from Anna and took the baby away. That night—only a few nights be-

Born a slave, Mary Kennebrew was about twelve years old when she was freed by the Union Army, for whom she cooked and washed clothes.

fore Christmas—my great-grandfather was carried across the plantation yard and placed naked in the hog pen.

"They did not let our grandmother see him," said my aunt Ruth. "She was kept locked away in her room. But throughout the night she cried and she prayed for her little boy."

"I was always told the baby cried very little—almost not at all," said my father. "He just lay still all night, and the hogs would not touch him."

The baby survived the night, and soon afterward both Anna and Jim were sold to a succession of slaveholders, named Weathers and Whitlow.

My father never heard his great-grandmother, Anna Weathers, tell the story firsthand. She died in 1923, the year my father was born. The fourteen children heard the story of their grandfather from their mother, Nancy Whitlow Moore, and my father first learned it from Jim Whitlow himself.

It was a story told rarely, and never with bitterness. "Yesterdays are days gone by," Jim Whitlow would say. "He wanted his children to love their neighbors as themselves—and vice versa." According to the U.S. Census of 1850, Jack Thrasher was at least sixty-two years old when he impregnated Anna, who was then twelve or thirteen years old. Though he is biologically my great-great-grandfather, I have extreme difficulty thinking of him as a member of my family.

During the Civil War, six-year-old Jim Whitlow, like other slaves, was required to give service to the Confederacy. Too young to do heavy manual labor, he fed horses, mules, and livestock for the Confederate army. There were times, too, when he was told to help carry dead soldiers. At age nine, he received word of the Emancipation Proclamation from a Union soldier while plowing a field with a mule. He then carried feed for Union livestock camped in the area.

"He learned to be careful not to be seen or caught helping the Yanks too much. White folks were watching to see who was being too helpful, because the Yanks were still the enemy no matter if the Rebels were whipped or not. When Jim Crow took over, a lot of folks [former slaves] caught hell for helping the North."

Whitlow married Mary Kennebrew who was known as "Pot Mammy" for her cooking skills. A *mambo,* or voodoo priestess, whose Louisiana ancestors likely arrived from Haiti or Martinique, "she had powers," said one uncle who remembered reverently both her glazed ham and her magical skill—which he dared not call witchcraft. "She knew roots. Planters would not plant without words from Mary." When the North took control of Macon County, Mary helped her mother cook and do laundry for the Union forces. "She said when she was a child she had a dream that her children would be free."

My great-grandfather did not have many opportunities, but he made the best of those presented to him. After the Civil War, he sharecropped until he earned enough money to purchase a grist mill. It was a successful operation and he built another. He hired a teacher to make sure his fourteen children were educated.

"Once at a land auction," said my uncle Dowell, "Jim was the only colored face in the crowd, and he said they laughed at him when he raised his hand to bid on a big piece of land—and they really laughed at him when he bid up the price to a dollar an acre. But when Jim pulled out a thousand dollars cash to buy the land, they stopped laughing."

By any standards of the times, my great-grandfather was a successful businessman and landowner. My father once told me, "Jim Whitlow himself couldn't read or write letters worth a lick, but he could write numbers. We had to read to him, but you didn't have to add for him."

Though he was not educated, he supported education. One of his

A nurse at the Veterans Hospital in Tuskegee during World War II, Ruth Moore Wynn later served as head nurse for the facility.

proudest days came when he met Booker T. Washington, an educator from Virginia who arrived in Tuskegee in June 1881 to set up a college for colored students. Washington spent at least one evening at Jim Whitlow's home and Jim felt honored to help the new principal. He loaned Washington the use of his personal carriage, and he and some of his children attended the school's opening ceremony on July 4, 1881.

My father and five of his brothers, Harvey (Sgt.), Cordell (Sgt.), Idell (Sgt.), Cicero (Sgt.), and Dowell (Maj.) served in the U.S. Army during World War II. My aunt Ruth worked as a nurse at the Veterans Hospital in Tuskegee.

My father and mother gave us a sense of patriotism. As parents have told their children stories over the centuries, my parents tried to help me find my place in the world.

FIGHTING FOR AMERICA

TWO AMERICAS?

[1776 TO 1941]

I once had a conversation with historian Stephen Ambrose, who was gracious enough to listen quietly as I made a complaint about the movie *Saving Private Ryan*. Ambrose had served as consultant on the movie, and so I asked him why black soldiers had been left out of the D-Day invasion. He told me he had provided the filmmakers with information about several hundred blacks at Utah and Omaha Beach on D-Day, but that the story was taken in a "different direction." Among the ablest historians of World War II, Ambrose believed that racism was at the heart of Nazi philosophy, and that its arteries extended to many nations, including our own. He assured me that military historians were taking a fresh look at the subject and that Americans would come to learn and appreciate more about the contributions of African-American soldiers throughout American history.

BLACK SOLDIERS AND AMERICAN FREEDOM

On the night of March 5, 1770, Crispus Attucks, a free black dock-worker, marched together with fifty laborers and sailors into a dangerous confrontation with British soldiers, whose presence in Boston was sharply

*Between 5,000 and 8,000 black
Americans fought for the patriot cause
during the Revolutionary War.*

resented. The soldiers fired into the crowd and Attucks fell instantly, becoming the first of five men to die that night. American patriots hailed
Attucks's heroism and declared the Boston Massacre the event that
sparked the American Revolution.

In January 1776, Gen. George Washington finally lifted a prohibition against black enlistment in the Continental Army, thus opening the
ranks to free black men. Some colonies also allowed slaves to win their
freedom by serving the American forces. Between 5,000 and 8,000
blacks fought for the patriot cause. At the climactic Battle of Yorktown,
about one-quarter of Washington's Continental Army was made up of
black soldiers. More than 10,000 enslaved men, women, and children
also provided labor for the Americans, transporting munitions, provisions, and constructing fortifications and barricades in the Thirteen
Colonies. Interestingly, many enslaved Americans took advantage of a

JUNE 15, 1775 The Continental Congress selects George Washington
to head the newly established Continental Army. Washington ordered
his officers not to recruit black troops but later rescinded the order.

British offer of freedom in return for military service, and more than 20,000 slaves fought and labored for the British side during the war.

By the time of the War of 1812, federal law restricted militia service to "free and able-bodied white citizens," and the U.S. Army and Marine Corps did not permit blacks to enlist. Although free blacks and slaves did fill support roles as laborers and teamsters in army camps, the navy was the only service that officially admitted blacks in a fighting capacity. Black troops served at the Battle of Lake Erie and at the Battle of New Orleans, under the command of Gen. Andrew Jackson, although they were excluded from later parades commemorating the New Orleans victory.

From the opening salvo of the Civil War, thousands of free blacks and fugitive slaves volunteered for the Union Army, only to be denied service by President Lincoln, who maintained that the war was being fought to restore the Union, not to end slavery. Believing the war would be short-lived and the Union successfully restored, Lincoln prohibited black soldiers from the Union ranks in order to avoid angering his own border states, Delaware, Kentucky, Maryland, and Missouri, where slavery was still protected by the Constitution.

However, as the war dragged on, President Lincoln's slavery policy (or strategy) changed profoundly. On September 22, 1862, he issued a preliminary Emancipation Proclamation, which effectively warned that if the South did not end its rebellion within 100 days (by January 1, 1863) all slaves in the South were to be freed. The edict also permitted former slaves and northern blacks to enter the armed services.

On July 18, 1863, the Massachusetts 54th, the first all-black regiment organized in the North, fought courageously during an attack on Fort Wagner in South Carolina. Though underpaid and often assigned hard labor, black men signed up by the thousands. Volunteers from South Carolina, Tennessee, and Massachusetts filled the first authorized black

1820 U.S. Congress prohibited the enlistment of blacks or "mulattoes" into the U.S. Army. Service in the army was limited to free white males.

Some 179,000 black men served as soldiers in the Union Army, about 10 percent of the total number. They were assigned to segregated all-black units such as the one pictured here, the 4th U.S. Colored Infantry stationed in Washington, D.C. in 1865. Another 19,000 black men served in the Union Navy.

regiments. By the end of the Civil War, about 179,000 black men served as soldiers in the Union Army (comprising 10 percent of that force), and another 19,000 served in the navy.

On April 9, 1865, at the Appomattox Court House, twelve "colored" regiments, or about 3,500 black soldiers, stood guard outside along with white Union soldiers as Gen. Robert E. Lee surrendered to Gen. Ulysses S. Grant. About 38,000 black soldiers died during the war. With nearly eighty black commissioned officers, black soldiers served in artillery and infantry and performed support functions that sustained the army. Black carpenters, blacksmiths, cooks, laborers, teamsters, nurses, scouts, spies, steamboat pilots, and surgeons also contributed to the war cause. Black women, who were not formally allowed to join the army, served as nurses, spies, and scouts—among them, Harriet Tubman, the Union's most famous scout.

BUFFALO SOLDIERS

So impressed were American military commanders by the bravery and valor of the Union's black soldiers that in July 1866, the first black post–Civil War regiments came into existence by an act of Congress, approved by President Andrew Johnson. By April 1867, six regiments of African-American soldiers were recruited into the regular peacetime army. Many were veteran U.S. Colored Troops from the Civil War, but among them were also newly freed slaves who wanted to serve their country. Organized as the 9th and 10th Cavalry and the 38th through 41st Infantries, each regiment consisted of approximately one thousand men. In 1869 the infantry regiments were consolidated into two, the 24th and 25th. All four regiments—two of cavalry and two of infantry— were sent to the western frontier to fight in the Indian wars.

In the winter of 1867–68, the newly formed 9th and 10th Cavalries were engaged in Gen. Philip Sheridan's campaign against the native Comanche, Kiowa, and Cheyenne in Texas and the western Oklahoma Territory. In the cold, harsh winters, the black soldiers wore coats made of buffalo hides. On account of the appearance of those coats and their own tightly curled hair, the Indians called them the "Buffalo Soldiers." According to legend, it was the fighting spirit of the black soldiers that reminded the Native Americans of the bison, and the soldiers accepted the name as a term of honor and respect. About twenty years later, when designs for regimental coats of arms were being prepared, the 9th Cavalry adopted a galloping Indian-on-a-pony as its emblem and "We Can, We Will" as its motto. The 10th Cavalry took the buffalo as its crest, and "Ready and Forward" became its motto.

Their duties were not limited to fighting. Known as "guardian an-

JULY 18, 1863 Sgt. William H. Carney's bravery under fire during the assault on Fort Wagner earned him the Congressional Medal of Honor. He was the first African American to receive the award. Fifteen black soldiers received the prestigious honor for their heroism during the Civil War.

gels," the Buffalo Soldiers protected frontier towns and farms, wagon trains, stagecoaches, and Pony Express riders. Guarding railroad work crews and cattle herds, the black troops also built and repaired frontier forts and outposts. Stringing hundreds of miles of telegraph lines, they explored and mapped vast areas of the Southwest and helped develop the early national parks. In garrison, the Buffalo Soldiers drilled, stood guard, and maintained horses, weapons, and equipment. Serving fifty-nine forts of the Old West, the black regiments developed into four of the most distinguished fighting units in the army during the remainder of the nineteenth century. Though completely overlooked in Hollywood's glamorization of the cavalry-to-the-rescue myth, black soldiers made up over 20 percent of the cavalry engaged in the Indian wars, fighting in 85 percent of the Indian battles.

In 1877, Henry O. Flipper became the first African American to graduate from the U.S. Military Academy at West Point. Promoted to lead a 10th Cavalry unit, he saw his promising career ended in 1881 with a dishonorable discharge. His commanding officer had charged him with embezzling $3,791.77 from commissary funds. Flipper denied the charge, claiming he was framed by white officers who disliked him because of his color. A court-martial cleared Flipper of the embezzlement charge but convicted him of conduct unbecoming of an officer and ordered him dismissed from the army. He died in 1940 without vindication. In 1976 the U.S. Army changed his discharge to honorable and a pardon issued by President Bill Clinton in 1999 completely cleared Flipper's name.

On the seas, Capt. Michael A. Healy, the highest-ranking black officer in the Revenue Cutter Service (precursor to the U.S. Coast Guard) commanded the cutter *Bear* from 1887 to 1895. In charge of patrolling Pacific waters from San Francisco to the Aleutian Islands, Captain Healy was considered by many the best sailor of the North Pacific. Commended by the U.S. Congress for his seafaring skills, an article in the January 28, 1884, *New York Sun* termed the black captain among the world's best seamen: "Captain Mike Healy is a good deal more distinguished person in the waters of the far Northwest than any president of the United States or any potentate in Europe has yet become."

By the 1890s, Native Americans had been defeated and confined to reservations. On February 15, 1898, the battleship *Maine* exploded in Havana harbor and twenty-two Buffalo Soldiers were among the 266 fatalities. Again, the U.S. Army's four black regiments were sent to war, distinguishing themselves in the ten-month-long Cuban campaign. In the famous charge up San Juan Hill, the black cavalrymen saved Col. Theodore Roosevelt and his Rough Riders from being massacred. Attacking through barbed wire and cannon fire, the 10th Cavalry charged up the steep hill to draw enemy fire away from the Rough Riders, capture the lethal blockhouse, and plant the flag of the 10th Cavalry on San Juan Hill.

Gen. John J. Pershing witnessed and later wrote about the heroism of the regiment's charge: "The losses of the day were heavy—the Tenth Cavalry losing half of its officers and twenty percent of its men. We officers of the Tenth Cavalry could have taken our black heroes in our arms. They had again fought their way into our affections, as they here had fought their way into the hearts of the American people."

In 1899, the United States sent troops to the Philippines to stop an insurrection. For the next three years, portions of all four regiments saw action in the Philippines. In 1903, the Buffalo Soldiers served as a presidential escort during President Roosevelt's visit to San Francisco—the first time black soldiers were assigned to protect an American president. The Buffalo Soldiers also patrolled and helped develop the Yosemite, Sequoia, and Kings Canyon National Parks.

In 1906, the black soldiers of the 25th Infantry Regiment were involved in a racially charged incident at Fort Brown in Brownsville, Texas. Several troopers were alleged to have "shot up the town," killing one resident. Although officials at Fort Brown confirmed that all black soldiers were in their barracks at the time of the shooting, local whites claimed that black soldiers were responsible. Without trial or hearing, President Roosevelt ordered 167 black infantrymen discharged without honor because of their alleged conspiracy of silence. In 1972 the U.S. Congress finally rescinded the less-than-honorable discharges and restored the members of the 25th Infantry Regiment to good standing. In 1916, when Pancho Villa crossed the border and invaded New Mexico, the 24th and 25th Infantries and the 10th Cavalry were sent to the border to assist General Pershing in his pursuit of the Mexican general. Between 1866 and 1912, twenty-three black soldiers won the Medal of Honor, the nation's highest military award.

SAVING THE PRESIDENT:
THE MCKINLEY ASSASSINATION

On September 11, 1901, President William McKinley lay in a Buffalo hospital bed, bleeding for a fifth day from two gunshot wounds to his stomach. A third shot would have killed the president instantly, the doctors surmised, and for one week, James Benjamin Parker, a black waiter from Georgia, was a national hero, for he had stopped the assassin from firing a third time.

On the previous Friday afternoon at 4:07 P.M., the president stood patiently greeting the first of more than one thousand well-wishers at the Pan-American Exposition in Buffalo, New York. Among those waiting to meet the president were Parker, the waiter, and Leon Czolgosz (pronounced: *showl*-golz), a son of Polish-German parents who had waited since morning to get near McKinley. At six feet six inches tall, Parker was likely more conspicuous than Czolgosz, who stood a few feet ahead of him in line.

Czolgosz, like many other people in the hot room—it was about ninety-five degrees—carried a white handkerchief, either to wipe their brows or wave at the President. Unnoticed by Secret Service agents, local police, and military guards, his handkerchief-wrapped hand concealed a five-shot .32-caliber revolver.

He fired two shots rapidly and the president grimaced and buckled to the floor. According to eyewitness accounts, Parker was the first to react—even before the security contingent. He lunged forward, knocked the gun from the attacker's hand, and tackled him to the ground.

Newspapers also circulated the story of the "Herculean Negro . . . Big Ben" who had saved the president's life. In a speech before 4,000 people in Charleston, Booker T. Washington hailed Parker's role as one of the greatest patriotic acts of any American. A black man, he emphasized, had risked his own life to save the nation's leader and an act of deadly violence had been stopped. A song was written honoring Parker. In the terrible national tragedy, he emerged as an authentic American hero.

"I am glad that I was able to be of service to the country," said Parker. But McKinley did not survive. Infection had caused the onset of gangrene in his pancreas, and on the fourteenth of September the president died.

The assassin's trial was a quick affair. A jury found Czolgosz guilty, and less than two weeks after McKinley's death he was executed in the electric chair.

Parker's heroic reputation lasted only briefly. He wondered why he was not asked to testify at the trial. No doubt it was because the Secret Service issued a statement declaring that he had played no role in the apprehension of the assassin. Many newspapers that had criticized the agency for failure to protect the president quickly retracted Parker's heroism. Many black newspapers took issue with the Secret Service's disavowal of Parker's "heroic" role.

Parker's dismissal as a hero angered Booker T. Washington. In an uncustomary and arguably the most militant statement of his public life, Washington directly associated the president's death with his perception of the growing and pervasive violence in America in 1901—aimed particularly at African Americans:

> In all sincerity, I want to ask, is Czolgosz alone guilty? Has not the entire Nation had a part in this greatest crime of the century? What is Anarchy but a defiance of law, and has not the Nation reaped what it has been sowing? According to records, 2,516 persons have been lynched in the United States during the past sixteen years. There are or have been engaged in this anarchy of lynching nearly 125,000 persons.

Violence could devastate America, warned Washington, if the nation did not take a stand against racial hatred.

Loyalty and love of country were unquestionable qualities of the average African American, wrote both Washington and W.E.B. DuBois in 1901. American historians described black loyalty as an admirable legacy from the slavery era, and the participation of black troops in America's wars was one of the richest veins of historic contributions to be mined by supporters of equal rights. Some of the oldest and best-known of the historically black colleges—Hampton, Howard, and Fisk—were founded by white Union generals, and retired black cavalry and infantry soldiers were often leaders in local black communities.

Yet by the turn of the century, the racial attitudes of many white Americans, led by Jim Crow politicians, businessmen, military leaders, and presidents, were hardening against blacks in the South and throughout the country. A prolonged internal war raged against the rights of African Americans, who were often cast as the enemy. Expected to be loyal in exchange for limited liberties, blacks were rarely viewed as patriotic, for doing so would implicitly qualify blacks for the full rights and privileges of American citizens. In a society that regarded blacks as rivals or foes, public recognition of their patriotism and heroism was out of the question. For a black man to be judged a hero seemed somehow to disgust or defame many white Americans. For much of the twentieth century, blacks would struggle even to be called American.

WORLD WAR I

In the East Room of the White House on the evening of February 18, 1915, President Woodrow Wilson gathered members of his cabinet and their families for a special screening of *Birth of a Nation,* D. W. Griffith's silent film based on *The Clansman,* a novel by Thomas Dixon.

After the movie was over, Wilson reportedly said the film was "like writing history with lightning. My only regret is that it's true." Others called the film a complete distortion of the historical truth. By any gauge, the Wilson administration was a step backward in the history of African Americans. A southerner by birth, Wilson's views on race were not always overtly racist, but whenever he needed southern support in Congress he conveniently turned away from civil rights. In 1913 he ordered the segregation of federal office workers. By the time of World War I, the standing of black soldiers in the American military was heading toward a new low.

Preparing for war, Congress passed the Selective Service Act of 1917, which called for whites and blacks to serve in segregated units. With the influx of 404,000 black soldiers, including eighteen army nurses, to the war cause, President Wilson's military directives changed the fundamental character of the black component of the U.S. military.

No longer assigned primarily to combat units (in units separate but equal to white units), most blacks were placed in labor battalions. Some black newspapers observed that President Wilson had personally forced Col. Charles Young, America's highest-ranking black officer, into retirement rather than promote him to general.

A notable exception to this trend was Gen. John J. Pershing, the commander of the newly designated American Expeditionary Force, who supported the use of black soldiers in combat. Known popularly as "Black Jack," a tag from his fifteen-year career attached to the all-black 10th Cavalry, the general was also known as "Results Pershing," for, as one officer observed, "Nothing counts with that son-of-a-gun but results." Pershing took a dim view of any racial policies that weakened the Allied effort in World War I.

In May 1918 General Pershing arranged the shipment of the all-black 92nd Division for infantry and machine-gun assignment with the British and French armies. Both nations had each deployed over 200,000 black soldiers from their African colonies into the war effort, but the British government refused to accept the black American force. In a letter dated May 5, 1918, Pershing admonished the British minister of war for his nation's bigotry.

The British Military Attache in Washington has made a protest against including any colored battalions [92nd Division] among the troops destined for service with your forces and that he has stated that this protest was made in behalf of your War Office. You will, of course, appreciate my position in this matter, which, in brief, is that these negroes are American citizens. My Government, for reasons which concern itself alone, has decided to organize colored combat divisions and now desires the early dispatch of one of these divisions to France. Naturally I cannot and will not discriminate against these soldiers.

I am informed that the 92nd Division is in a good state of training and I have no reason to believe that its employment under your command would be accompanied by any unusual difficulties. I am informing my Government of this letter to you. May I not hope that the inclusion of the 92nd Division among the American troops to be placed under your command is acceptable to you and that you will be able to overcome the objections raised by your War Office?

Though ready to continue his campaign, Pershing learned quickly that he had no support from the White House or his military cabinet. "The [U.S.] War Department evidently did not wish to insist upon it, as the division came over shortly afterwards and was not included among those assigned to the British," lamented Pershing. "I was surprised that they should take this attitude in as much as the French were anxious to have colored troops assigned to their divisions." He then transferred the division to France, which welcomed the black soldiers. From elements of the U.S. Army's two black sectors, the 92nd and 93rd Divisions, about 40,000 black American combat troops fought under the French flag.

One of the war's most highly decorated units, the 369th Regiment, known as the Harlem Hellfighters, spent 191 days in combat—longer than any other American unit. The first Americans to win the prestigious Croix de Guerre, Pvts. Henry Johnson and Needham Roberts of the 369th, together held off a German raiding party, killing or wounding twenty of the enemy attackers. The French awarded the 369th Regiment the honor of being the advance guard of Allied troops in the triumphal march to the Rhine on November 17, 1918. The Americans, however, refused to allow any black American soldiers to march with

Eighty-two black soldiers of the 24th Infantry were found guilty at a military court-martial in November 1917 for their alleged participation in a Houston riot that left sixteen whites and four black soldiers dead. Nineteen black soldiers were executed and sixty-three received life sentences at Fort Houston, the largest murder trial in the history of the U.S. Army.

other Allied soldiers, including black colonial troops, in the victory parade up the Champs-Élysées on Bastille Day in 1919.

In December 1917, when the 369th departed from New York City,
they were not allowed to march in the farewell parade of New York's
National Guard, the so-called Rainbow Division. The reason given was
that "black is not a color in the Rainbow." Returning to America in

*Lt. James Reese Europe conducts the 369th Infantry Regiment's "Harlem Hellfighters Band."
The all-black military musical ensemble entertained French, British, and American troops and
introduced jazz to many European civilians during World War I.*

February 1919, the heroic 369th were not to be denied the honor of returning heroes. Crowds thronged New York City's Fifth Avenue as the 369th marched north to Harlem, to the music of its regimental jazz bandleader, James Reese Europe.

Like his fellow Americans of the Harlem Hellfighters, ace pilot Eugene Bullard shared the patriotic but thankless assignment of defending American freedom under a foreign flag. The son of slave-born parents, Bullard left his Georgia home in 1914 at the age of eighteen and traveled to France to pursue a boxing career. After the outbreak of World War I, Bullard joined the French Foreign Legion, where he first distinguished himself as an extraordinary soldier, then qualified for the elite French Flying Corps.

The only black American in the French air force, Bullard flew more than twenty missions against the Germans, fought in many dogfights, and shot down at least five enemy aircraft—certifying his "ace" status. After the United States entered the war, American pilots in the French corps were given the opportunity to transfer into the U.S. Army Air Corps. Bullard applied but his application was denied: "This hurt me deeply. Then, as now, my love for my own country was strong. I got

American Eugene Bullard was not allowed to fly combat for America. He became an ace pilot for the French army during World War I.

some comfort out of knowing that I was able to go on fighting on the same front and in the same cause as other citizens of the United States. And so in a roundabout way, I was managing to do my duty and to serve my country."

Denied entry into the American Air Corps, Bullard next transferred to the French 170th Infantry, where he continued to serve until the armistice. By the end of the war, Bullard had distinguished himself both in the air and on the ground. Wounded five times, he received more than ten French military decorations, including the Croix de Guerre, and was made a Chevalier (knight) of the Legion of Honor—France's highest military and civilian honor.

In his autobiography, *The Black Swallow of Death,* Bullard attributed his success to his slave-born parents who never let him "know that white people looked down on Negroes. I know how wise our parents were to give me [a] head start without a single doubt that I was as nice as anybody and as smart. This, I feel sure, is one reason that I developed enough self-confidence to let me dare to get ahead later in life."

AFTER WORLD WAR I, official reports of the black regiments overwhelmingly rated black officers and soldiers as inferior. Most reports were strikingly at odds with the assessment of Pershing. In his memoir, *My Experiences in the World War,* winner of the 1932 Pulitzer Prize for History, General Pershing again defended and supported the wartime abilities of black soldiers:

> My earlier service with colored troops in the Regular Army had left a favorable impression on my mind. In the field, on the frontier and elsewhere they were reliable and courageous, and the old 10th Cavalry (colored), with which I served in Cuba, made an enviable record there. Under capable white officers and with sufficient training, Negro soldiers have always acquitted themselves creditably.

Other military reports concluded that blacks should be assigned to subordinate positions, as they were in civilian life. Army planners took note that the U.S. Navy no longer employed blacks in peacetime at all, except as messboys, because of the problem of "mixing the races" aboard ship. Black peacetime army regiments were reduced and demobilized. Black career soldiers were denied reenlistment. In 1931 *The Cavalry Journal* forecast the end of the last remaining Buffalo Soldiers of the 10th Cavalry:

> The passing of the 10th Cavalry as a combat regiment is an event of note and will come as a shock to many distinguished officers and soldiers who have served with it. The 10th Cavalry *returns saber* with a proud consciousness of duty well done. The past will preserve for it a record second to none. For the future we can confidently predict that it [Buffalo Soldiers] will carry on in its new role with the same loyalty and high spirit that has given its motto a living means, Ready and Forward.

By 1935 the total number of black officers in the army was four, of whom three were chaplains.

In 1936, the Army War College produced a study that would shape the use of black soldiers in the next war. Intelligence testing placed nearly 80 percent of blacks in the army's lowest classifications. The fact that blacks from northern industrial states scored higher than whites from southern agricultural backgrounds did not, however, cause the army to consider the effects of environment and opportunity on their test results. The report's purported scientific summary consigned the majority of incoming blacks to the military's most subordinate positions. The study spoke of "the negro" as if he were another species:

> As an individual the negro is docile, tractable, lighthearted, care free and good natured. If unjustly treated he is likely to become surly and stubborn, though this is usually a temporary phase. He is careless, shiftless, irresponsible and secretive. He resents censure and is best handled with praise and by ridicule. He is unmoral, untruthful and his sense of right doing is relatively inferior. Crimes and convictions involving moral turpitude are nearly five to one as compared to convictions of whites on similar charges.
>
> On the other hand the negro is cheerful, loyal and usually uncomplaining if reasonably well fed. He has a musical nature and a marked sense of rhythm. His art is primitive. He is religious. With

proper direction in mass, negroes are industrious. They are emotional and can be stirred to a high state of enthusiasm. Their emotions are unstable and their reactions uncertain. Bad leadership in particular is easily communicated to them.

RACIAL SUPERIORITY IN GERMANY, JAPAN, AND THE UNITED STATES

On June 19, 1936, German führer Adolf Hitler received the satisfying news that his nation's finest athlete, boxer Max Schmeling, had defeated the promising young African-American fighter Joe Louis in the twelfth round of a nontitle match-up. Though a relatively inconsequential bout (Louis would not become champion until 1937), the fight made international headlines when American Jewish groups, protesting Germany's enactment of the Nuremberg Laws of 1935, which stripped German Jews of their citizenship, demanded that Schmeling be prohibited from entering the United States.

On the night of the Schmeling–Louis fight, German minister of propaganda Joseph Goebbels stayed up much later than normal. He was listening to the radio, following the contest round by round. At 3:00 A.M. he made this self-satisfied entry in his diary: "In the 12th round, Schmeling knocks out the Negro. Wonderful. A dramatic, exciting fight. Schmeling has fought and won for Germany. The white man over the black man, and the white man was a German."

Goebbels declared Schmeling's triumph a victory for Hitler's social policies. The Nazi weekly journal *Das Schwarze Korps* (The Black Corps) glowingly reported the fight's outcome in similarly racial terms: "Schmeling's victory was not only sport. It was a question of prestige for our race." But the Aryan athletic chest-thumping was short-lived. Within two months, African-American track star Jesse Owens's astonishing performance at the summer Olympics quieted white-supremacy theorists on both sides of the Atlantic—briefly.

By the early 1930s, African-American jazz bands were banned from Germany. The music of black artists and entertainers who toured German cities and towns was considered immoral, decadent, and "excessively erotic." Performed by musicians of an "inferior" race, Hitler and the Nazis found jazz dangerously seductive and threatening to Aryan racial purity. Jews, whom Hitler believed were responsible for many of Germany's economic and social problems—among them inflation, unemployment, communism, and Marxism—were likewise deemed responsible for the importation of jazz and other allegedly decadent and bohemian arts. Hitler's intense hatred placed Jews at his highest priority for elimination, but he desired, too, to defeat, enslave, and destroy the Slavic peoples, Gypsies, homosexuals, the disabled, blacks, and other people of color. A 1933 Nazi law made legal the forced sterilization of handicapped persons, Gypsies, and blacks.

Hitler's greatest influence regarding eugenics and pseudoscientific racism was likely Dr. Eugen Fischer, a German anthropologist and prominent racial theorist who had studied the "cross-breeding" between European males and African women that occurred in Germany's African territories. In 1908 he traveled to German South West Africa to study the so-called Rehoboth Bastards, descendants of mixed-raced parents. Fischer sought to prove that "negro blood" was a weakening agent in the Aryan race. In 1923 he hypothesized the presence of negro blood in Jews, thus establishing "Jewish inferiority." Hitler used the Fischer study as scientific justification for his plans to rid Germany of Jews.

Fischer and other Nazi scientists claimed to find traces of Africa in Italy, France, and Spain, but only among Jews was the amount intolerable. In a 1938 seminar on the "Jewish question" in Munich, Fischer suggested that the gene pool of several European nations was tainted with Negro and Asian blood, but that among the Jews the African influence was unacceptably high. "There is no doubt about its presence among the present-day Jews. Occasionally one sees Negroid hair, lips, and even subdued Negroid nostrils."

At the core of Nazi policy was anti-Semitism, and Hitler's hatred of the Jews was certainly deep and went beyond anything remotely resembling scientific reasoning. Nevertheless, the opinions of Fischer and the supporting racial theories of other Nazi "scientists" provided the sole "proof of inferiority" and rationalization necessary to send more than six million Jews to their deaths.

Interestingly, it was only in one other nation that Hitler observed an admirable attention being paid to notions of racial purity:

Of course, it is not our model German Republic, but the American Union [the United States], in which an effort is made to consult reason at least partially. By refusing immigration in principle to elements in poor health, by simply excluding certain races from naturalization, it professes in slow beginnings a view which is peculiar to the folkish [Aryan] state concept.

THE BERLIN OF 1936 was a massive parade of Nazism. Enormous red-and-black swastika flags decorated the Olympic Stadium, and brown-shirted soldiers goose-stepped as Hitler settled ceremoniously into his box seat in the reviewing stand. On the first day of competition, August 2, Hitler watched the opening shot-put event and then publicly congratulated the Finnish athletes who had swept the event, taking the gold, silver, and bronze medals. He also congratulated the German women who won gold and silver in the javelin. The führer then watched the men's high jump competition, but quickly exited the stadium at the conclusion of the event, before the medals were awarded. To Hitler's obvious annoyance, the gold medal winner, Cornelius Johnson, and the silver medalist, Dave Albittron, both Americans, were black. As if that weren't enough, Jesse Owens then qualified for the finals in the 100-meter race with a world-record 10.2 seconds, winning the thunderous acclaim of 110,000 people at the Reich Sports Field Stadium. As one American sportswriter noted, "If Hitler is going to avoid the Afro-Americans, he is going to have his work cut out for him."

On the second day of the Olympic competition, Owens learned that his world record was nullified due to a trailing wind. In his autobiography, Owens, the son of a sharecropper and the grandson of slaves, recalls beginning his stretches and warm-up for the start of the 100 meters: "I remember seeing Hitler coming in with his entourage and the storm troopers standing shoulder to shoulder like an iron fence. Then came the roar of 'Heil, Hitler!' from 100,000 throats. And all those arms outstretched. It was eerie and frightening."

Hitler watched silently as Owens won the 100 meters, trailed by his black-American teammate Ralph Metcalfe. Again, Hitler left the stadium before the African-American athletes received their medals. On August 4, John Woodruff won the 800 meters, and Jesse Owens beat

Lutz Long of Germany in a close contest in the long jump. Owens and Long, who had become friends during the competition, were walking arm in arm after the event when Hitler called Long, but not Owens, over to his box to congratulate him on winning the silver medal. Owens won his third gold medal the next day, setting a new world record in the 200 meters, followed by silver medalist Mack Robinson, older brother of Jackie. The führer was nowhere to be found in the stadium when Owens was awarded his unprecedented fourth medal for the 400-meter relay. *New York Times* correspondent Frederick Birchall noted that it was not until the fifth day of competition, August 6 that "an American Negro was entered in an event that wasn't won by a Negro. Fritz Pollard Jr., in the high hurdles, came in only third."

For the first time, African-American athletes as a group had defeated whites in head-to-head athletic competition. Although Germany won the greatest number of medals of any nation, African-American athletes dominated among medal winners. By winning four gold medals, Owens had personally subdued Hitler's braggadocio about his unbeatable Aryan supermen of the German track-and-field squad, but so did the others. Of the 312 athletes from the United States, eighteen black athletes gar-

A slide for a lecture on genetics and race in Nazi Germany shows the daughter of a German woman and a colonial African soldier. Some 500 mixed-race teenagers were forcibly sterilized as part of a Nazi policy to "purify" the German population.

nered one-quarter of the American medals. While American newspapers singled out Owens, only black newspapers hailed the extraordinary performances of the other black members of the squad. The continuing social and economic inequality that the black medalists faced upon returning to the "home of the free and the brave" underscored the irony of their victory in pridefully racist Germany. Hitler's racial theorists, of course, were quick to put a face-saving spin on the contest results. German commentators speculated that America's blacks were adept at running "because of a peculiar formation of their bones"—and certainly, they argued, there could be no question about Aryan intellectual superiority.

"When I came back to my native country, after all the stories about Hitler, I couldn't ride in the front of the bus, I had to go to the back door," said Owens. "I couldn't live where I wanted. I wasn't invited to shake hands with Hitler, but I wasn't invited to the White House to shake hands with the President, either."

In June 1937, young Joe Louis finally delivered on his promising talent. The twenty-three-year-old gained international acclaim when he fought world heavyweight champion James J. Braddock in Chicago and captured the title with an eighth-round knockout. After the victory, Louis silenced his well-wishers, insisting "I don't want nobody to call me champ until I beat Schmeling."

FDR's reticence about inviting an African-American athlete to the White House had changed by the time Louis gained the heavyweight championship (and began a string of title defenses that would span the next twelve years). At the president's invitation, Louis visited the White House prior to his June 1938 rematch with Schmeling. Roosevelt proclaimed what most Americans hoped would result from the upcoming return match. On greeting Louis, FDR grasped the champ's biceps and said, "Joe, we're depending on those muscles for America."

Louis's defeat of Schmeling in two minutes and four seconds in the first round at Yankee Stadium served as the decade's final athletic refutation of Hitler's argument that German Aryans constituted a "master race." Ironically, America's seemingly weakest and most beatable target—its Constitutionally second-class black citizens—caused Hitler's greatest international embarrassment on the eve of World War II. Per-

Propaganda illustration from a Nazi filmstrip captioned "The Jew Is a Bastard." The diagram links Jews with others whom the Nazis considered inferior, including Arabs, Asians, and Africans.

haps the bout's conclusion obliquely supported Hitler's supremacist strategy that the only way to guarantee defeat of an "inferior" race was to destroy it.

On November 9–10, 1938, anti-Jewish riots raged in Germany and Austria. The overnight destruction, dubbed Kristallnacht (the "Night of Broken Glass") for the litter strewn in the aftermath of the attacks on Jewish property, left ninety-one dead, hundreds injured, and thousands terrorized. The pogrom was a harbinger of the "Final Solution," Hitler's profound and deadly attack upon the Jews, the religious and racial group he most despised. The race war that smoldered in the United States raged in Germany and eastern Europe.

IN 1939, CONCERT promoter Sol Hurok approached the Daughters of the American Revolution (DAR) about renting its Constitutional Hall in Washington, D.C., for a performance by Marian Anderson. The DAR, which operated the concert facility, denied the request, citing Anderson's race as the reason. In a historically unprecedented response, Eleanor Roosevelt, wife of President Roosevelt, resigned from the DAR

During a visit to Tuskegee Airfield in March 1941, pilot Charles Anderson flew First Lady Eleanor Roosevelt over the area. Within a few days, the Army announced the formation of a black pilot-training program to be based at Tuskegee.

to protest its racist stance (though as recently as 1938 FDR had thrilled the DAR by attending its annual convention). Mrs. Roosevelt then used her cabinet influence to persuade Harold Ickes, Secretary of the Interior, to arrange an open-air concert at the Lincoln Memorial on Easter Sunday. The outdoor concert attracted 75,000 people, and millions more listened by radio, focusing much attention on Anderson and subsequent cases of racial discrimination.

> It stands almost in the shadow of the Lincoln Memorial, but the Great Emancipator's sentiments about "race, creed, or previous condition of servitude" are not shared by the Daughters, for contracts of a commercial nature, the use of these halls contains a clause banning any member of the Negro race. Prejudice rules to make the Capital of the Nation ridiculous in the eyes of all cultured people and to comfort Fuehrer Hitler and the members of our Nazibund.
>
> *Washington Times Herald,* January 15, 1939

In 1930, Anderson had studied in Berlin, living with a German family in order to absorb and master the German language. Building her international reputation at the major European opera houses, she sang in

Paris, Berlin, and Austria, where her performance at the 1935 Salzburg Festival thrilled conductor Arturo Toscanini, who declared that "a voice like hers is heard only [once] in a hundred years."

After Hitler took power and the Nuremberg Laws were passed, which, in addition to their provisions against Jews also included restrictions concerning black and bohemian music and non–Aryan culture, Anderson's Stockholm manager received an inquiry about her availability to perform in Berlin in 1936. There was a possibility, the German was told, because Anderson would also be appearing in Poland, and a day was set aside for a possible Berlin appearance. Fine, came the reply from Germany, but also a question about Anderson's race, which, incredibly, the German booking agent did not appear to know.

Is she an Aryan? he asked. Like many African Americans, she knew her racial heritage to be a mix of African, Native American, and European. Her manager deftly replied that she was part but not 100 percent Aryan. "That ended the correspondence," said Anderson.

As 1939 wore on, Hitler grew determined to conquer Poland. Though Poland had guarantees of French and British military support and expectations that the Soviet Union would oppose German invasion, Hitler had made a secret deal that kept the Soviet Union out of the fray. Germany's September invasion triggered the start of World War II. After the fighting started, a policy that FDR had already initiated—to make the country "an arsenal of democracy" and build U.S. strength—sped forward.

Japan and Race

In 1941, Japan closely watched the German army move across Europe and eastward into the Soviet Union. A treaty with Germany eased Japan's concern that Hitler's long-range goal might lie beyond the Russian front, all the way to the hemisphere's Pacific shore. Japan's leaders reasoned privately that its tripartite pact with Germany and Italy forestalled the possibility of the führer making a grab for all of Asia.

Wary of Western culture and geopolitics, Japan assessed Hitler's racial-superiority tirades as consistent with an international "white supremacy" ideal, which had created colonial empires for Europe and foreign territories and protectorates for the United States. The Nazis and America's southern politicians may have been racism's best-known advocates, but the Japanese were well aware that much of the West held firm to a belief in Asian, as well as African, inferiority.

After World War I, as the racial-superiority debate became more global, several black American scholars and editorial writers looked upon Japan as the leader of the world's "colored races." African-American scholars like W.E.B. DuBois considered Japan's industrial modernization proof of the fallacy of white supremacy. And in a Japanese bestseller of the 1920s, *If Japan and America Fight,* Lt. Gen. Sato Kijori predicted that America's fifteen million "colored people" would not take up arms to defend America in a war against Japan—a war Kijori prophesied would start with a Japanese attack on the U.S. naval force stationed in Hawaii.

Beyond the racial-superiority debate, most threatening to Japan was the U.S. policy of Manifest Destiny, a doctrine that openly challenged Japan's protectionist policy for the western Pacific region. Most of all, Japan wanted to stop the westward expansion of U.S. trade and military interests in Asia, which now included military bases in Guam, Wake Island, the Philippines, and Hawaii.

In 1940, Roosevelt broke from the tradition of presidents serving two terms and ran again for president. (The two-term limit has been law only since 1951.) On October 25, one week before the November election, Roosevelt sought to bolster his support among African Americans by promoting Benjamin O. Davis, Sr., to the rank of brigadier general, making Davis the first black to reach that status. On the same day he also appointed William Hastie, dean of the Howard University Law School, as his Civilian Aide on Negro Affairs. Earlier in the fall, the president had signed the Selective Training and Service Act, the first peacetime draft in U.S. history. The act contained an antidiscrimination clause establishing a 10 percent quota system to ensure African-American participation—though blacks would, however, remain in separate units.

On June 22, 1941, twenty-two thousand blacks rallied at Madison Square Garden in support of labor leader A. Philip Randolph's demand that the federal government act to end employment discrimination. On June 25, President Roosevelt issued Executive Order 8802 prohibiting racial discrimination in federal government employment.

The same year, Dr. Charles Drew, an African-American scientist who had developed a system to produce plasma, separating it from the blood matter, arranged for large amounts of plasma to be shipped to war-ravaged England. Blood banks were set up in England and Drew established a blood bank program in the United States under the auspices of the Red Cross. However, when the U.S. Department of War adopted the Red Cross Blood Bank program, which Drew had established, the U.S. military command insisted that black and white blood be segregated.

Though scientifically indistinguishable, blood from blacks was labeled "AA"—for Afro-American—an official designation solely for the comfort of any "patient who holds a prejudice against the injection of Negro whole blood or plasma processed therefrom," stated a Red Cross advisory. Drew, whose genius helped save the lives of thousands of American soldiers and countless other victims of war, resigned in protest from the very program that he had established.

READY FOR WAR

A big boost to the black pilot program came from First Lady Eleanor Roosevelt, who visited the Tuskegee pilot project in March 1941. While there she asked to be taken on a ride in an airplane with a black pilot at the controls. Mrs. Roosevelt then insisted that her flight with pilot Charles "Chief" Anderson be photographed and the film developed right away so that she could take the picture back to Washington with her. A half-hour flight in Anderson's Piper J-3 Cub convinced Mrs. Roosevelt that blacks could fly just as well as the best white pilots.

Using the photograph as visual evidence in her personal civil rights campaign, Mrs. Roosevelt presented it to FDR to urge him to reject the opinion of his very capable but bigoted military advisers who staunchly opposed the presence of black pilots in the U.S. military.

On May 22, 1941, a squadron of African-American male college students were activated at Tuskegee Airfield in Alabama. Dubbed the "Tuskegee Airmen," they became part of "the experiment"—schooling

Pilot candidates report to Capt. Benjamin O. Davis, Jr., commandant of cadets at Tuskegee Airfield, in September 1941.

black students in a fully equipped aeronautical program for training as fighter and bomber pilots, navigators, gunners, radio specialists, mechanics, and ground engineers. Candidates for training as commissioned pilots were selected in the same manner as prescribed for white candidates, with, however, a quota system to limit the number to thirty-three pilots and a ground crew of 276.

Opinion surveys of the era commonly found whites favoring segregation and blacks against racial separation. Upward of nine out of ten whites felt that white and black troops should be kept separate, while eight out of ten blacks were opposed to segregation in the military. In 1939, fewer than 4,000 African Americans were serving in the military and only twelve African Americans had become officers. By November 30, 1941, black enlisted strength had risen to 97,000 troops. By the end of December 1942, black enlisted strength had grown to more than 467,000 troops. By 1945, more than 1.1 million African Americans were serving in uniform, about half overseas.

Many black leaders urged a dual response to the war effort in America. Known as the "Double V" campaign—for victory at home and victory abroad—they urged African Americans to support the war effort as a way to fight racism. Once again, black Americans hoped their patriotism and military contributions would break down segregation and racial barriers. With their increased influence as voters, moreover, African-American demands for equality were having greater impact than ever before. It was a moment in American history when the "color line" seemed likely to soon fade from sight. Humorist and writer Art Buchwald once recalled that as a kid he was sure of three things: "Franklin Roosevelt was going to save the economy . . . Joe DiMaggio was going to beat Babe Ruth's record, and Joe Louis was going to save us from the Germans."

PEARL HARBOR

[1941–42]

I just grabbed hold of the gun and fired.

DORIE MILLER, U.S. NAVY

When Japanese planes roared down on Pearl Harbor, the enemy undoubtedly believed that, in addition to striking a shattering blow at the U.S. Navy, they would also fracture the morale of the American people. We were a disunited people, they thought—a people inclined to dislike one another based on racial, religious, and ethnic differences—and disinclined ever to work together or ever to fight for one another's interests.

At 7:55 A.M. on December 7, 1941, a Sunday morning, the first wave of Japanese bombers attacked the U.S. naval fleet. Airfields and battleships anchored in the harbor were the enemy's principal targets. By 8:50 A.M., not a single American plane had successfully made it into the air. The attackers were unopposed, except for the efforts of a few soldiers who had managed to get to battle stations. Aboard the smoldering USS *West Virginia,* Doris "Dorie" Miller was below deck, collecting laundry, when the ship was struck by the first of five aircraft torpedoes and two one-thousand-pound bombs.

Adm. Chester W. Nimitz pins a naval decoration on Doris "Dorie" Miller, in a ceremony aboard the USS Enterprise *on May 27, 1942.*

Miller scrambled from below to assist on deck but was knocked down by the force of another explosion. He recovered and, under a hail of strafing machine-gun fire from enemy planes, carried several wounded soldiers, including his mortally wounded captain, to greater safety. He then took up a position at a .50-caliber antiaircraft machine gun.

A naval messman, he had never been taught how to fire a gun, but he quickly figured out how it worked and began firing. Miller later said: "It wasn't hard. I just pulled the trigger and she worked fine."

Miller shot down four, possibly five, Japanese planes before being ordered to leave the badly damaged ship. After continuing to assist in the rescue of shipmates, he dove into the harbor and swam to safety, part of the way underwater, beneath the burning oil leaking from the USS *Arizona* and other neighboring vessels.

When the last attacking Japanese planes returned to their carriers, at about 9:45 A.M., Pearl Harbor was a smoking shambles. Every American airplane was either destroyed or disabled; the battleships were sunk or disabled; and other naval craft in the harbor were badly damaged. Of the personnel in the area, 2,403 were dead; the wounded totaled 1,176.

In the wake of the Japanese victory that momentarily stunned America, the government, military, and news media searched for heroes from our side to present to the American public. Most American sailors and soldiers had been unable to fight back at Pearl Harbor, but some had. Newspapers carried stories and printed the names and actions of local heroes. Except for one national story about the heroics of an unnamed "negro messboy," all of the acts of bravery belonged to white Americans.

More than three months passed before Dorie Miller's name became known and he was brought to national attention. His identity was announced by Lawrence Reddick, director of the Schomburg Center for Research in Black Culture, in Harlem. Suspecting that the navy might purposefully have withheld the name of this black hero, Reddick wrote an amicable letter requesting that the soldier's name be released so that he could be acknowledged in the Schomburg Center's "Honor Roll of Race Relations." The navy provided Reddick with Miller's name, and on March 12, 1942, Reddick's announcement made public the war's first African-American hero.

Polite, powerfully built, and soft-spoken, Dorie Miller, the twenty-one-year-old son of Waco, Texas, sharecroppers, quickly became the model of a black war hero. That he was of low military rank, had risked his life to save a white officer, and was humble about his heroics made Miller acceptable even for navy recruitment posters. Commonly, newspapers acclaimed him as "Dorie Miller, the first negro hero," as if none had preceded him in American history. At a special ceremony aboard the USS *Enterprise,* Adm. Chester W. Nimitz, the Commander in Chief of the Pacific Fleet, personally presented the Navy Cross to Miller. Pinning the metal to Miller's chest for his extraordinary courage in battle, Nimitz remarked: "This marks the first time in this conflict that such high tribute has been made in the Pacific Fleet to a member of his race and I'm sure that the future will see others similarly honored for brave acts."

In black communities, Dorie Miller buttons were sold, and folk songs told of how he was "peeling sweet potatoes when the guns began

JANUARY 8, 1942 Joe Louis scores a first-round knockout over Buddy Baer at Madison Square Garden. Louis donates his $800,000 purse to the Navy Relief Fund.

to roar," and how he forgot he was a messman and grabbed a gun when he saw his captain "lying wounded on the floor."

"Some say we colored people have nothing to fight for," said Mrs. Conery Miller, mother of the naval hero, before a Harlem "Unity for Victory" rally of 6,000 people in June 1942. "We all have something to fight for. We have freedom to fight for. But we can't fight this war by ourselves. We've got to put Jesus into it, for He has never lost a battle."

But black Americans did not need to know Miller's name before they responded to the national emergency of December 7. Within twenty-four hours of the Pearl Harbor attack, the NAACP issued a statement of its unqualified support for the war effort:

> Though thirteen million American Negroes have more often than not been denied democracy, they are American citizens and will as in every war give unqualified support to the protection of their country. At the same time we shall not abate one iota our struggle for full citizenship rights here in the United States. We will fight but we demand the right to fight as equals in every branch of military, naval and aviation service.

DECEMBER 8, 1941

Within hours of Miller's action, another African American became part of the history of the first day of the war. Ten hours after the morning attack on Pearl Harbor, more than one hundred Japanese bombers and fighter planes flew high in the sky over the Philippines. Pfc. Robert H. Brooks, a twenty-five-year-old African American, likely heard the first distant sound of airplanes approaching his base, Fort Stotsenburg. It was lunchtime, 12:30 P.M. (already December 8 in the Philippines because of the international dateline), and Brooks and about sixty other soldiers of Company D of the 192nd Tank Battalion were waiting for a "chow truck" to take them to mess hall.

At breakfast they'd been told that Pearl Harbor had been bombed but "there was little information and no orders," said post commander Maj. Gen. Jonathan Wainwright. The base was to "take every precaution against a possible Jap paratroop landing." Brooks and the 192nd Tank Battalion spent the morning unpacking weapons that were still in crates

The grave site of Pfc. Robert H. Brooks, the first American soldier killed in action following Pearl Harbor, is located at the Manila American Cemetery in the Philippines.

since their arrival on Thanksgiving, November 21. Sgt. Robert Stewart recalled that the guns were still in Cosmoline. "They were still all sticky and greasy—and nothing was operational. There were no machine-gun belts loaded, so you had to put the bullets in the belt by hand and our thumbs got raw pushing those in." The battalion was told to expect to be bombed by noon. But activity at the base and the presence of American planes flying in and out all morning lulled many of the soldiers into a false sense of security.

In the clear, sunny, blue sky overhead, several V formations of bombers and escort fighter planes appeared. A fine sight, recalled one soldier who remembered thinking the planes were "ours," but then, squinting his eyes in the sun, he saw the bright red circles on the sides of the planes. The "beautiful" shiny-metallic reflections cascading from the sky "like tinfoil" were bombs. The air-raid siren sounded just as the bombers were almost directly overhead. Enemy pilot Saburo Sakai was almost as surprised as the Americans below:

The sight which met us was unbelievable. Instead of encountering a swarm of American fighters diving at us in attack, we looked down and saw sixty enemy bombers and fighters neatly parked along the airfield runways. . . . The Americans had made no attempt to disperse the planes and increase their safety.

Suddenly, "buildings, people, airplanes, and everything else [were] going up in the sky." Though the bombs rained downed, Brooks ran across the landing field to a combat tank positioned in the woods, about fifty yards away from the airstrip. Mounted on the tanks were .50-caliber antiaircraft guns, with which he may have hoped to bring down the attacking planes.

Brooks made it to a tank just as a bomb exploded behind him. Shrapnel severed his arm and part of his face. Soldiers who saw him soon after knew that he would not live. The Japanese bombs hit with precision. Immediately after the bomber assault, the smaller Japanese fighter planes flew in low to strafe the field.

Commander Wainwright saw Brooks fall, his face "a bloody blob. A bomb splinter had streaked all the way over from Clark Field, whose edge was twelve hundred yards from us." Wainwright gave orders to get the soldier to the Stotsenburg hospital. The general recalled: "We were in a war for which we were no more prepared than a child is to fight a cruel and seasoned professional pugilist." A soldier recalled: "There was a garbage can outside the surgery section at the Stots hospital with arms and legs sticking out of it; we had one hell of a cleanup job."

Of the ninety-three American deaths at the Clark and Stotsenburg fields that afternoon, Brooks was the first recorded fatality. Dead on arrival at the Stotsenburg hospital, he became the first member of a U.S. armored unit killed in World War II. About twenty-four hours later, on December 8th in the United States, President Roosevelt declared war on Japan, effectively making Brooks the first army casualty of the war.

That he was also the first African American to die was not an issue, as he was officially, though erroneously, listed as white. In Scott County, Kentucky, black and white childhood friends remembered Brooks as light enough to pass for white. A few white fellow soldiers said he had confided in them. "I knew he was black all the time," said one white soldier. Another believed Brooks lied about his race. "We was all white. . . . And he lied to get into a white outfit," said another soldier. "I called him Nig all the time, and didn't know he was a nigger." Kentucky soldier Kenneth Hourigan insisted no one in the battalion suspected Brooks was black. Hourigan said he learned the truth only when he returned home after the war. "We always thought he had a colored man's laugh, but he wasn't as dark as some colored people."

But Sam Wood of Sadieville, who grew up with Brooks, said he knew Brooks well enough to know that he would never try to pass for white. Rather, Wood said he thought the army simply assumed Brooks, the oldest son of Roy and Addie Brooks, was white and assigned him to a white unit.

Likewise, William McIntyre, a black childhood friend of Brooks's younger brother, Oram, believed Robert's chief desire was to serve his country. "When the time came and he wanted to join the army, he simply let them write him up as white. So I don't believe for a minute Robert was passing any more than to say, 'Hey, this enlistment guy wrote me up as white, so unless someone asks me point-blank, I won't say anything. I won't say I am and I won't say I am not, because I want to serve my country like any man should be able.' "

Only after the U.S. Army took steps to name a parade ground at Fort Knox in honor of Brooks did his race become an issue. Maj. Gen. Jacob L. Devers, chief of the U.S. Armored Force, issued the order to honor Brooks, sending a letter of condolence to his parents.

MR. AND MRS. ROY BROOKS
RFD #1
SADIEVILLE, KY

My Dear Mr. and Mrs. Brooks:
    It is with the deepest regret that I have learned of the death of your son, Robert, who gave his life in the defense of his country, December 8, 1941, in a battle near Fort Stotsenburg, Philippine Islands.
    With appreciation of your suffering, my sincere sympathy goes out to you.
    Robert was the first battle casualty of the Armored Force, and be-

cause of this, and because of his excellent record, I have directed that the main parade ground at Fort Knox be named Brooks Field in honor of your son.

In 1991, a fiftieth-anniversary story in the *Lexington Herald Leader* continued the mystery of Brooks's enlistment and death—and the question of whether or not the Brooks family had been invited to the naming ceremony. Local historian Anne Bevins recalled two theories as to what happened. "One is that the army didn't push very hard to get them to come. The other is that they didn't go because they were upset at [their son for] passing himself off as white." However, childhood friend McIntyre remembered otherwise: the Brooks family did go to the ceremony but, as he recalled it, they were not acknowledged by the military brass.

> There have been a lot of martyrs,
> And we read of them in books.
> Ev'ry martyr gives his life to stay his cause.
> Now Kentucky mourns the latest,
> Private Robert Harold Brooks.
> In his honor let the entire nation pause.
>
> SONG LYRICS TO "PRIVATE ROBERT HAROLD BROOKS,"
> HANDY BROTHERS MUSIC CO., 1944

In the twenty-four-hour period that encompassed Pearl Harbor and Brooks's death, the Japanese had made the most ambitious assault in the history of the Pacific region, attacking Singapore, Thailand, Malaya, Guam, Hong Kong, Wake Island, and the Philippines.

On December 11 President Roosevelt declared war on Germany and Italy. Both white and black newspapers in America deplored the Japanese attack—and most supported the president's response against the Axis alliance.

FIRST TO WAR

Less than twenty-four hours after the Pearl Harbor attack, American forces were deployed to the Panama Canal, a region considered vulnerable to enemy attack from east or west—either by Germany from the Atlantic or Japan from the Pacific side. By December 8, 400 black soldiers of the 275th Signal Construction Company were on their way to the Panama Canal. To the American military command the Panama Canal seemed a likely "next target," and its protection became one of America's first military priorities.

In the hot, humid jungle of Panama, the black crew began work immediately. Slashing brush and digging holes to put up poles and string lines for telegraph and telephone systems, the 275th worked night and day to secure communication lines. Lt. Gen. Daniel Van Voorhis of the Caribbean Defense Command was pleased with their work, and the 275th were among the first Allied units commended in the war. They were first, too, to experience the hostile reception often extended to black Americans—even those trying to help the Allies win the war.

Black American servicemen perform duties on Canton, the first base station in the island-hopping strategy to defeat Japan, which was completed in January 1942. Ironically, the island was named after the Canton, a nineteenth-century New Bedford, Massachusetts, whaling ship that had been seeking "oil and bone" in Pacific waters when its crew, which included black American and Cape Verdean sailors (en route to Guam, the Philippines, and China), ran ashore on the atoll on March 4, 1854. The island's spelling changed to Kanton in 1973 when it became part of Kiribati. Artist: Paul Sample.

Despite the urgent needs of war, black American soldiers were not welcome in Panama. Panamanian law prohibited the immigration or long-term visitation of non–Spanish-speaking blacks. Though emigration was never an American military tactic, local leaders expressed fear that the higher wages paid to the black American soldiers would be a bad example for the local population—a reason expressed by more than a dozen Caribbean and Latin American countries, including Barbados, Trinidad and Tobago, Jamaica, Honduras, Guyana, Venezuela, Chile, and Brazil.

Still, Voorhis kept the black crew in Panama long enough to finish their assignment. Throughout the rest of the war, he sidestepped military and political pressures to keep black Americans out of the conflict. Believing that black troops were "peculiarly adaptable" to the extreme heat and humidity of Central America and the Caribbean, he regularly rotated black labor battalions into the region for the duration of the war. Regarding the Panamanian request that they keep blacks out, Secretary of War Henry Stimson remarked: "Tell them they must complete their work. It is ridiculous to raise such objections when the Panama Canal itself was built with black labor."

THE FIRST STEP TOWARD JAPAN

About 1,800 miles southwest of Pearl Harbor, Canton Island, a white coral island three miles long and a half-mile wide, became the first of many stepping-stones in the war against Japan, thanks in part to the yeoman efforts of a small group of black American aviation engineers. Since 1938, Canton Island had served as a Pan American Airways base for its airmail and passenger service to New Zealand and Australia. In early November 1941, a squadron of forty-three engineers was assigned to build shipping facilities and runways on Canton capable of handling B-17s. Taking construction equipment, a fresh water supply, and orders to construct a 5,000-foot runway, the Canton engineers were reported "striving very hard" to improve the airbase and blast a passage for ships into the island's lagoon. A supervisor's report, dated December 6, expressed confidence that the runway would be ready for medium and heavy bombers by January 15, 1942—to thwart any possible attack from Japan.

But the Pearl Harbor disaster drastically altered Canton's military role. Though the island was untouched during the enemy's December siege of many Allied stations in the Pacific, communications were knocked out between Hawaii and Canton, and on December 14, all civilians on Canton Island were evacuated and the engineer unit was left alone to both construct the base and now, if necessary, defend the island. Aware that the American command had virtually lost touch with Canton, the enemy declared during a Christmas Eve broadcast over Japanese radio that the base there had been attacked and "all installations demolished and all personnel killed." But despite their claim of victory, the enemy never appeared and the American crew kept working resolutely. Their job was made tougher by the heat and the hard, sharp coral, which could puncture gloves and shoes, causing cuts and scrapes that easily became infected. But in early January, contact was restored. By January 16, the field was ready for the first combat patrols by aircraft in the South Pacific. Two days later, six B-17 aircraft landed at Canton. On Friday, February 13, more than 1,100 reinforcements arrived aboard the troop carrier USS *President Taylor* to continue developing the island. Unfortunately, the ship struck a reef during its arrival and had to be abandoned; but this bad experience served to reinforce opinions that new—amphibious— landing crafts would have to be designed for the war.

Within bombing range of the Japanese-held Gilbert Islands, Canton Island, with its labor battalion of about 200 African-American soldiers in 1942, emerged as one of the first battle-ready air and naval stations. American planes flew daily searches of the waters between Canton and the Fiji Islands, and preparations were under way for the pending strikes against the Marshall and Gilbert Islands. About 3,000 more black American engineers were quickly and quietly dispatched in early 1942 to other Central Pacific islands that Admiral Nimitz deemed essential to kick-start the American offensive, including Christmas (Micronesia's largest island, at thirty-five miles long and twenty-four miles wide), where black soldiers worked on airfields, docks, and a network of roads across the coral terrain. On the islands of Penrhyn, Aitutaki, and Tongatapu, black American soldiers comprised upward of 50 percent of the total American military workforce.

THE PHILIPPINES

Following the attack on Pearl Harbor, Japanese planes pounded the Philippines for the next several days, reducing all American naval and army bases, airfields, and ports in the islands to ruins, except for two bases at Bataan and Corregidor. With American defenses badly weakened, the enemy came ashore north of Manila on December 22 with 47,000 well-equipped and well-trained soldiers.

Gen. Douglas MacArthur, the American commander in the Philippines, then implemented an old, though questionable, strategy called War Plan Orange 3, declaring Manila an "open," or neutral, city to avoid massive casualties and destruction. To keep from engaging the enemy too soon, he retreated all military personnel to the Bataan peninsula and Corregidor Island. There they were dangerously bottled up, but MacArthur planned to defend Manila Bay from the two positions until Washington could send help. However, aid was not forthcoming. On December 23, President Roosevelt and his military advisers agreed that Europe would be the primary theater of war for the United States, not the Pacific. MacArthur was told to use the forces at hand to hold off the Japanese offensive.

On New Year's Day 1942, bleary-eyed party-goers leaving Tom's Dixie Kitchen, an all-night bar and restaurant in Manila owned by a black American war veteran, watched signs going up announcing: OPEN CITY, BE CALM, STAY AT HOME, NO SHOOTING. The next day more than 50,000 Japanese troops marched triumphantly into the capital city.

"I was just a teenager," said Thomas McCremens, son of a black American soldier and a Filipino mother. "And I was away from home when the Japanese came."

As he approached his house, a family member motioned for him to go away.

"I ran into the hills and joined the guerrilla forces and fought with them until Liberation."

Twenty-one-year-old Beatriz Valdez Brook, the daughter of a black American, barely escaped with her life when a Japanese soldier slashed her head with a sword. Civilians of every racial and ethnic background were in a general panic as the Japanese army took control of Manila.

AFRICAN AMERICANS IN THE PHILIPPINES

More than one thousand black American soldiers from the turn-of-the-century Spanish-American War had stayed in the islands. Tom Pritchard, the huge and affable owner of Tom's Dixie Kitchen, which attracted the city's elite, including President Manuel Quezon, was one of many black Americans living in the Philippines. Another, Lt. Col. Walter H. Loving, served as bandleader of the famous Philippines Constabulary Band.

Most had married Filipino women and many prospered as farmers, chefs, merchants, and businessmen. Some obtained U.S.-government contracts and sold their products to the U.S. Army. Isaac Lloyd, a black veteran of the Philippine wars and a prosperous farmer and sawmill operator, supplied the U.S. Army with rice, vegetables, pork, chickens, and logs. In 1933 Robert T. Browne, an African American with nearly twenty years' service as U.S. Army procurement officer, arrived in the Philippines.

In January 1942, Pritchard, Loving, Lloyd, and Browne were among the more than two hundred black Americans and their families who were rounded up and questioned by the Japanese. Many were classified as "enemy nationals" along with many other foreigners—Americans, Australians, Britons, Canadians, Dutch, French, Poles, and Norwegians. Over 3,800 men, women, and children were imprisoned at the Santo Tomas Internment Camp, or STIC, as it was called by the internees. These American civilians were the first in this country's history to be placed in a foreign concentration camp.

Pritchard's connection to President Quezon helped him get released. Like Quezon, Pritchard was able to convince the Japanese of his neutrality, while secretly aiding the guerrilla underground. Browne, Lloyd, and Loving and his wife were confined to the camp.

"THE LOVING TOUCH"

At six feet one inches tall, the sixty-nine-year-old Lt. Col. Walter Howard Loving still cut an impressive figure, pumping his baton as the most famous conductor in the Philippines and the entire Pacific. The son of former slaves, Loving spent much of his adolescence in the guardianship of his older sister Julia. In the 1880s she worked in the Washington, D.C., household of future president Theodore Roosevelt, who frequently tutored young Walter in mathematics. He was introduced to music through the Second Baptist Church and became conductor of its choir at age eighteen.

In 1893 Loving enlisted in the U.S. Army and became a member of the 24th Infantry Regiment Band. In the next decade he did three tours of duty in the military, and after his second enlistment he enrolled in the New England Conservatory of Music, where he studied harmony, conducting, and cornet. Reenlisting in 1899, he was sent to the Philippines, where he was promoted to chief musician and appointed second lieutenant.

Loving's bandleading talent so impressed William Howard Taft, an island commissioner in 1901, that Taft promised that if he ever rose to higher office, he would pick Loving to set up an official commonwealth military band. Appointed governor, Taft made good on his pledge and named Loving, who was fluent in Spanish, conductor of the Philippine Constabulary Band. In 1909, Taft summoned the band and its conductor to Washington—to add "the Loving touch" to his inaugural parade from the Capitol to the White House.

Loving led the band until 1910, when he suffered a severe bout of tuberculosis. Returning to the United States, he was hospitalized and subsequently retired from the military. In 1916 he married Edith McCary, the daughter of an army friend, and soon afterward they settled in Los Angeles, where she gave birth to a child, Walter Jr. By 1917 Loving had made a full recovery, and when World War I broke out, he was called upon to serve in the Office of Intelligence in Washington, D.C. Appointed a major in the U.S. Officers Reserve Corps, Loving was assigned to investigate potentially subversive activities of African Americans.

For two years Loving kept dossiers on several black leaders regarded by the Woodrow Wilson administration as seditious. In a January 5, 1919, memo to Brig. Gen. Marlborough Churchill, director of U.S. military intelligence, Loving drew a bead on Marcus Garvey:

> Considerable attention has been paid to Mr. Garvey's talks on street corners in New York lately where he urges the darker races of earth to get together and form one great alliance. . . . He has been recently making frequent trips out of New York, and has spoken in Chicago, Baltimore and Newport News. Strict watching is being kept over all his meetings to see that he does not try to incite race prejudice. . . . Messrs. Phillip Randolph and Chandler Owen, colored, Socialists from New York, are arranging a conference in this city during the third week in this month. It appears that all of these New York "soap box orators" are beginning to invade this city, and their presence must carry some significance.

His fifteen-page analysis, "Final Report on Negro Subversion," fingered Garvey, Randolph, Owens, and others, including journalist Ida B. Wells-Barnett and even his friend W.E.B. DuBois. An earlier report submitted by Loving had kept DuBois from receiving a special officer's commission during the war. Although Loving did author memos criticizing the army's treatment of black soldiers and federal Jim Crow laws, the military intelligence director regarded him as a "white man's negro" and the nation's best Negro spy whose few critical comments simply gave him more credibility in the army's effort to thwart potentially seditious movements among African Americans. Considered so thorough and sound in its scope, Loving's report became the obvious primary source of another federal report released in 1919, "Radicalism and Sedition Among Negroes as Reflected in Their Publications," submitted to the U.S. Attorney General by a rising young investigator—J. Edgar Hoover.

Loving left the War Department in November 1919 and returned to the Philippines, where he again led the Constabulary Band until 1923. Returning to California, he entered the real estate business in Oakland, where he and his family lived until 1937, when, at age sixty-four, he was once again offered his old job by President Quezon. Promoted to lieutenant colonel in the Philippine army, Loving became a fixture in the musical and social life of Manila, conducting concerts and attending elegant parties with his wife.

DURING THE JAPANESE capture of Manila, many black American veterans fled with their families to the hills to join the guerrilla forces. James Coleman, a captain in the Filipino and American resistance force, led sabotage teams and surveillance squads to spy on enemy camps. A bounty of 5,000 pesos was placed on his head. His twenty-year-old wife, Rose, went with him to fight alongside the underground U.S. Allied Forces.

In mid-January, Gen. Douglas MacArthur confidently sent a message to the troops on Bataan, just two miles across the bay from his headquarters on Corregidor.

HEADQUARTERS
UNITED STATES ARMY FORCES
IN THE FAR EAST FORT MILLS, P.I.

January 15, 1942

Help is on the way from the United States. Thousands of troops and hundreds of planes are being dispatched. The exact time of arrival is unknown as they will have to fight their way through Japanese attempts against them. It is imperative that our troops hold until these reinforcements arrive.

No further retreat is possible. We have more troops in Bataan than the Japanese have thrown against us; our supplies are ample; a determined defense will defeat the enemy's attack.

It is a question now of courage and determination. Men who run will merely be destroyed but men who fight will save themselves and their country.

I call upon every soldier in Bataan to fight in his assigned position, resisting every attack. This is the only road to salvation. If we will fight we will win; if we retreat we will be destroyed.

MacArthur

MacArthur's exhortation was in vain, and everyone knew it. Within weeks more than 200,000 well-trained and disciplined Japanese soldiers came ashore and were within striking distance of the American and Filipino forces on Bataan.

General MacArthur was ordered to leave the Philippines and go to Australia, which had become the Allies' priority. The Japanese were setting up bases on neighboring New Guinea and had already bombed Darwin, the northern Australian port. A landing on Australia appeared imminent, and the American and Filipino armies were left to fend for themselves. Many officers in the War Department, including General Eisenhower and Chief of Staff George Marshall, felt that MacArthur had failed miserably and should be relieved of his command.

On March 11, General MacArthur, along with his wife, son, and staff, left Corregidor aboard PT boats. At Mindanao they boarded two B-17s that flew them to Darwin, Australia, where MacArthur issued his famous statement, "I shall return." His staff suggested the line should be changed to "We shall return," but MacArthur stuck with his original.

BATAAN DEATH MARCH

The troops left behind braved on for only a few weeks more. Among the 20,000 American troops were about 250 African-American soldiers, most of whom had been assigned to engineering, quartermaster, trucking, ordnance, laundry, and kitchen details. Without food supplies—for every one supply ship that made it to Corregidor, two were sunk—the army relied upon its service units to forage for any kind of meat. Near starvation, they slaughtered horses, mules, dogs, monkeys, and snakes for food. Ill fed, they were ravaged by tropical diseases.

MARCH 1942 The U.S. Coast Guard recruited its first 150 black volunteers, who underwent basic training at Manhattan Beach, New York. Over 5,000 African Americans served as Coast guardsmen in WWII. Among their duties was the horse patrol unit, which kept watch on the beaches in New Jersey.

On April 9, 1942, the first surrender in American history made front-page headlines around the world: BATAAN, WORST BLOW TO AN AMERICAN ARMY, newspapers reported. Over 70,000 American and Filipino soldiers started the sixty-five-mile march to a waiting prison camp, but about 16,000 died on the trek. Men were bayoneted, beaten with rifle butts, or shot for stumbling or falling behind. Thousands died from disease and exhaustion, or from Japanese brutality in what became a metaphor for wartime atrocities—the Bataan Death March.

READY TO SERVE, BUT UNWELCOME

> When the Japanese bombed Pearl Harbor, that particular Sunday, all of the whites at McDill Field [Florida] were running around with loaded guns. We had no guns and no idea as to what was going on, so you can imagine what was running through our minds until we learned of the Japanese attack. Even with this knowledge it was of no comfort to be practically penned in our area with armed patty boys all over everywhere. We trusted them just about as much as a coiled rattlesnake.
>
> Master Sergeant Warren Bryant, 812th Aviation Engineers

Irrationally and incredibly, many of America's top military commanders and politicians did not want to send black soldiers abroad. With black Americans potentially able to make up 10 percent of America's fighting force, the leadership was clearly risking the nation's defense against Germany and Japan by holding fast to racist notions that blacks were either cowardly or not smart enough to serve. So poisoned was the reputation of American blacks that even in Africa, where nearly all nations were governed by European colonial powers, America was told to keep black soldiers home. In the midst of war, more than thirty nations indicated their unwillingness to accept black soldiers.

In Australia, which Japanese forces were preparing to strike by the summer of 1942, black American soldiers were officially prohibited. A "whites only" immigration policy that prohibited Asians, southern Europeans (dark-complexioned French, Italian, and Spanish), and Africans, led to a government protest to keep black American soldiers out of Australia. American commanders—those who saw the enormous value of black soldiers as well as those who did not—were ultimately forced to devise ways to use the wealth of black talent while keeping racists, in and out of the military, political, and diplomatic spheres, at bay.

Black Americans carrying weapons, either as infantry, tank corps, or as pilots, was simply an unthinkable notion in 1942. More acceptable to southern politicians and much of the military command was the use of black soldiers in support positions, as noncombatants or laborers.

Although it was the Japanese attack on Pearl Harbor that brought the United States into the war, America's primary focus was on Europe. President Roosevelt and the American military chiefs agreed on a strategy with Great Britain and the Soviet Union, to first defeat Germany, the most powerful and dangerous of the Axis powers. The war against Germany was planned and coordinated by the three national powers. Strategic decisions were argued and agreed upon by American, British, and Soviet chiefs of staff, and on occasion, directly by Roosevelt, Churchill, and Stalin.

The Pacific war differed fundamentally in strategy and command. Although the United States had some Allied support in that theater, particularly from England, Australia, and New Zealand, Russia was honoring its April 1941 neutrality pact with Japan and would not help in the Pacific campaign. In the Pacific war, the ratio of U.S. to other Allied forces was much higher than in Europe; consequently black soldiers, whom various U.S. military and political leaders were reluctant to deploy in Europe, were especially needed in the Pacific.

It would take over two years to build up the armed forces to meet Germany head-on, so the Pacific war was confronted first and most directly by the United States. With almost the entire British navy deployed in the Atlantic to stop the German U-boat attacks, little U.S. offensive naval power was required there. U-boat defense primarily required small, fast escort vessels. Thus, American offensive naval power—especially its battleships and the aircraft carriers and warplanes—could be committed to the Pacific.

The first six months of the war, from December 1941 to May 1942, were a time of unbroken Japanese military victory. Singapore crumbled before the Japanese Imperial Army on February 15, 1942. The defeat of this strategically critical island in Southeast Asia rapidly led to the fall of the Netherlands East Indies. By early April 1942, the Japanese had completely occupied Burma. But at the height of Japanese expansion, in mid-1942, the tide turned—thanks in large part to the presence of white and black soldiers in the Pacific war.

Thousands of American men, women, and children gave of themselves unselfishly and without acclaim during the war, but perhaps the most unsung were the nation's African-American soldiers. Treated as incompetent outcasts fit only to clean kitchens and latrines, throughout the war their actual work was unheralded yet critical to the nation's success.

In the early years of America's participation in the war (1942–43), the role of black soldiers was virtually unknown and unaccounted. Rare were pictures or news releases about black troops stationed at home or abroad. More common were wire-service reports of white and black soldiers scuffling with each other. In the public perception, any possibility, even remote, that black Americans would or could begin to contribute soon to the war effort was embodied in the promising but untested class of black student pilots at a Tuskegee airbase.

Not until July 1942 did the American military command release photos of black soldiers stationed in Great Britain, yet by then blacks were deployed to more than a dozen overseas stations. In 1942 and 1943, Americans were left with the impression that few if any blacks were contributing to the cause. The public was not aware that more than 100,000 blacks were deployed overseas by December 1942. Stationed in Alaska, Australia, Iceland, Africa, and islands in the Caribbean and South Pacific, in many places black soldiers were the dominant American presence.

In some cases, particularly in Asia and the Pacific war zone, black soldiers were the first to arrive on foreign soil. Long before American combat divisions hit the beaches of the South Pacific islands, white and black construction battalions were at work. To achieve the main military objective—to bring the war to Japan—the massive preinvasion labor campaign in the Pacific, Asia, and Africa proved critical and decisive. In the Pacific war, America's black soldiers were a truly secret weapon.

AFTER PEARL HARBOR

Following Pearl Harbor, American military racial policy became simple: black soldiers were not generally asked to carry guns, but they were ordered to carry nearly everything else. For the next four years, black soldiers would be called upon to build, transport, or carry virtually every element of the military's combat campaign. They built bases, airfields, and roads. They transported artillery, ammunition, troops, and airplanes. They drained swamps and shorelines for docks and piers. In order for the country to succeed in WWII, even the most bigoted politicians and military commanders would yield to the strength of the military's black labor force—but their concession was cloaked in silence and denial. A nondisclosure policy about black labor and combat achievements and heroics became a de facto secret strategy.

No press releases would herald Herculean work tasks in Alaska, Africa, Burma, France, Great Britain, Iran, New Guinea, or dozens of islands in the Pacific. From December 1941 until August 1945 black soldiers were the veritable backbone of the American military's labor needs. Neglected for more than sixty years as "noncombat service units," most black WWII veterans have gone to their graves with no public recognition, or even awareness, of their sacrifices and deeds.

AMERICA'S SECRET WEAPON

[1942]

WAR IN THE PACIFIC

On the blustery cold Friday night of January 23, 1942, eight gray troop-carrier ships slipped quietly out of New York Harbor. Because of the threat of German U-boats along the entire Atlantic seacoast, the vessels in this top-secret military maneuver were headed "somewhere in the world." The soldiers aboard were all members of combat, engineering, service, and medical battalions known as the Americal Division, one of the few army divisions known by a name rather than a number.

Equally secret was the presence of black soldiers aboard. They were among the few American units considered ready for war. Only days before, the 1,500 black soldiers—members of the 810th and 811th Engineer Aviation Battalions (EABs) unloaded and loaded ships at the Brooklyn Navy Yard. At night they bivouacked in segregated quarters aboard the SS *America,* which was being converted to a troop ship.

As aviation battalions, they were trained to build airfields in swamps, forests, and jungles, but neither cadre had much training. While white aviation battalions had had a full year or more of training with the best and newest equipment available to the military, the 810th EAB (Negro) had trained less than six months, since August 1941. With old trucks, broken tractors, and World War I–era equipment, most of which was badly in need of repair, the 810th trained in some of the most dangerous and arduous conditions in the States.

In Florida, a report of the 810th's work near Tampa Bay gained the attention of a military command badly in need of work battalions capable of transforming remote and undeveloped territories into modern airfields. Draining swamps, cutting palmetto trees and brush, the 810th cleared a snake-infested and mosquito-ridden forty-acre island, "losing track of the number of rattlesnakes they killed though they preserved the skins to make shoes and belts for their wives and sweethearts." Black historian Ulysses Lee detailed the 810th's training: "They repaired the island's long unused rain-catching equipment to provide a water supply. They acquired an old sixty-foot tug from the district engineer office, patched and painted it up, and operated it with their own crew, carrying supplies and men back and forth."

In six months the 810th built air landing facilities in North Carolina, South Carolina, Louisiana, and Georgia. On New Year's Day 1942, the 810th performed a special assignment in Georgia, constructing a runway in the red mud and steady rain of Savannah.

The 810th's buddy unit, the 811th EAB, had even less training—a mere six weeks. All of the 760 men of that battalion were relatively new to the army, arriving on December 7, 1941, at Langley Field in Virginia—where much of the 811th's instruction was interrupted by an unusually heavy snowfall. With minimal preparation, the 811th were ordered to New York City, where they arrived in January to await their next assignment.

At the Brooklyn Navy Yard, the two black battalions boarded the USAT *J. W. McAndrew*—where they bunked in quarters apart from the white soldiers for the mission—destination unknown. Because their officers, all of whom were white, credited a rumor that they were destined for a cold climate, the battalions took only their warmest clothing and embarked for overseas duty in their winter uniforms. But once they passed the ice floes in the New York bay, the temperatures climbed steadily as the convoy moved southward.

At the Panama Canal, the ships entered the locks, one after another. A steel cable attached to an electric donkey did most of the work, tow-ing the vessels through the canal. As the final huge gate opened, they saw a vast calm ocean ahead. With consistent blue skies, sunshine, and temperatures ranging from 85 to 110 degrees for the next four weeks, the men sweltered as the convoy made its way to Australia, arriving in Melbourne on February 26. The black soldiers were to be kept on board. The Australian government did not want nonwhites on its soil.

THE ALLIES CHOSE Australia as the place to organize for a counterattack, and the buildup there under General MacArthur was moving fast. The U.S. Navy was moving planes, guns, and troops in impressive numbers across the Pacific. Germany may have been the priority target according to official U.S. strategy, but in the first half of 1942 about four times as many men and twice as many ships and supplies were being sent to the Pacific as to Europe. Because the Australian government did not want black soldiers, General MacArthur was asked to make the call: would the United States support its own black troops or send them back home, as the Aussies were asking? On March 29, General MacArthur wrote to Washington with a plan to circumvent the Aussie request:

I will do everything possible to prevent friction or resentment on the part of the Australian government and people at the presence of American colored troops. Their policy of exclusion against everyone except the white race known locally as the "White Australia" plan is universally supported here. The labor situation [here] is also more acute perhaps than any place in the world. I believe however by utilizing these troops in the front zones away from great centers of population that I can minimize the difficulties involved and yet use to advantage those already dispatched. Please disabuse yourself of any idea that I might return these troops after your decision to dispatch them. You may be assured of my complete loyalty and devotion and my absolute acceptance of any decisions that you may make. I visualize completely that there are basic policies which while contrary to the immediate circumstances of a local area are absolutely necessary from the higher perspective and viewpoint. You need never have a doubt as to my fulfilling to the maximum of my ability whatever directive I may receive.

29 March 1942

General Douglas MacArthur

MacArthur's solution allowed the United States (and ultimately Australia itself) to take advantage of its full labor force, although the black battalions carried the extra weight of the agreement. Unlike white soldiers whose "rest and recuperation" were routinely at Australian ports over the next three years, R&R for black soldiers became limited to short stays or none at all. While white soldiers disembarked and went quickly to a variety of local taverns, shops, and servicemen's clubs, MacArthur's policy allowed for black soldiers to go no farther than their daily work area at the pier.

The American command also took pains to describe the black forces in Australia as specifically trained ground troops, not as combat units. Australian reporters were told the black troops were working on a multitude of construction jobs necessary to the U.S. war effort. Australian officials claimed that their policy was intended to protect white workers "from the competition of any peoples, black, brown or yellow, who might accept lower standards than the whites" would accept in a nation of strong labor unions. But when questioned by British and American reporters, Australia's war minister, Francis M. Forde, ultimately summed up the official policy of his government toward black Americans in these words:

> We look upon the Negro troops as part of the United States Army and we would not be so presumptuous as to place any bar against any form of assistance to the defense of this country. We have been assured by your generals that these men are good soldiers.

The Builders

The racial edict was not yet created when on February 27, white and black American troops walked down the ship plank to an enthusiastic welcome from the citizens of Melbourne. The Australians in general were receptive to all of the soldiers, and they greeted everyone warmly. However, most of the black soldiers were loaded aboard trains out of Melbourne the same day. As they passed through the countryside to rural camps, crowds of Australian men, women, and children gathered at rail crossings to cheer the men on—and on they went, out of town.

Detachments of the 810th and 811th that were left behind in Melbourne were kept busy on the docks, unloading ships and reloading them with ordnance supplies. When not working they were taken on cross-country marches out of Melbourne. A bus tour of the city was made available to some of the men, but they were not allowed to go off on their own.

First to New Caledonia

The first black American soldiers to arrive in Australia were also the first to leave. Their heavy construction equipment still had not arrived before the two battalions received new orders. They were heading to an island that, as with most of the places in the developing Pacific war, few Americans had ever heard of before. On March 7, the 810th and 811th boarded the USAT *Erickson* and headed for the French-controlled territory of New Caledonia, with the first contingent of American troops arriving at the harbor of Noumea on March 12.

New Caledonia lay directly across the Coral Sea from Australia, and construction of naval and air bases on the island was critical for Australia's protection. Together with a French crew, and using local equipment, four companies of the two black battalions began work immediately to construct New Caledonia's first military runway and facilities for fighter planes and bombers, while others were assigned to unload the fourteen vessels that were waiting to dock in the Noumea harbor. Both tasks were accomplished with commendations from the army brass, as the ships were unloaded and the airfield was ready in four days. On March 17 the new field received a squadron of twenty-five fighter aircraft. Still awaiting their "real equipment"—bulldozers and graders—for the next three weeks the two battalions unloaded cargo ships, often under Japanese strafing and bombing. The work of the black and white construction battalions was crucial. New Caledonia would become a staging area for major battles at the Coral Sea and Guadalcanal.

In the spring of 1942, Japan controlled the largest empire ever known in the world. Although mostly water, the new Japanese realm spanned from the Aleutian Islands in the North Pacific, encompassing almost the entire eastern edge of Asia. Its western boundary extended from the Manchurian-Soviet border through eastern China, Burma, and India, and south through Indochina, Sumatra, Java, Timor, Philippines, the Solomon Islands, and half of New Guinea.

Although Secretary Stimson and members of the Operations Division were determined to move black troops overseas, the War Department followed a policy of sending black soldiers only to countries where they would be "tolerated." Some commanders canceled their requests for additional personnel when they learned that only black units were available. But by May 1942, over 15,000 black troops were deployed abroad.

JUNGLE AIRPORTS

Airfields were critical if the Allies wanted to launch more planes than aircraft carriers could accommodate. To close in on Japan, construction battalions were assigned to frontline staging areas before combat forces arrived. Once combat was engaged, service units, including quartermasters, truck drivers, and maintenance crews, were used to expand and maintain roads, airfields, and bridges, and generally to support the army afield.

In 1942, most military airplanes could make do with turf runways. But the larger planes being developed for the war, like the B-17 and B-24, required a harder surface. Even asphalt, then a recent innovation for commercial airlines, was inadequate for planes weighted down with heavy bomb loads. A mixture of crushed rock or iron slag mixed with creosote and tar, called tarmac—a surface that was both hard enough and waterproof—was found to be best for airplane operation.

On Pacific islands, neither cement nor asphalt were plentiful, so the engineer aviation battalions began using coral. The construction crews soon learned that coral, like limestone, could be crushed and rolled, and that when wetted with either salt- or freshwater it was hard enough to use for runways. When tar was not available, innovative construction battalions used molasses to bind the surface stone—manufacturing their own from the wild sugarcane.

Engineer Aviation Battalions (EABs)

The job of the engineer aviation battalion was to literally bring the American war machine as close to Japan as possible—to clear jungles and construct runways to accommodate American P-40 fighters and B-17 bombers. But first the 810th and 811th built roads. When their machinery finally arrived at New Caledonia in April, the two battalions transported it across more than one hundred miles of mountainous terrain to Plaines des Gaiacs, on the northern side of the island.

In the process, they cleared forests and leveled the land enough to transport their heavy equipment (diesel tractors, bulldozers, carry-all scrapers, graders, gasoline shovels, rollers, mixers, air compressors, drills, trucks, trailers, asphalting and concreting equipment, rock crushers, draglines, and pumps).

Reinforcing bridges and building new ones when necessary, they moved to the northern end of New Caledonia, where the 810th was assigned to take over the airbase project at Plaines des Gaiacs. There, they

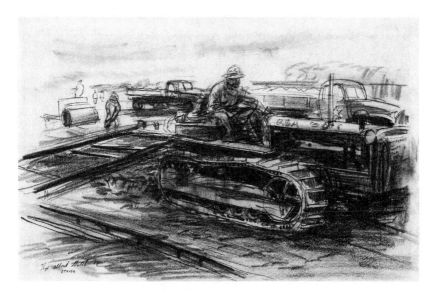

Bulldozers were the "tanks" used by white and black construction crews to build airfields, roads, and ports in the Pacific, as well as elsewhere in the global military strategy against the Axis powers. Artist: Albert Gold.

cleared a wide jungle area, draining and leveling the land into a major airfield. Once the dirt runway had been leveled, engineers laid pierced steel planking (PSP) to create an all-weather runway. It was now ready for fighter planes for the coming Battle of the Coral Sea.

The 811th moved on to Tontouta, the most important airbase on the island, and they transported crated airplanes thirty-five miles through the jungle. A friendly rivalry developed when the black regiment began working with white Seabees (as the navy's construction battalions were known) on various projects. The 811th set the island record for B-24 hangar construction. Promised one day off for every day under the existing Seabee record for constructing radio-antenna and broadcast facilities, the black crew beat the Seabees' time by thirteen days, despite heavy rains.

AUSTRALIAN SECURITY BECAME the first goal of U.S. forces in the South Pacific, and defense of Australia meant protecting the 7,000-mile island supply route and communications links between Sydney and San Francisco. Key to protecting the Aussies were the Melanesian Islands. Called the "black islands," for their habitants, they included New Caledonia, New Guinea, New Hebrides, and the Solomon Islands (Guadalcanal).

The 810th astounded army brass, and Secretary of War Stimson in particular. The American success at the Battle of the Coral Sea hinged significantly on their work. They kept the work going twenty-four hours a day, moving equipment inland and then constructing an airfield and airdrome for the army and navy aircraft. Stimson commended the 810th for performing "exceptionally meritorious" service in New Caledonia.

Finishing the airfield projects at Plaines des Gaiacs, the black engineers then unloaded gasoline from a supply ship that had anchored offshore. They transported the fuel ashore in rafts and moved it rapidly to the airdrome, just in time to service aircraft in the Coral Sea engagement.

In July, the all-black 91st Engineers arrived with the 808th Engineer Aviation Battalion, a white unit. Along with the 810th, the units com-

Off-duty in Noumea, New Caledonia. Black and white construction battalions built airfields, roads, and docks in New Caledonia in preparation for the Battle of the Coral Sea in May 1942. Artist: Aaron Bohrod.

pleted construction of an airport, surfaced with iron ore transported by trucks from an ore pit seven miles away. After completion they received orders to enlarge the runway to accommodate B-17s. The field was finished on time, and on August 1 a squadron of B-17s landed at Koumac. The next morning they took off to bomb targets in the Solomon Islands.

BLACK SOLDIERS DOWN UNDER

Lt. Hyman Samuelson, who was assigned to the 96th Engineer Battalion since training camp in 1941, swore by the talents and abilities of his men. A Jewish officer from New Orleans, he kept a diary about his personal life and everyday experiences with the 96th Engineers. So, too, did Lt. Roy Weaver, a white Texas officer with the 585th Dump Truck Company. The black engineers and two black dump-truck companies had trained at Camp Claiborne (Louisiana), then traveled to New York City to board ships to an unknown destination.

Shipping the trucks and heavy construction equipment in separate vessels, the soldiers packed ammunition, rifles, canvas cots, mosquito nets, tents, and field kitchens aboard the troop ships. The 585th boarded the *Santa Lucia,* a large converted luxury liner, while the 96th and the 576th Dump Truck Company traveled on the smaller *Santa Clara.* For part of the voyage the comfortable officers' cabins were no relief from the rough Atlantic waves, recalled Lieutenant Weaver, as the crowded ship and its odors and unpleasant saltwater showers made for a miserable journey for everyone. It was even worse for his men:

> My 585th Engineer Company was assigned to the forward hold on the lowest deck ("E" Deck). It was the worst place on the ship, with no portholes, because it was at or below the waterline, and it was right in the bows of the ship so it rose and fell like a runaway elevator with each wave the ship encountered. Most of the men got very seasick as soon as we left the dock and encountered the swells of the Atlantic.

Passing through the Panama Canal and entering the calmer Pacific waters made for a more relaxed journey. All the men on board did daily cleanup chores of their living quarters and toilets, then played cards, read, or talked among themselves. As the trip concluded and the convoy approached Brisbane, Lieutenant Samuelson stood on deck with 1,500 members of the 96th Engineers and the 576th Truck Company. In his diary entry for April 6, 1942, he wrote about the battalion's dismay upon learning that after a 12,000-mile journey in the service of their country, they were not allowed to leave their ship:

> Brisbane looked pretty from the boat. We crowded the rail. Our equipment and clothing were all assembled, and we were ready to debark. At last we were at journey's end. There was no telling what lay ahead, but that didn't matter. Then came a message. The 96th and 576th were not to get off the boat! It had been a terrific anticlimax, and morale fell through the floor. Men had to carry their clothing and equipment back to their quarters; everyone had to return to the life which he endured for five weeks and had hoped to be leaving.

Bishop John Andrew Gregg of the African Methodist Episcopal Church in the United States visits a military base in Australia. Bishop Gregg fondles a pet koala bear owned by one of the surrounding soldiers of the 630th Ordnance Company. Black soldiers first arrived in Australia in February 1942.

"Now it seems a wonder to me that we were able to keep control," said Lieutenant Weaver. "That was a bitter disappointment. We were tired of the ship. . . . On the one hand we were regarded as saviors from the Japanese, and on the other hand as a menace to their society."

On April 8, the 96th Engineers were sent to Townsville, 800 miles up the Australian coast, with no equipment. Two days later the 91st Engineers boarded four trains, with no equipment, arriving in Townsville on April 11, 1942. The 91st Engineers relocated to a railway siding called Woodstock about thirty miles south of Townsville, where they were assigned with the all-white 46th Engineers to build landing strips for fighter aircraft at Woodstock and Giru—using nothing more than hand tools.

On April 16, white and black soldiers brawled outside of a dance hall in Townsville. "Over a hundred of our men had been rounded up by white soldiers armed with bayonets and loaded guns," reported Lieu-

Capt. Charles H. Dubra introduces Bishop John A. Gregg (seated in silhouette), who is about to address a gathering of African-American troops in Port Moresby, New Guinea.

tenant Samuelson in his war diary. "A corporal thrust a cocked rifle at me when I stopped his truck and gave instructions to his negro 'prisoners' on the back of it."

He later wrote: "It is a dirty shame the way the white American soldiers treat our boys. The Australians are wonderfully tolerant, but the Americans, especially the Southern boys, are a problem. The only solution will be to send our battalion away from any town."

Clarence Toomer, who enlisted in 1942 and served in a quartermaster unit in Australia agreed with Samuelson's take on the locals:

> You hear all kinds of stories about Australians not liking blacks, but the citizens were cordial. They received us with open arms. The people in Melbourne had Sunday teas in their homes and churches and would invite the black troops, and we went. They also had skating rinks in the city, but the white Americans identified a recreation area for black troops only. The American government, the American military did that—not the Australians.

AUSSIE BASEBALL: THE MACARTHUR CUP

Yelling loudly to the crowd of some 6,000 people on Sunday, April 26, 1942, before the start of the first-ever baseball game between an Australian team and a squad of black American GIs, the stadium announcer apologized that Sunday regulations prevented him from using the public-address system to describe the games. Playing any organized sports on Sunday was, in ordinary times, against national law, but now a war accommodation was made to help boost morale. The league's willingness to include the U.S.A. Services, a black team, was popular among Australian fans. Leave was arranged on weekends for the U.S.A. Services, with its roster that included several semipro and former Negro League players, to play in the Australian league.

They won their first game over the Aussies, 7 to 2, and one local newspaper reported the U.S.A. Services team had played the game like the Australians had never seen before: "The barrage of verbiage, shouts of encouragement to each other, and trick tossing of the ball among the infielders whenever an opposing player is declared 'out' provide the scintillating interludes that the crowd enjoys."

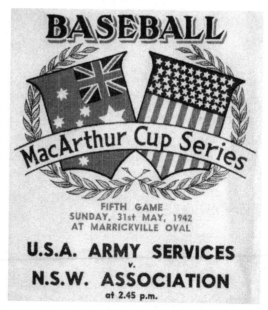

Black soldiers win MacArthur Cup, May 1942: Sports contests were often the first time black and white soldiers faced one another in equal competition.

The crowd especially enjoyed one player who dropped to his knees, palms together, praying to the umpire for mercy in the batter's box. A week later the Services team had qualified for the country's biggest baseball series—called the MacArthur Cup, named for the American general.

Nicknamed the "Wildcats," the black soldiers played every Sunday in May, sometimes to crowds of more than 10,000, winning the best-of-seven MacArthur Cup series four games to one. Behind the pitching of ace left-hander Richard Cureton, the Wildcats won the decisive fifth game, 3 to 1, on May 31. Sadly, before they could bask in the honor and glory of receiving the winning cup from General MacArthur the following Sunday, the team's players were transferred to the war front in New Guinea.

WAR IN THE Pacific was unlike the fighting in Europe. The European war was typified by huge ground forces driving overland into the heart of the enemy's country. The Pacific war was based on a strategy of island-hopping campaigns, naval and air confrontations, and amphibious landings on hundreds of beaches. The Pacific war required an enormous engineering effort to bring the war closer and closer to Japan. General MacArthur referred to the leapfrogging war in the Pacific as the "engineer's war."

To most military historians, the Pacific war was even more brutal and deadly than the war in Europe. Japanese defenders always dug in and fought to the death, dedicating their lives to their country's cause in ways hitherto unknown to Americans. Suicide assaults—the kamikazes, or human bombs—were a new way of fighting war, and the Japanese almost never surrendered.

FIRST TO NEW GUINEA

MacArthur's aim was to deploy the 96th and 576th to Port Moresby, on the southeastern coast of New Guinea, 700 miles from Australia. On Tuesday, April 28, the 96th Engineers became the first American troop unit in New Guinea. With Japanese forces at Lae and Salamaua, on the northern coast of New Guinea, the black engineers were sent to the southern coast to establish airfield bases. In the evening Japanese planes strafed the camp, making the battalion the first American unit to come under fire in New Guinea.

Port Moresby was now becoming a buildup area for the fighting to come in New Guinea. The goal of the 96th was crucial: to build airbases to receive supplies from Australia. New airfields were needed to make Port Moresby a base to support operations elsewhere in New Guinea. To improve the port, which could handle only one ship at a time, the 96th built a causeway from the harbor to Tatana Island, six miles away. On Tatana the 96th built docks capable of handling six, and later nine, ships at a time.

Most of the black soldiers stationed in New Guinea were surprised at how much "the people here looked so much like us," in the words of Cpl. J. T. Judson, a truck driver from Mississippi. Even the sugarcane that grew wild across the country reminded him of home. But the wildlife—fish, animals, birds, rodents, snakes, and insects—was of a far different order. The mosquitoes, especially the malarial mosquitoes in the Pacific region and Asia, were troublesome. At times 25 percent of the regiment would be hospitalized or receiving outpatient treatment for malaria. In islands such as Espiritu, black maintenance units sprayed DDT in an attempt to control the malaria problem.

New Guinea was settled by Asians more than 50,000 years ago; likely followed by African travelers and, more recently, Portuguese and Dutch ships carrying consignments of enslaved Africans and Asians. In 1527 a Portuguese explorer named the island Ilhas do Papuas (Island of the Wooly Hairs). A Spanish explorer later called it Nueva Guinea (New Guinea) because he thought the people similar to those of Guinea in Africa. From 1920, New Guinea was held by Australia as a mandate, or protected colony—with more than 40,000 natives laboring as indentured servants for Australian and other foreign businesses.

Many New Guineans welcomed the Japanese takeover in

the northern region of the island nation, as Japanese leaflets proclaimed "Asia for Asians" and instigated distrust of whites. Even those who remained loyal to the Australians were not allowed to enlist because of the Australian requirements that enlistees be "substantially of European origin." Still, many natives volunteered as laborers, mess orderlies, cooks, and stewards. An Australian officer stationed in New Guinea reported on the valuable assistance of the New Guineans in the war effort:

> There is little doubt that, in the years to come, school children in various parts of the world will read in their history books accounts of the great deeds performed by the Papuan natives in this War. It is really a little beyond the author to place on paper his real thoughts regarding the amazing work done by these dark-skinned people.
>
> *C.G. Bowman, 1942*

WAR LETTERS

The army's policy to withhold information about black service battalions was, ironically, somewhat compatible with editorials in African-American newspapers, which demanded that black soldiers be used in combat. In effect, the black papers were also keeping silent about noncombat troops. Concerned that either attitude might ultimately diminish the rightful place of all black soldiers in the history or the war, the Schomburg Center's Lawrence Reddick started a "War Letters" campaign. Convinced that more heroics of African Americans like Dorie Miller and Robert Brooks might be kept silent by the War Department, Reddick initiated a campaign to gather information about the experiences of blacks in the military from the black population itself—in the form of letters either to or from the soldiers themselves.

> The trip over was quite interesting, having crossed the equator, the international date line, also lost a day. We are now on the northern coast

of New Guinea on a high hill over looking the sea. It is now winter here, but is hot and rains all of the time. The mud is awful. The jungles are dense and spooky looking. Cocoa nut trees are plentiful. The natives are very primitive in their dress and customs. Some are very intelligent. This base was held by the Japs a few months ago. There is plenty of evidence of the Japs being here. Write soon.

Sgt. J. L. Hawkins
395th AAA
New Guinea

Letters like this were collected as part of a letter-writing campaign at Prairie View College in Texas. In 1946 the college forwarded the correspondence to the Schomburg Center. Letters like the following from Chaplain Charles H. Dubra were sent to Reddick soon after the war:

In April, 1942 my unit, 96th Engineer General Service Regiment, was ordered to New Guinea. We were the first American troops to land there [Port Moresby]. As its chaplain, I was the first American chaplain there. One of my first tasks was that of providing for the burial of any and all casualties. At that time the only setup the U.S. had that far north was our unit. I won the commendation of the Graves Registration Service for that work, as not a single soldier was buried "Unknown," and every grave was in order. . . .

Here is my story: In April, 1942 my unit , 96th Engineer General Service Regiment, was ordered to New Guinea. We were the first american troops to land there (Port Moresby). As its chaplain, I was the first american chaplain there. One of my first task was that of providing for the burial of any and all causalties. At that time the only setup the U.S. had that far north was our unit. I won the commendation of the graves Registration Service for that work, as not a single soldier was buried "Unknown", and every grave was in order. The next problem was that of recreation. During these days there was not much time, but then they came and something had to be done about it. As we were short of line officers the task fell to me. We set up concert parties, using the talent of the soldiers in the area. Through the Red Cross we were able to get some old picture films and put on the first movie in that area. We got soap, toothpaste, and other amenities through the Australia Comfort Fund as the Red Cross had not yet reached us. This was secured by me for all american troops.

My real task was spiritual. Being the only american chaplain in the forward area for a short while, it was my job

Letter from Chaplain Charles H. Dubra to Lawrence Reddick, February 10, 1946.

My real task was spiritual. Being the only American chaplain in the forward area for a short while, it was my job to provide for the spiritual welfare of our troops. I did it by conducting religious services for all units, sometimes holding ten to twelve services a week, in addition to visiting the hospital and counseling, comforting, and performing the burial rights at the cemetery; visiting the stockade to counsel with the men therein, also holding religious services for them. . . . This work was carried on in behalf of both white and colored troops. I even held many services for Australian troops in isolated spots. In October Chaplain T.R. Firerson was sent to New Guinea with his unit and he shared the work with me. In the meantime, white chaplains were coming with units or to be assigned to units. I was affectionately called the "bishop of New Guinea." As our forces moved forward elements of my unit was sent also. This caused it to be scattered over a wide area. Col. George T. Derby, regimental commander, ordered me to visit every group. I took to the air, traveling more than 13,000 miles by that method. Boat travel not counted. Wherever I went my services were given to all units without the services of a chaplain, both white and colored. In several instances I was asked by commanding officers of white troops to serve their troops. Many times I would bring back large sums of money from these forward groups to be sent to the States. . . . It amounted to something like $100,000.

When leaves were first given, I was sent to Australia to look into the facilities for and treatment of colored troops. The facilities were nil and the treatment was one not to be mentioned. I spent about three weeks in Brisbane working on the problem, and was instrumental in getting set up the George W. Carver Club in Brisbane, it was the finest club for the enlisted personnel in Australia, and the improvement of the Booker Washington Club in Sydney. My work was also responsible for Sydney being added as a leave center. The War Correspondents referred to me as a "one man NAACP."

I faced danger on many occasions, but there was nothing heroic about any of it. I was not required to go into the front lines or in any place of danger. But I could not serve my men in some place of safety when they were up there facing all hell and death. Wherever my men were there I was. I was strafed by a Japanese fighter plane, had my slit-trench crushed in by bombs, while in it, dodged machine gun fire and mortar fire and had a plane in which I was traveling attacked by Japanese fighter planes. . . .

I sincerely hope that you will be able to tell the whole story of the Negro as a soldier. He has wrought well in spite of the fact that most of the time he was wondering why he was fighting and what for. I wish that you could get the story of the 96th. It is a saga of valor, courage, heroism, and hard work. One phase of the fight against tyranny is over, but there remains yet, the second part. With the same courage, fortitude, determination, and faith I now turn my face to the task remaining.

Charles H. Dubra, Roxbury, Mass., February 10, 1946

After the war, upon obtaining his master's degree from Boston University, Charles Dubra attempted to become the first black student at the University of Mississippi School of Law in 1953 but was denied admission. Dubra was followed by Medgar Evers, who was denied admission at Old Miss in 1958.

ALASKA TO
GUADALCANAL
[1942]

"We e were totally surprised to find ourselves in Alaska, that's for sure," said an Alabama soldier who discovered a vast new and different region of the world in his first war assignment. The wilderness terrain and climate were nothing like "down home," though there were some similarities. Salmon could be just as tasty as catfish—and easier to catch—and snow as pretty as cotton, "but cotton never froze anybody's fingers," said Sgt. William E. Griggs, regiment photographer of the 97th Engineers.

Both Hawaii and Alaska—the two territories that would become the forty-ninth and fiftieth states some years after the war—were found to be extremely vulnerable to Japanese invasion. Closer to Japan than Pearl Harbor, Alaska had long been a concern of the United States. An overland link between Alaska and the lower forty-eight states had been studied as early as 1930 under President Herbert Hoover. Most problematic was the rugged, largely dirt, road that weaved its way over mountains, swamps, and tundra for nearly 2,000 miles. A one-week run from Seattle to Fairbanks was quick time for a mail or supply truck, and any plan for a convoy of military supplies was unthinkable. Yet not until the bombing of Pearl Harbor was the construction of a trans-Canadian

Chow line in Alaska: more than one-third of the 10,500 soldiers who built the Alcan Highway were African American. Artist: Joe Jones.

highway deemed a military necessity. FDR wanted to cut the time drastically, from seven days to one.

In February 1942, FDR ordered construction of a highway from Washington State to the Alaskan territory. Over 1,600 miles long and with a completion time of less than one year, the project was an engineering nightmare. But to block the threat of a Japanese attack from the northwest, Alaska needed fortification and a communications link with the United States. In April 1942 over 10,500 soldiers began arriving by ship in Alaska and Canada, and more than one-third of them were African American.

As in Australia and Panama, Alaska governor Ernest Gruening had asked to receive no black soldiers and was overruled. Construction of the highway began on March 8, 1942, and ended eight months and twelve days later, on October 25, 1942.

The soldiers' bulldozers plowed snow and earth, toppled trees, and shaped hundreds of miles of Alaskan wilderness. Following the ancient trails of Native Americans and caribou, the engineers carved a two-lane highway through rugged mountains, valleys, swamps, and permafrost. Most of their tools and clothing were of World War I vintage. "They gave us the worst equipment but expected us to do the best job," said Griggs. Swarms of mosquitoes tormented the workers in the summer, replaced in the fall by gnats "a thousand per square foot." In the winter, the troops had to contend with snow and freezing temperatures. "We had to wrap mosquito nets around the old helmets just to be able to work," recalled Griggs.

The deployment of black troops to Alaska angered many military leaders, including Gen. Simon Bolivar Buckner, the U.S. Army commander in Alaska. In a letter to his superior, Brig. Gen. C. L. Sturdevant, Buckner, the white-supremacist son of a Confederate general, wrote: "I have no objection whatever to your employing them on roads if they are kept far enough from the settlements and kept busy and then sent home as soon as possible." Buckner's chief concern was to keep black troops out of the towns and cities and prevent them from settling in Alaska "after the war, with the natural result that they would interbreed with the Indians and Eskimos and produce an astonishingly objectionable race of mongrels which would be a problem here from now on."

From Dawson Creek, British Columbia, to Fairbanks, Alaska, three of the seven engineer regiments building the road through the northern wilderness were African American. In April the 97th Engineer Battalion and 93rd General Service Regiment were the first black units to arrive. In June the all-black 95th Engineer Battalion joined the effort. The 95th followed the white 341st Engineer Battalion, grading and pouring concrete road-fill. The 95th Engineer Battalion pushed through glacier and rugged terrain for more than 500 miles.

From the south, the white 341st Engineers worked to meet the 97th Engineers south of the Alaska-Canada border. When the bulldozers of lead drivers finally broke through to close the last gap in the road on October 25, 1942, the meeting between white and black soldiers symbolized to a hopeful country the kind of unity and cooperation that foretold eventual victory. For months to come, public speakers and radio programs made much of its potential significance.

After finishing the "Pioneer Road," as it was initially called, the black regiments stayed in the region for more than a year, maintaining and expanding the highway. The 97th worked on roads and operated terminals for trucks on the "Fairbanks Freight," a truck supply line that ran along the highway. One company worked "glacier control," hacking creeping glaciers off the highway by hand or building bypass roads around them when they encroached too far. All three regiments later served in other regions: the 95th in Europe, and the 97th and 93rd in the Pacific.

Road construction teams were followed by the Army Signal Corps, which next began work on an aerial version of the Alcan Highway. White and black corpsmen, including men of the 255th and 258th Signal Construction Company, installed communications facilities and strung radio and telephone lines. The army's weekly publication *Yank* cited the new 2,000-mile-long radio-telephone line, which helped link Washington, D.C., to Alaska, as the longest communication system of its type in the world.

THE 24TH INFANTRY REGIMENT

On May 1, 1942, the troop ship carrying the all-black 24th Infantry Regiment entered the waters of New Hebrides. From miles out at sea, the bright red glow of the Yasur volcano produced a false dawn for ships approaching at night. They passed Pentecost Island, where, in an annual ritual, men and boys leaped head-first from ninety-foot towers, a long liana vine tethered to their ankles to stop them just before hitting the ground. The 24th Infantry Regiment became the first all-black combat unit to face the Japanese when it disembarked at Efate on May 4, just in time to provide backup ground support for the Battle of the Coral Sea. Arriving on Efate, the regiment became part of the island's perimeter defense. But mostly the regiment performed labor duties, including loading and unloading ships, guarding airbases, building roads, and spraying and draining, as part of mosquito control.

> I was inducted in Service January 30, 1941. I served in the states at Fort Benning, GA until April 13th, 1942, On the above date we sailed [to] New Hebrides, after 21 days on sea, we landed on 4th May 1942. This was the same day Coral Sea battle started. On 18th May my battalion moved to the north side of this island. . . .
>
> Here on this island we ran 600 miles of telephone and telegraph wire to be laid through the jungles to near by islands. With many opinions that [this task] was impossible, I said it could be done. With a group of 18 men we started out without transportation and food. Wire was dropped by airplanes, we then worked all most 24 hours per day. . . .

This was how I was awarded the Legion of Merit for outstanding couregeous duties.

Official Citation for Dennis Holt

Staff Sergeant. Infantry, United States Army, for exceptionally meritorious conduct in the performance of services of a considerable degree of merit, as chief of a battalion wire section from May 4, 1942, to April 20, 1943, at a base in the south Pacific Area. His leadership, skill, cheerfulness and devotion to duty in the installation, maintenance, and operation of a wire net in many respects comparable to that of a division, assured continuous communications. Without transportation, he led his men in cutting wire up to a mountain top observation post and in crossing several miles of water to nearby islands, in all kinds of weather. After an operation for hernia, brought about by strenuous work, he was assigned to light duty, but disregarding his own personal welfare, he continued his work with unfailing spirit and devotion, and caused the reopening of his surgical wound. Home address: 3600 Douglas Road, Birmingham, Alabama.

AMERICAN GODS

"To the people of our islands, black American soldiers were gods," said Chief Kissak of Vanuatu (formerly known as New Hebrides), who lived near an encampment of the 24th Infantry in 1942. "Some of our people actually worshipped black soldiers as deities. We believed they had come to deliver us from the European devils who had ruled us for four centuries."

Controlled and governed jointly by the British and French in a colonial mix known as a "condominium," the natives regarded the relative power exercised by black Americans who drove vehicles and ate meals with whites—two practices forbidden to the natives themselves—as a sign that great changes were coming to them, both spiritually and physically. American officers were quick to squelch local rumors that black American troops were anything other than normal men. White and black Americans were unaware of a religious group (known to anthropologists as the John Frum Cult) in which thousands of islanders believed that one day a great black man named John Frum would come to liberate the islands from French and British control. Seeing the Americans, especially the black American soldiers, arriving in ships, and with so much material wealth, bolstered the local belief that a black man with an army of black soldiers was coming from America to lead them to independence. "When we saw the black soldiers, we knew that our savior was John Frum."

Islanders dressed like American soldiers, carried wooden guns, and built their own "landing strips" for John Frum's plane. Bamboo sheds were constructed to hold the cargo he was expected to bring. Believing "if you build it, he will come" they strung rope between trees and used tin cans as "earphones" through which they hoped to hear messages from John Frum. Although American commanders were, for the most part, indulgent of this peculiar religion, British troops frequently arrested John Frum priests and followers. In December 1943 an uprising inspired by John Frum believers was put down by British and American military

Baseball in the New Hebrides: soldiers play baseball or relax during off-time in the Pacific islands. Labor performed by white and black American soldiers in the New Hebrides aided in the Battles of the Coral Sea and Guadalcanal in 1942. Artist: Aaron Bohrod.

forces on Tanna. By the 1950s, in an attempt to attract tourists, island officials downplayed the black savior notion in favor of fabricated expectations of a white messiah. This was bolstered by worldwide interest in the South Pacific (largely due to the popularity of *South Pacific,* the stage musical and, later, movie based on James Michener's *Tales of the South Pacific*).

Many Pacific island natives shared more than a kinship of skin color with black Americans. Ironically, the American Civil War, which marked the emancipation of four million enslaved African Americans, marked the enslavement, indenture, or forced emigration of more than one million Pacific islanders and Asians. The destruction of American cotton and sugar production during the Civil War prompted international investors to establish plantocracies on many islands and to use islanders as cheap or slave labor. Indentured Indian and Chinese workers were exported to the Americas, Africa, and the Pacific islands. Slave traders raided every known island chain from the western to the central Pacific, and the captives were sold to foreign plantations. From 1862 to 1865 Peruvian slave traders captured several thousand islanders, boarding them on "labor ships" to South America.

"People have waited nearly two thousand years for Christ to return, so we can wait a while longer for John," a mission-educated village chief declared. According to Chief Kissak, simply listening to black soldiers speaking day after day, and singing joyously at Sunday church services "week after week," from April 1942 until December 1945, left many people with a powerful and lasting impression. "We knew these cousins of the Vanuatu were very special, like us. We are special."

REMINISCENT OF DORIE Miller at Pearl Harbor, another unlikely hero emerged at the Battle of the Coral Sea. On May 8, 1942, Elvin

JUNE 1942 The U.S. Navy began accepting black draftees for the first time. About 167,000 blacks served in the navy in WWII, and 12,500 African Americans served in the Seabees, as the navy's construction battalions were known.

World-famous singer Paul Robeson leads workers at the Moore Shipyard in Oakland, California, in singing "The Star-Spangled Banner" in September 1942. "We have to be together," said Robeson, who served as a shipyard worker in World War I.

Bell, a mess attendant, voluntarily joined a repair crew fighting blazing fires aboard the USS *Lexington*. "Bell," according to his official citation, "although emerging in exhausted condition unhesitatingly entered the most dangerous section of the stricken carrier and assisted in removing injured personnel who had been trapped belowdecks. His courageous initiative and utter disregard for his own safety were in keeping with the highest traditions of the United States naval service." For his heroic action, Elvin Bell received the Navy and Marine Corps Medal.

BATTLE OF GUADALCANAL

In July 1942 the Japanese were discovered building an airbase on Guadalcanal, a small island in the Solomon Island chain, close enough to put land-based Japanese bombers within striking distance of Australia and the Allied bases in New Guinea. On August 7, exactly eight months after Pearl Harbor, the U.S. Marines attacked Guadalcanal, quickly gaining control of the unfinished airstrip, which they renamed Henderson Field. For the next six months, the Japanese kept hammering away at the island.

Ninety miles long (on a northwest-southeast axis) and an average of twenty-five miles wide, Guadalcanal presented forbidding terrain of mountains and dormant volcanoes up to 8,000 feet high, steep ravines and deep streams, and a generally even coastline with no natural harbors.

As the army's black construction crews helped pave the way in the early Pacific battles against the enemy, so, too, did the African-American crewmen aboard the navy ships. Like Dorie Miller, many were messmen and laundry workers, who distinguished themselves as heroes in the summer and fall of 1942.

Commendation

September 5, 1942
Charles Jackson French
Mess Attendant Second Class, U.S. Navy

[A resident of Foreman, Arkansas, French was commended by Admiral William F. Halsey, U.S. Navy, Commander South Pacific Area and South Pacific Force, for heroism, while serving on a destroyer in the Pacific area. His commendation reads:] *For meritorious conduct in action while serving on board a destroyer transport which was badly damaged during the engagement with Japanese forces in the British Solomon Islands on September 5, 1942. After the engagement, a group of about fifteen men were adrift on a raft which was being deliberately shelled by Japanese naval forces. French tied a line to himself and swam for more than two hours without rest, thus attempting to tow the raft. His conduct was in keeping with the highest traditions of the naval service.*

Commendation

October 26, 1942
William Cook Pinckney
Cook Third Class, USS Enterprise, U.S. Navy

[The son of Mr. and Mrs. Renty Pinckney of Beaufort, South Carolina, he was awarded the Navy Cross for outstanding heroism. His commendation reads:] *For extraordinary heroism while serving aboard the USS* Enterprise *during the engagement with enemy Japanese naval forces near Santa Cruz islands on October 26, 1942. When a heavy bomb exploded in the vicinity Pinckney, standing at his battle station in the ammunition handling room, was knocked unconscious. With several compartments completely wrecked and four of five companions killed, Pinckney regaining consciousness groped his way through the burning and tangled wreckage to a point under an open hangar deck hatch. When the man fell unconscious, either from his wounds or from smoke and fumes, Pinckney, unmindful of his own danger, lifted his comrade through the hatch to safety before he himself battled his way out of the burning and smoke-filled compartment. By his dauntless courage in saving his comrade's life at great risk to his own, Pinckney upheld the highest traditions of the United States Naval service.*

Commendation

November 12 and 13, 1942
Leonard Roy Harmon
Mess Attendant First Class, U.S. Navy

[A resident of Texas, he distinguished himself when he rendered valuable assistance to wounded personnel during a combat opera-

Navy recruitment poster honoring heroic seaman Leonard Roy Harmon, who was killed during a naval battle in the Pacific in November 1942.

tion. He was awarded the Navy Cross posthumously. On June 8, 1943, Frank Knox, Secretary of the Navy, asked Mrs. N. Harmon Carroll of Cuero, Texas, to sponsor the destroyer escort USS *Harmon,* which was launched July 10, 1943, and was named in honor of Mrs. Carroll's son, the late Leonard Roy Harmon. Citation of Harmon's Navy Cross reads:] *For extraordinary heroism while serving aboard the USS* San Francisco *during action against enemy Japanese forces in the Solomon Islands area on November 12 and 13, 1942, with persistent disregard for his own personal safety, Harmon rendered invaluable assistance in caring for the wounded and evacuating them to a dressing station. In addition to displaying unusual loyalty in behalf of the injured executive officer, he deliberately exposed himself to hostile gunfire in order to protect a shipmate and as a result of this courageous deed, he was killed.*

A sergeant directs soldiers unloading war materials at Guadalcanal in 1943. General service, ordnance, and quartermaster battalions were essential to the buildup of military supplies in the Pacific. Artist: Aaron Bohrod.

. . . About my soldiers medal. Well the best I can remember. Here it is. I had some papers on this. But threw a mistake burnt them up. So I have forgotten the date. But I believe it was in Aug, or, Oct, but any way late and afternoon about 6 o'clock. I was lying in bed. Listing to the sound of that motor. Not that it was the motor. That made me wandering it was, what was going to happen that man life. What I was to try to save. And didn't no what it was. But when the plane struck the earth that was it. I was on my feet. I didn't take time to fully dress before I was out there fighting to save the life of this white man. Not the man that made me fight. It was his life. And neither was it his color. I feel everybody wants to live if some one can help them save their life in danger an I felt as tho I was doing a part of my duty towards my fellow man. An that goes with me with any body I don't care who they are. I don't hate no body. Because I hate the word hate, I wasn't looking for a medal or nothing else. Because there is not a medal that mean what a man's life do to him. Noing I have one myself. I may fall ill any where an need help. So it matters not who it's from that is my fealing towrds human being. An I pray that the world all people see it that way then we will have an America of love and friendship between all people . . . an not discrimination.

Pfc. Frank Earl, Mobile Alabama

In late summer or fall 1942, Pfc. Frank Earl, an army ordnance supply worker, saved the life of a pilot whose plane malfunctioned and crashed shortly after takeoff from Port Moresby, New Guinea. For pulling the pilot to safety from his burning plane, Pfc. Earl received a Bronze Star.

JUNE 1, 1942 The U.S. Marine Corps began admitting African-American recruits. Of the nearly 20,000 blacks who trained at the segregated facility near Camp Lejeune, North Carolina, about 13,000 served overseas, primarily in defense battalions and combat support companies or as stewards.

The Atlantic War

[1942]

The U.S. Navy fought hard to limit both the presence of and the opportunities for African Americans within its ranks, but the U.S. Coast Guard made progress toward achieving integration in 1942. Since 1922, a Coast Guard policy specified that new black enlisted men could advance no higher than the rank of steward. In March 1942 black recruits were made eligible for a wider range of duties, including navigation, engineering, and patrol. Alex Haley, who signed on as a steward in 1939, advanced to duty as a writer for the Coast Guard's public relations office. New recruit Jacob Lawrence, an artist from Harlem, obtained the rating of Public Relations (PR) PO3/c and was assigned the painting of documentary works of Coast Guard life during the war. Other recruits served on lighthouse duty or on horse and dog patrols as lookouts for enemy infiltration along the Atlantic Coast.

THE CARIBBEAN

In July 1940, President Roosevelt bargained with British prime minister Churchill for the right to establish American naval and air bases in seven British possessions in the Western Hemisphere. In exchange for fifty

Mounted soldiers of a Coast Guard Horse Patrol unit patrols beaches along the New Jersey shore.

naval destroyers, the U.S. gained ninety-nine-year leases on new bases in British Guiana, the Bahamas, Bermuda, Jamaica, St. Lucia, Trinidad, and Newfoundland.

More than 7,500 black soldiers were deployed to Central and South America and the Caribbean, where they constructed airfields, barracks, and docks and transported, loaded, and unloaded fuel, supplies, and ordnance (ammunition). Bermuda, a British island territory 600 miles east of the Carolinas, served as the anchor of the United States' Atlantic defenses. To increase the size and capability of air and naval bases private contractors and army engineers dredged 29 million cubic yards of coral, filling in Castle Harbor to create Kindley Field.

In the Arctic—despite local government requests for white troops only in Greenland and Iceland—Gen. George Marshall authorized deployment of black service units. Bases in the North Atlantic protected shipping lanes, and in Greenland, white and black service units built a 6,500-foot concrete runway and a 5,000-foot asphalt strip over the frozen terrain. In Iceland about two hundred black soldiers worked on air-base and hangar construction in the cold weather and rocky terrain of Keflavik. In Reykjavik, air bases were constructed, as well as housing and hospital facilities for the more than 30,000 troops who arrived by December 1942. With bases in Canada, Greenland, and Iceland, planes could fly from Maine to Scotland with no leg of the trip longer than 850 miles. In this way, American bombers and fighter planes manufactured as far west as Seattle were able to "hopscotch" across the United States and the Atlantic. More than 10,000 planes crossed the North Atlantic to Europe in this fashion by 1944.

AFRICA: GETTING SUPPLIES TO THE FRONT LINE

German U-boats and submarines had taken control of the central Atlantic Ocean corridor, making shipping to Europe and the Mediterranean extremely hazardous. Transport across the North Atlantic was easier, but it was little help in getting materials and manpower to North Africa, where Great Britain and Germany were battling in the desert. The route to Africa went through Brazil, which, being less than 1,600 miles from West Africa, allowed for some nonstop flights, but only the best military planes could make the flight from Brazil to Africa.

ASCENSION ISLAND

In March 1942, about 200 African-American soldiers in service units accompanied the 38th Engineer General Service Regiment to Ascension Island, a tiny outcropping midway between the Brazilian bulge and Accra in the Gold Coast territory (now Ghana). A craggy peak rising 10,000 feet from the ocean floor, the island was nearly solid volcanic rock. Unloading supplies, machinery, and construction materials from their three freighters was a tough assignment, as a projecting shelf of volcanic rock prevented the vessels from making a close approach to shore.

Supplies were unloaded by barge, but the job was made nearly impossible by continuous rough waves. Construction work got under way in late April, and less than three months later, on July 10, a 6,000-foot runway was ready for traffic. In the meantime, the task force also constructed roads, barracks, a hospital, underground gasoline storage tanks, a seawater distillation unit, an electrical plant, gun emplacements, and ammunition dumps, all carefully camouflaged.

The strip at Wideawake Airfield was more tunnel than runway, as it was blasted and carved from the rock. Along the sides of the narrow landing strip were vertical rock walls, which in some places rose six to ten feet high. Named for an island bird, Wideawake became known to pilots as one of the scariest runways in the war. Pilots and soldiers aboard Ascension-bound planes joked, "If you miss Ascension, your wife gets a pension."

A large tern rookery at the end of the runway offered a serious threat to air traffic at Ascension Island, as takeoffs commonly flushed flocks of birds into the flight path. A smoke generator, dynamite blasts, and a planeload of unlucky cats were among the futile efforts to encourage the terns to relocate. The island's strong-beaked booby birds found the cats an appetizing treat.

"Well, the birds started eating the cats, so that was a dumb idea," said Cpl. Joseph Delgado. Only the destruction of some 40,000 eggs, at an ornithologist's suggestion, induced the birds to leave the runway area. (Green sea turtles, born on Ascension Island, swim as hatchlings more than 1,000 kilometers to Brazil, then return to Ascension as adults to mate and continue the cycle.)

Though G-2, a War Department troop deployment committee, had tried to keep black soldiers out of Wideawake, an estimated 500 of the 4,000 troops were African American. "I really do not know why they wouldn't recommend black soldiers," said Delgado. "They did a good job like everybody else. And there were really no women to fight over, which is probably why everybody got along. For the most part, we all suffered equally.

"Everything moved through Wideawake," he recalled. "Boats, planes, submarines, ammunition, supplies, and casualties going home for treatment, either to recover or to die."

The Ascension air station made South Atlantic crossings possible for twin-engine planes in two fairly easy hops with a normal gas load. Four-engine bombers and transports could fly directly from Natal (in Brazil) to Liberia, Sierra Leone, or Accra. By using refueling facilities on Ascension, four-engine transports could take on a much lighter load of gasoline at Natal, increasing proportionately the amount of payload carried. Equally important, with a stop at Ascension, it was even possible to ferry fighter aircraft to Africa, as would soon be done with P-38s and P-39s.

In Africa, as elsewhere in the world, vehement arguments were raised against the use of black American forces. Colonial governments argued that black soldiers would cause social upheaval among the local populations. But among the corps of political advisers concerned with America's role in Africa was thirty-eight-year-old Ralph Bunche, a Howard University professor who had taken a job with the U.S. State Department in 1941. Bunche argued for the presence of black troops in as many places as possible on the African continent.

Bunche wrote the army training manual that was distributed to all American soldiers sent to Africa. By December 1942, more than 3,000 blacks were in Africa, including Liberia, Sierra Leone, Gold Coast (Ghana), Libya, and Egypt. American troops, including Company C of the 27th Quartermaster Truck Regiment, arrived in Matadi, Belgian Congo, on August 29, 1942.

NORTHERN IRELAND

"Colored units should not, repeat not, be sent to British Isles," cabled Gen. James E. Chaney, the U.S. Army commander in Britain, on April 17, 1942. But the War Department instructed that "Colored Troops may

Black soldiers draw rations at the camp cookhouse at a military base in northern Ireland.

be included in reasonable proportion for any type of Service Units." By May 1942, there were about 800 black GIs in Britain, and officials on both sides of the Atlantic tried to keep the number from rising. Foreign Secretary Anthony Eden tried to cloak his own anti-black recommendation in a seemingly humane gesture, stating: "Our climate was badly suited to negroes."

Pressure from President Roosevelt, who was clearly listening to the agitation of civil rights organizations and black newspapers, plus military advisers who saw the benefit of deploying black soldiers to a fuller extent, overruled the persistent opposition to black troops. Per Roosevelt's endorsement, more black soldiers were assigned to the next wave of American soldiers to Great Britain in June.

FIRST CONTINGENT OF AMERICAN NEGRO TROOPS ABROAD read the June 14, 1942, Associated Press headline, announcing the arrival of black GIs in North Ireland. They were part of the first major U.S. military contingent to be sent to Europe, some 20,000 soldiers of the "greatest American convoy which ever crossed the Atlantic." The AP report continued: "For the first time since World War I, Negro troops were landed on British soil. An Army statement said their number was small and that they were intended for 'services of supply.' "

Most African-American commentators welcomed the inclusion of black soldiers in the convoy, but many criticized the War Department for not including black infantry. Editorials in black newspapers ripped the army and the Roosevelt administration for not deploying combat-ready black soldiers. Roosevelt, in turn, skewered the army publicists for political incorrectness, WWII-style:

> This is your No. 1 headache. The Army people are dumb when it comes to a matter of information that Negro troops landing in Ireland are for "service supply." In other words it is the same old story of publicizing the fact during the World War that Negro troops were sent to France as "labor battalions."
>
> FDR in a memo to Elmer Davis, Director of Office of
> War Information, June 17, 1942

Roosevelt further demanded that all military service branches pick up the pace at training black recruits for combat roles.

A Northwest British Port, August 16, 1942 (United Press)

Negro Troops Hold Ball
Their First in Britain Shows Some Expert "Rug Cutting"

The hot licks of "Darktown Strutters' Ball" opened the United States Army's first all-Negro military ball in Britain last night, giving North England its first look at genuine rug-cutting by experts from Harlem, Basin Street and Water Street.

Seventy-five Negro women from the African Church's mission in this port were invited to attend the ball, which was sponsored by the United States forces' special services branch in cooperation with British officials.

Music was provided by the Negro troops' own band—it already has the reputation of being the hottest on this side of the Atlantic—conducted by Corporal Douglas Palmer. Officials said they hoped to organize a number of other similar dances and entertainments soon.

In his August 5, 1942, directive "Notes on Relations With Coloured Troops," British general Arthur Dowler ordered that British soldiers "should not make intimate friends with them, taking them to cinemas and bars." And "white women should not associate with coloured men" at all. Dowler wanted "the British, both men and women, to realize the problem and adjust their attitude so that it conforms to that of the white American citizen."

General Eisenhower responded with an idea of his own: why not recruit and send over several thousand black members of the Women's Army Auxiliary Corps (WAACs) to staff special clubs for black male soldiers? On the advice of Mary McLeod Bethune, the suggestion was disregarded by WAAC commanders as a demeaning use of WAAC personnel, and General Eisenhower subsequently dropped the idea.

But Eisenhower did address the issue again in a letter to Washington, September 1942:

To most English people, including the village girls—even those of perfectly fine character—the negro soldier is just another man, rather fascinating because he is unique in their experience, a jolly good fellow and with money to spend. Our own white soldiers, seeing a girl walk down the street with a negro, frequently see themselves as protectors of the weaker sex and believe it necessary to intervene to the extent of using force, to let her know what she's doing.

By the end of 1942, a plan was devised to keep white and black soldiers apart at dances, bars, and any off-duty activity or entertainment that involved women: "While color lines are not to be announced or even mentioned, entertainments such as dances should be 'by organization,' " determined the army's chief of Service of Supply, the company to which most black GIs belonged. "The reason, if any, given for such an arrangement should be 'limitation of space and personnel,' not race," read the order. About 7,500 black American soldiers were stationed in the British Isles by year's end.

London, September 27, 1942 (United Press)

Negro Troops Praised
Americans Win British General's Applause in Maneuvers

Yelling "Up and at 'em! Let's get 'em!" American Negro troops stole the show at the weekend anti-invasion maneuvers at Merseyside and were praised by the British general in charge.

WAAC soldiers Ruth Wade and Lucille Mayo (left to right) demonstrate their ability to service trucks at Fort Huachuca, Arizona.

"They showed great style and ability," the general said. "They had to defend a bridge and a factory. Although the enemy was successful in his first attack, the Americans counter-attacked, took the enemy by surprise and recaptured the strong points. Their initiative was splendid."

The Negro troops were commanded by a white officer, Captain James T. Stewart of Winifred, Mont. It was the first time that American forces had participated in British military and Home Guard defense maneuvers.

Belfast, Northern Ireland, October 1, 1942 (United Press)

U.S. Soldier Killed in Brawl in Ireland
Negro Stabbed to Death as Military Police Intervene

A Negro American soldier was stabbed to death and a white American soldier suffered serious gunshot wounds last night when United States military police had to use force to break up a brawl outside a pub in the village of Antrim, it was revealed today.

Witnesses reported "many shots were fired" and that residents fled from the town, which is on Lough Neagh, eighteen miles northwest of Belfast, when they heard the volley. Several soldiers were reported arrested in connection with the incident.

The argument was reported to have started as Negro troops left the pub. The military police rushed up, but the Negroes refused to disperse and the police were forced to draw their revolvers.

Headquarters of the United States Army in Northern Ireland issued the following statement on the affair:

"There was a disturbance in the streets of Antrim last night shortly after 9 o'clock involving United States military police and United States soldiers.

"Several shots were fired before the disorder was ended. One soldier was killed, the victim of knife wounds. Another soldier was seriously wounded. No civilians were involved."

Ready for Combat

[1942]

93RD INFANTRY DIVISION

In 1942, the army activated two all-black infantry divisions, the 92nd and the 93rd Infantry Divisions. Supported by aircraft, ships, and armor, infantry divisions were the most fundamental element of any military: the foot soldier. Arming black soldiers was a major policy change, and because divisions were large, the army now had the problem of where to base its two black units. At full strength, each division would number almost 20,000 soldiers, and according to official army policy large numbers of black soldiers were not to be placed at any one post, and in no case were blacks ever to outnumber whites.

Destination: Fort Huachuca

"Some came with scars of shackles stamped into their eyes. They came with college degrees and parole papers," wrote Nelson Peery, a veteran of the all-black 93rd Infantry Division, about his fellow soldiers who arrived at Fort Huachuca.

"They came with pockets full of loaded dice. They came damning

America, her Jim Crow, and her lynch law. They came cursing Hitler and the Fascists and eager to do battle for human rights."

In January 1942 the Army Chief of Staff adopted a policy that stated: "No Negro unit larger than a brigade [3,000–5,000 men] shall be stationed at any post within the continental limits of the United States, except one infantry division [18,000–20,000 men] may be stationed at Fort Huachuca, Arizona." Too many armed black American soldiers were considered a serious threat to the small towns near bases throughout the South.

In April 1942, the first soldiers of the 93rd Infantry Division began arriving in Arizona. The best location for the nation's first all-black infantry division was the army's most remote training facility. A military reservation encompassing about one hundred square miles of desert and mountain terrain, Fort Huachuca, with its environmental variety of hot weather, dust, poisonous snakes, spiders, and chiggers, was considered "hell on earth" by white and black recruits alike.

Segregation at every level was the rule at Fort Huachuca, including separate post exchanges, hospitals, and officers' clubs. "Having separate clubs follows a traditional pattern not only as pertains to the relationship between the white and colored races, but between all races. It has been the custom throughout the world for people to organize clubs according to their races," responded post commander Col. Edwin Hardy to a *Pittsburgh Courier* question about Fort Huachuca's separate officers' clubs. "With the urgent and important problems which have to be solved in these critical times, the problem of separate officers clubs fades into comparative insignificance."

The Blue Helmets

The 93rd Infantry Division wore a patch showing a blue French helmet on its shoulder-sleeve insignia, a reminder of the division's heroism during World War I. But the 12,000 men of the division wanted a more exciting symbol. A contest was devised to come up with a new insignia design and the winner was a black panther. The popular request was turned down, however, by the division commander, who cited reasons of cost to replace the old insignia.

By the end of 1942, 18,000 black soldiers were based at Fort Huachuca. The soldiers adopted as their division mascot "Myrtle," a thirty-three-year-old mule that had served with General Pershing and the 10th Cavalry during the Pancho Villa raids in the Huachuca Mountains.

92ND INFANTRY DIVISION

Organized in October 1942, the 92nd Infantry Division trained at four different locations around the United States. Unlike the "Blue Helmets" and all other army infantry divisions, which trained together in one location, the 92nd "Buffalo Soldiers" were housed at Alabama's Fort McClellan, Indiana's Camp Atterbury, Kentucky's Camp Breckinridge, and Arkansas's Camp Robinson. In 1943, only after the 93rd vacated Fort Huachuca to go on maneuvers, the 92nd was finally assembled and moved to Arizona.

ELSEWHERE IN THE global war in 1942, about 5,000 black troops were deployed to Iran. In the Persian Gulf Command, more than 90 percent of the American troops were African American. Black units like the 345th Quartermasters drove the thousand-mile run from the Persian Gulf through Iran to the Russian border. Loaded with ammunition and tank, truck, and plane parts, the black drivers transported crucial war supplies, and black maintenance and engineering units repaired, maintained, and built roads in Iran, to aid the Soviet defensive effort to stop the German campaign on the Russian front.

In Tehran, Evi Sassoonian, a sixteen-year-old Iranian boy, gave fresh fruit and vegetables to black American mechanics at a base near his home. "They were no different to me than my brothers or my father," he later recalled. "They were very kind and they did not look at us as inferior as did some of the white American soldiers."

In the last two months of 1942, the Allies shipped more than 5,500 tanks, 2,100 planes, and 54,900 trucks to the Soviet Union. In late 1942 and 1943, the efforts of white and black engineer, ordnance, and quartermaster battalions provided the lifeline for the Soviet Union.

LIBERTY SHIPS

"Liberty Ships" were built as an emergency response to the shortage of cargo ships. The Liberty Ship *Booker T. Washington* was the first named after an African American. Built in Los Angeles, the vessel was launched in 1942 and christened by Marian Anderson. The ship made its first trans-Atlantic crossing in early 1943, from New York City to Great Britain, commanded by black Capt. Hugh Mulzac. Operating as a merchant ship, the crew was completely integrated with sailors of seventeen nationalities aboard. In all, seventeen Liberty Ships would be named for African Americans.

VALAIDA SNOW: AN ENTERTAINER ABROAD

On Tuesday, June 9, 1942, Valaida Snow arrived at a Hudson River pier in New York City aboard the Swedish liner *Gripsholm*—"the only colored person among the 194 passengers." She then took a taxi uptown to the Theresa Hotel aka "the Waldorf of Harlem" on 125th Street, where she first told the story of her overseas experience.

The leader of an all-female band, she sang, too, and could play every instrument in the orchestra. She was often billed as "Little Louie" in recognition of her virtuosity on the horn.

During a European tour that took Snow to England, Ireland, France, and Scandanavia, she was working in Denmark when that country was invaded by the Nazis in April 1940. Prevented from leaving, she continued to perform in Danish clubs until January 1941, when the death of a close female friend, apparently by suicide, led to an investigation of Snow on charges of illegal drug use. Charged by the Danish police with illegally obtaining an opium derivative, her work permit was revoked. Unable either to work or leave the country, she was remanded to Vester-Faengsel, an internment facility in Copenhagen for petty criminals, political detainees, and the indigent. After six months, through her theatrical contacts, she was able to find work in Sweden where she resided for a few months until she was returned to Denmark. Following Germany's declaration of war against the United States in December

Musician and singer Valaida Snow was detained in Nazi-occupied Denmark for several months, then was returned to the United States in June 1942.

1941, she was interned until the Danish authorities could arrange for her repatriation, via Sweden, in June 1942.

On her first day back in the United States, Snow told the *Amsterdam News* of the struggles of "the fine brave Scandanavian people, suffering under the yoke of Hitler's tyranny. Each night," she said, "they pray for help from across the seas. They regard the United States as their savior."

She said nothing about losing work because of illegal drug charges, nor did she say anything about spending time in a concentration camp—the details of which she revealed only later. Still, she was judged by one reporter to have been through an ordeal. "She is her old self, except for the fact that she is a bit more streamlined than previously," the newspaper reported. "The curves just aren't there," he said of Valaida's figure, at a time when the entertainer was down to ninety pounds. "What could you expect of one who has lived more or less on a rationed boiled potato diet for the past six months," she said. When she had returned to Denmark, the Germans were in complete control, and her working days had ended. She had managed to save some money during her tour, she said,

JULY 30, 1942   President Roosevelt authorizes formation of the Women Accepted for Voluntary Emergency Service (WAVES), the women's auxiliary of the U.S. Navy. The Secretary of the Navy excluded black women from the organization until October 1944. Fewer than one hundred black women served with the WAVES during WWII.

"and it was a blessing, because if I wouldn't have had money, I'd still be in Europe, most likely in a prison camp."

For five days before she left Sweden, she said she was compelled to sleep in a prison, though she explained pointedly that she was not a prisoner. She could not leave her quarters until after 7:00 A.M. and she had to be in before 11:00 P.M. It was a great day, she said, when she was told she could go home. Through the help of Danish friends, she secured passage, and on May 23 she flew to Sweden. The *Gripsholm* was sched-

Hirohito, Hitler, and Mussolini were the comic targets of the trio known as "Three Loose Nuts," appearing here at a New York City club.

uled to sail that day, but was delayed until May 28, when the homeward voyage began. Snow said she was permitted to bring only her jewelry and a small amount of money. She was forced to leave more than $1,500 behind, she told reporters.

"On the day she left Gothenburg, the two leading [Scandinavian] newspapers published front page pictures and stories of Valaida's departure," wrote Julius J. Adams of the *Amsterdam News*, "which she proudly displayed while the reporter struggled through the text and translated enough words to understand that the articles were not mere news stories, but were tributes—tributes to a great little star from a grateful people to whom she had brought much happiness and joy."

In a later article titled "I Came Back from the Dead," Valaida's own account of her Danish experience revealed considerably more. Whether she recalled more details or simply embellished her experience, she now had had all of her money and belongings taken from her, including jewelry, $7,000 in traveler's checks, and a gold trumpet that she said had been given to her by Queen Wilhelmina of the Netherlands. Adding still more new information, she claimed that one day, unable to bear to see a child being beaten, she threw herself in front of a guard to protect the child. For her compassionate act, she said she was struck by the guard

```
Sir;
     We see by the papers, that our so called racial
leaders, are piqued because the chocolate soldier,
in thier opinion is not getting enough opportunity
to dodge bullets, in this present conflict.
     Question please, after they, the Negro Leaders
maneuver us, the chocolate soldier behind the eight
ball, just what are they prepared to offer us, in the
way of post war planning???
     Until they can answer that question, we suggest
that they leave the affairs of war, to the War Dept.

                              Signed;
                              Btry.A,A.P.O; 961
```

Unsigned letter from a black soldier questioning the wisdom of black leaders demanding that "chocolate soldiers" be sent into combat.

and received a deep gash along the side of her head, and that she now had to carefully style her hair to conceal the scar. Though the story Valaida told was not entirely forthcoming, she had clearly been through a dramatic and perilous experience.

FBI

Federal Bureau of Investigation reports of a seditious movement among African Americans were pervasive throughout the war. In 1941, Elijah Muhammed, leader of the Nation of Islam, was convicted and jailed in Detroit. In 1942 Ralph Bunche, who had left his teaching position at Howard University to take a job in the U.S. State Department, was personally categorized by J. Edgar Hoover as a "stage 2" dissident—meaning not dangerous enough to be jailed but "a suspected menace who should be watched closely."

The same year, an FBI report branded W.E.B. DuBois as a Japanese sympathizer who "had stated in a speech made while in Japan that the Japanese were to be complimented on their progress and especially upon their military prowess. Further, that in the Japanese he saw the liberation of the negroes in America, and that when the time came for them to take over the United States, they would find they would have help from the negroes in the United States."

By 1943 Malcolm Little (later Malcolm X) and others thought up creative ways to avoid the draft:

> In those days only three things in the world scared me: jail, a job, and the Army. I had about ten days before I was to show up at the induction center. I went right to work. The Army Intelligence soldiers,

AUGUST 1942 U.S. Army Chemical Warfare Service activates inordinately high number of black soldiers to potentially dangerous chemical units. Over 14 percent, or one in seven soldiers, were assigned to seventy-five all-black units in decontamination, chemical processing, and chemical-smoke-generating companies.

those black spies in civilian clothes, hung around in Harlem with their ears open for the white man downtown. I knew exactly where to start dropping the word. I started noising around that I was frantic to join . . . the Japanese Army.

Malcolm X, from *The Autobiography of Malcolm X*

"FIGHTING FOR THESE UNITED SNAKES"

In the view of some, black soldiers like Dorie Miller and thousands more were unwise and foolish to fight for the "United Snakes"—better they should disobey orders and shoot the man next to him if "given a gun." So went the reasoning of four black defendants charged with sedition in New York City in December 1942. A federal jury listened to a phonograph recording of the four made by FBI investigators who had monitored a Harlem meeting of the Ethiopian Pacific Movement.

Confronted with the prosecution's audio evidence, the defendants (three of whom were from the West Indies) claimed their accents had rendered their statements far more sinister than intended. Asked what he meant by "we" in the statement "We are going to knock out Pearl Harbor again and then we are coming into Vera Cruz and then into Arizona," defendant Leonard Robert O. Jordan answered, "I speak very broken English."

"Are you willing to fight for the United States without any modification?" Jordan was asked by his attorney.

"Yes, the only modification I have is as long as the United States government is willing to give the black man equal rights according to the Constitution," replied Jordan, who was dubbed the "Black Hitler" by the press. Convicted of treason, for discouraging blacks from fighting in the U.S. Army, Jordan was fined $10,000 and sentenced to ten years in federal prison.

7

The Road to Burma

[1942–43]

Native Asian nationalism in Burma and India initially favored Japan; however, Hirohito's brutal sweep through Indochina and China would make European and American imperialism seem welcome by comparison. Since April 1941, America had sent fighter planes, spare parts, and fuel to help China defend itself against Japanese aggression. In May 1942, Japan cut off the Burma Road—the 1,041-mile land supply line between India and China. The only way for the Allies to supply the Chinese then was by the risky air route over the Himalayas known as "the Hump." Losses were high (over 800 pilots and crew were killed in crashes during "Hump" flights), and Allied military engineers proposed a new road—a construction challenge even more daunting than the Alcan Highway. The route would traverse the mountain ridge (8,000–10,000 feet high), be constructed during the monsoon season, and be located in the war zone with the enemy nearby.

Approximately 275 miles of road were required to connect Ledo, India, with existing routes to China. New construction would be needed for about half the distance, and major improvements of existing trails thereafter. So vital was the land route to China that the United States assigned 15,000 American troops to construct the Ledo Road, which ran 271 miles from Ledo in Assam Province, India, to a junction with the old Burma Road. Deployed to India were some of the finest roadmakers in the Allied military units, including Chinese, Indians, West Africans, British, and Americans. Sixty percent of the American troops were African Americans.

African-American soldiers were the first American units assigned to the Ledo Road. The 45th Engineer General Service Regiment and the 823rd EAB arrived in December 1942 to begin construction and to rebuild bombed-out sections of the roadway. The winding road's first section ascended a steep trail through unsurveyed territory from Ledo, across the Patkai Mountains, and down to Shingbwiyang, Burma. The crews removed 100,000 cubic feet of earth every mile along the 103-mile trail, which rose to 4,500 feet. In 1943 four more black EABs (the 848, 849, 858, and 1,883) were brought on to the Ledo project. On December 27, 1943, the lead bulldozer reached Shingbwiyang three days ahead of schedule.

Despite a widely distributed statement within American military circles that Chinese general Chiang Kai-shek did not want black soldiers in China (allegedly because the Chinese had never before seen black people), relations between Chinese and African-American soldiers were good, both along the Ledo route and later in China.

On one special project—the construction of the Namchik Bridges—two bridges, one a Chinese and the other an American bridge, were built within a few hundred yards of each other. The "Chinese Bridge," the smaller of the two, was made of wood and built by the Chinese 10th Engineers. The "American Bridge" was steel-rigged by the 45th Engineers. A friendly rivalry had developed on the job, and a gala celebration was planned for the simultaneous opening of the bridges on July 2, 1943.

At the celebration, the Chinese prepared dinner, and the 45th Engineers' band played the "Star-Spangled Banner" and the Chinese National Anthem. Special invited guests of the two work battalions were Chinese and American nurses from field hospitals nearby. The festivities concluded with the selection of a Chinese and an American nurse, each to sit on a jeep fender and be driven across the new bridges. The crowd cheered as ribbons were snipped in unison across each roadway, and a cocktail afterparty was hosted by the 45th Engineers. A day later, a flood washed out both the log and the steel bridges, and the Americans and the Chinese started the project all over.

Along the India-Burma border, the all-black 21st Quartermaster Regiment operated a dropping ground at "the Bum"—the highest peak on the upper road. There they maintained a depot for supplies flown into the sector. In an unofficial capacity, the 21st also operated an "alpine resort," a place for food and drink with its own radio station strong enough to pipe in news and music from around the world. At 4,808 feet, it provided a picturesque, though dangerous, overlook of the tea plantations along the Ngalang Valley. At the site, the troops lived in "bustees"—thatched houses on tall stilts that were cooler than most quarters and provided relief from many ground insects.

"In the morning the hill stuck up out of a snowbank of clouds at our feet," said one black GI who remembered waking one day to a stunning view and good news about the war before starting daily chores. "Just as we left, [the radio] picked up the news flash that Italy had surrendered. We had not even heard that the invasion from Sicily to the mainland had taken place."

In the Burmese jungle, American-trained Chinese troops and American guerrillas under Brig. Gen. Frank D. Merrill were sustained mainly by airdrops loaded by the quartermaster corps. Known as Merrill's Marauders, with a reputation as the toughest of combat troops, the Marauders were generally well liked for their camaraderie with black troops along the Burma trail.

Flying Quartermasters: Bundles for Burma Boys

The plane's nosing over now. You're heading down towards the jungle. As the plane circles lower, your eyes keep searching the unbroken green of the jungle trees and growth for a little white spot, the cleared area. Suddenly, you see it—a tiny little patch in the solid field of forest. You're heading toward it and you stand ready by the open door. Then as the C-47 swoops over the clearing you push out the loaded chutes.

Down they go—little white and colored dots sailing straight for the target. You see the first two or three hit. They were the heavier ones. A generator, parts for a truck motor, and an Army field range were contained in those bundles. Looking back you hold your breath as you watch the wicker basket chutes settle. Wrapped separately in cotton, and surrounded by rice husks are delicate medical supplies and instruments, urgently needed by the jungle fighters below. Then the packs sit down nicely and you're sure they're OK. That's because you also know that all those bundles were packed tenderly and expertly by men who really know their jobs. Now the cargo ship heads for home and another haul and you settle back to take it easy 'til the next flight. This trip is just part of the everyday experience you would have as a member of the CBI flying Quartermasters, self-styled "Bundles for Burma Boys." (Recently, the CBI has been divided into the China and Burma-India theaters.) These QM's are members of a colored battalion of QM truck drivers, retrained in Northeast India to prepare and supply entirely by air men and installations in country inaccessible to all standard land supply routes.

The battalion has been, and still is, the basic organization conducting air dropping activity for the Services of Supply in Northeast India.
FROM PLASMA TO HOWITZERS   Theirs is no routine supply job. In addition to supplying the standard cargoes of clothing and ammunition, they've been called upon to drop delicate medical supplies and instruments, bulky and heavy operating tables, blood plasma, fresh meats and vegetables, tons of highly sensitive wet gun cotton, dynamite, nitrostarch, and TNT. Along with food they've parachuted typewriters, radios and radio parts, motors, lights, generators, field ranges, rifles, machine guns, mail, tank and truck parts. They also packed and "pushed over the side" the first 75mm pack howitzers known to have been parachuted down in the theater—and all with an extremely low percentage of losses and in some cases no losses at all!
COMMENT FROM THE TOP   But the real evidence of air supply's significance comes from a staff officer attached to the staff of the former commander of the CBI, General Stillwell. Says he, "Air supply has undoubtedly been one of the greatest single factors contributing to the success of the North Burma campaign to date. Conditions on lines of

communication, particularly during the monsoon season, has resulted in almost total dependence upon air drops and landings for support of the entire force in forward areas. From a tactical standpoint, certain operations have been successfully accomplished, which without air supply, would have been difficult, if not impossible of achievement."

Quartermaster Training Service Journal

November 24, 1944

(From the archives of the U.S. Army Quartermaster Museum, Fort Lee, Virginia)

Its been only 7 months since I left the States but after 5 months in India I'm low enough to walk under a cobra's belly (if I ever see one). . . . I'm convinced that this is no place for one who has been schooled in modern living.

Pvt. G. Blackstone

India

ca 1942

Troops stationed in India take a break and get around in rickshaws. Some are on their way to take in a new movie, Tarzan's New York Adventure.

8

BLACK WOMEN AT WAR

[1942–43]

My girlfriends and I were at a Sweet Sixteen party on the Sunday afternoon when we heard on the radio that Pearl Harbor had been attacked. I never in a thousand years thought I might wind up in the army.

PFC. NORMA K. MOORE

In May 1942 the U.S. Congress established the Women's Army Auxiliary Corps (WAAC) with the promise that it would be open to women of all races. But black organizations protested quickly when President Roosevelt appointed Oveta Culp Hobby, a Texas socialite and wife of that state's former governor, as director of WAAC. Her background guaranteed that she would discriminate against black women, her opponents argued.

When Hobby appointed forty black women among the first 440 candidates enrolled for officer training at Des Moines, Iowa, black opposition to her appointment lessened. Thirty-nine of the black women made it through the process, including Charity Adams, who arrived at the Iowa training center in July 1942. She recalls:

When we left the mess hall we were marched two-by-two's to the reception center. A young, red-haired second lieutenant said, "Will all the colored girls move over on this side." He pointed to an isolated group of seats. There was a moment of stunned silence, for even in the United States of the forties it did not occur to us that this could happen. The integration of our trip did not prepare us for this. What made things worse was that even after the "colored girls" had been pushed to the side, all the rest of the women were called by name to join a group to be led to their quarters. Why could not the "colored girls" be called by name to go to their quarters rather than be isolated by race?

Almost 80 percent of black women officers were college educated, and the army quickly learned that discrimination had a dramatic impact on recruitment. By January 1943 the 10 percent ratio of black women officers dropped to less than 3 percent. An army study revealed that because of discrimination or perceptions of racism, the best qualified black women stopped volunteering for the WAAC.

General enthusiasm among all women, white and black, toward the WAAC dimmed further in 1943 because of negative public opinion regarding women in the military. Rumors of rampant pregnancies and unfounded charges of prostitution, venereal diseases, and homosexuality brought enlistment to a near halt.

The role of women in the military was challenged primarily by men (military and nonmilitary). Sexism was a major problem confronting women in the military, noted Hobby, who in June 1943 vehemently defended the WAACs against the onslaught of slanderous reports:

Five hundred [WAACs] were said to have been returned from Africa to have babies. Three actually returned. One was legitimately pregnant before she left, one was ill with a gall bladder, the other was suffering with a concussion from a bomb. One hundred WAACs [were] said to be in St. Elizabeth's [Hospital]. No truth in this statement. Nor was there any truth in the statements that a trainload of WAACs had been sent to Walter Reed [Hospital] to have babies, 86 discharged from Fort Devens with babies (3 were discharged), 172 lesbians in a hospital. Out of 65,000 women there [are] 7 illegitimate pregnancies, 9 cases of syphilis, and 41 cases of gonorrhea.

The WAAC slogan "Release a Man for Combat"—found by some to be a double entendre—was changed to "Replace a Man for Combat." National columnist John O'Donnell's claim that a "super-secret War Department policy authorized the issuance of prophylactics to all WAACs before they were sent overseas" was not true, but the allegations sounded a death knell for WAAC recruitment as women feared for their reputations—as did their fathers, brothers, boyfriends, and husbands.

On July 3, 1943, WAAC was folded into the Women's Army Corps (WAC), a branch of the army itself rather than a mere "auxiliary" to it. Designed to give a new name and a fresh start to the women's military campaign, the WAC conversion emphasized the critical and positive role women were playing in the war. Women served in numerous capacities, including accountant, auditor, baker, cashier, chauffer, cook, cryptanalyst, dietitian, technical draftsperson, fingerprinter, linguist, light truck driver, mathematician, meat inspector, medical personnel, meteorologist, motorboat operator, motor vehicle mechanic, photographer, shipping clerk, storekeeper, and typist, as well as in such fields as public relations and radio communications.

A contingent of fifteen nurses, newly arrived at the 268th Station Hospital in Australia in November 1943, receive their first batch of mail from home.

On July 14, 1943, the first contingent of WACs, all white, landed in England. Nearly a year and a half passed before the first black WACs were sent overseas.

NURSES

The Army Nurse Corps (ANC) accepted only a small number of black nurses during World War II. To join the ANC, a woman had to be a registered nurse and a member of the American Red Cross. When war mobilization began, the National Association of Colored Graduate Nurses urged its members to enroll in the American Red Cross, the agency that served as recruiter for the Army Nurse Corps. However, black nurses were not accepted and were snubbed by the Army Nurse Corps, which told them, quite plainly: "Your application for appointment to the Army Nurse Corps cannot be given favorable consideration as there are no provisions in Army regulations for the appointment of colored nurses in the Corps."

In World War I no black nurses were allowed to serve in the war; only after the armistice was signed were eighteen black women admitted into the nursing corp. In 1941 a campaign initiated by Mary McLeod

In 1941, pilot Willa Beatrice Brown became the first black woman officer in the U.S. Civil Air Patrol. Throughout the war, Lieutenant Brown served as an instructor in the Civilian Pilot Training program.

Bethune and Eleanor Roosevelt for the recruitment of black women caused military officials to give in, and a quota for the limited recruitment of black nurses was set. The army approved about fifty per year, with the stated condition that they would "serve in hospitals or wards devoted exclusively to the treatment of Negro soldiers."

The first black nurses were deployed to West Africa in 1943 and served at the 25th Station Hospital in Liberia. The unit of thirty nurses provided medical care for the black U.S. troops. In January 1944 the superintendent of the Army Nurse Corps, Col. Florence A. Blanchfield, wrote: "Colored nurses have a definite contribution to make to the nursing services of the Army, and careful consideration is now being given to determine how their services may be fully realized." In June 1944 a unit of sixty-three nurses went to the 168th Station Hospital in England to care for German prisoners of war.

By the end of the war, black nurses had also served in Australia and the Southwest Pacific. Along the Ledo Road the nurses served at the 383rd and 335th Station Hospitals near Tagap, Burma. In the Southwest Pacific, black nurses served at the 268th Station Hospital in New Guinea, which had a 250-bed capacity and was commanded and staffed solely by black officers. At war's end in September 1945, there were only 479 black nurses in a corps of 50,000.

Mary McLeod Bethune

Born on July 10, 1875, near Mayesville, South Carolina, the fifteenth of seventeen children, Mary McLeod Bethune was the highest-ranking black woman in the federal government and had significant influence in President Roosevelt's New Deal government. Regarded as the president's "race leader at large," she served as director of African-American affairs for the National Youth Administration and as special assistant to the secretary of war. With the help of President and Mrs. Roosevelt, Bethune fought for better conditions for African-American men and women in the military.

Bethune supported the Women's Army for National Defense, an all-black women's organization founded on November 15, 1942, by Lovonia H. Brown to "provide an instrument through which our women could serve in this great crisis, with dignity and pride." Their motto, "Working for Victory, Planning for Peace," was echoed in Bethune's greeting at its first national meeting. "We are aware of the profound and worldwide significance of this war and the postwar era that is rapidly emerging." (Bethune became the organization's National Commander in 1944.)

Founder of the Daytona Normal and Industrial Institute for Negro Girls (now Bethune-Cookman College) and the National Council of Negro Women, Bethune also served as vice president of the NAACP and on President Truman's Committee of Twelve for National Defense.

Bethune died in Daytona Beach on May 18, 1955, of a heart attack. She was buried on the campus of Bethune-Cookman College.

August 2, 1942 (Associated Press)

Alabama Senator Wants Northern Negro Troops out of the South

Senator John D. Bankhead has suggested to General George C. Marshall, Army Chief of Staff, that Northern Negro soldiers be quartered in Northern States only, the Senator revealed today in a letter to John Temple Graves of The Birmingham Age–Herald. *The letter, quoted in Mr. Grave's editorial, says: "The best friends of the Negroes in the South are very much concerned about the growing anxiety that race conflicts may break out and lead to bloodshed. Our people feel that the government is doing a disservice to the war effort by locating Negro troops in the South in immediate contact with white troops at a time when race feeling among the Negroes has been aroused and when all the energies of both the whites and the blacks should be devoted to the war effort."*

August 20, 1942 (Associated Press)

Negro Candidates Picked
Tryouts for Selected Players Planned by Pirates

The [Pittsburgh] Pirates disclosed today that Club President Bill Benswanger had authorized the sportswriter of a Negro newspaper to pick some Negro baseball candidates who might be considered by the Pirates.

The sportswriter Wendell Smith of the Pittsburgh Courier *said he had suggested catcher Josh Gibson and outfielder Sammy Bankhead of the Homestead (Pa.) Grays and shortstop Willie Wells and pitcher Leon Day of the Newark Eagles. The tryouts may not take place until after close of the season, as Bob Rice, Pirate farm director who will supervise them, is busy with the farm teams.*

October 30, 1942 (Associated Press)

Roosevelt Mum on Liberia
Declines Comment on Reports of Landings by American Troops

President Roosevelt today said he preferred to withhold any comment on the possibility that American troops had been stationed in Liberia. He said it came under the classification of troop movements and operational movements and that he would not dare comment without consulting his military authorities. It is an operational movement of troops, if it exists, he asserted, so any statement should come from these authorities.

He had been asked at a press conference whether he could confirm stories from British sources that both white and Negro troops from the United States had taken up stations in the Negro republic on the African coast.

AUGUST 15, 1942 In a letter to the *Chicago Defender,* a writer from Los Angeles remarks: "Let the Negro have his name in the casualty lists of Pearl Harbor or Bataan or Midway. But, for heavensakes, let's keep his name out of the [sports] boxscores."

THE NORTH AFRICAN CAMPAIGN:
OPERATION TORCH

On the eve of November 8, 1942, over 100,000 American and British forces were approaching the African shore, in a maiden invasion known as Operation Torch. For the 85,000 Americans soldiers, it would be the first American combat unit landing on African soil. Coming by sea from three separate points of origin, England, Sierra Leone, and Norfolk, Virginia, all of which were a considerable distance, many of the soldiers were seasick and exhausted as the ships neared the morning landing. The invasion was a potential disaster for the Allies, even in the judgment of its chief planner, Gen. Dwight D. Eisenhower, who feared its outcome. Eisenhower later wrote of the history-making event: "The venture was new. . . . Up to that moment no government had ever attempted to carry out an overseas expedition involving a journey of thousands of miles from its bases and terminating in a major attack."

Apart from the soldiers' readiness, General Eisenhower knew that the Allies' best hope rested on another important but unknown factor: would the French colonial (mostly black African) troops lower their weapons and join the Allied cause? Much of Eisenhower's confidence relied on the efforts of a black African leader, Félix Eboué. Eboué, the French Guyanese-born governor of Chad, had been the first colonial French leader to support the Free French army of Charles de Gaulle. His bold and swift decision in 1941 led to a Vichy court condemning him to death. Eboué now diplomatically urged other African colonies to follow the Free French and the Americans. Eisenhower agonized over the reliability of his intelligence reports, and, finally assured that the French colonial forces would not resist, sent the order to "play ball," and Operation Torch was under way.

In the Sunday-morning landing at Casablanca and Oran, to the Allies' unhappy surprise, French shore installations opened a heavy arsenal of machine-gun fire on the invading force. The fighting was sporadic, and for several hours the position of the fourteen French colonial divisions remained uncertain. Within two days the French command officially switched sides and Adm. Jean Darlan surrendered French North Africa to Eisenhower. Had Eboué not been persuasive, and the well-armed and

-trained French and African colonial army been thrown full-force against the sea-weary Allies, the invasion would have almost certainly been a disaster. Thanks to its newfound friendship with black African colonial leaders, America's first plunge into the European war was a success.

THE REAL *CASABLANCA*

The 1942 Hollywood movie *Casablanca* forecast a detail of the actual secret American plan. In the film's memorable conclusion, Humphrey Bogart's character and his French friend, the former Vichy-installed chief of police, are headed for Brazzaville, Congo. The film's concluding line, "Louis, I think this is the beginning of a beautiful friendship," reflected the real-life espionage network in Paris, Casablanca, Algiers, Brazzaville, and Dakar that was working to sway France's 350,000 colonial African troops to the side of the Allies. (Eboué died of pneumonia in May 1944. De Gaulle later wrote to his widow that "Félix Eboué was my friend and nothing can make me forget the man, the companion, the brother in arms that he was to me during the greatest struggle of our time.")

By November 10, combat engineer and quartermaster units, including white and black soldiers, were at work repairing and building new ports, roads, airfields, and hospitals. The necessary and demanding labor routine involved white and black soldiers in virtually every landing-force invasion throughout the rest of the war.

BATTLING ROMMEL: THE DESERT FOX

The aim of the Operation Torch campaign was to drive the Germans off of the African continent. The same week of the Allied invasion of Morocco and Algeria, the British army in Libya, aided by more than 100,000 British colonial African soldiers, plus attachments of white and black American units, took aim at German Field Marshal Erwin Rommel's desert brigade. In June 1942, Rommel, the "Desert Fox," had scored a near-devastating victory over the British in Libya at Tobruk. The enemy seized a huge depot of ammunition, food, and gasoline, enough supplies to move toward its main objective—the capture of Egypt and the Suez Canal. Led by Gen. Bernard L. Montgomery, the

OCTOBER 15, 1942 The U.S. Army reactivated the all-black 92nd Infantry Division at Fort McClellan, Alabama, for duty.

British 8th Army had launched an offensive in late October that pushed Rommel's forces out of Egypt. Attached to the British forces were an assortment of American units, including black American engineer and quartermaster battalions, whose presence in the campaign against Rommel neither the U.S. Army nor President Roosevelt had publicly acknowledged.

> [We] traveled a hundred miles a day through the desert. Our destination was Benghazi. Some of our men went on to Tobruk, where they took part in the final driving out of Rommel's forces.
>
> Master Sergeant Warren Bryant, 812th Aviation Engineers

With more than 2,500 black American troops stationed in Egypt, supplies were kept moving to the front lines. In desert war, the flow of gasoline was absolutely vital, and the black American troops assigned to the desert task were largely responsible for the movement of supplies to Montgomery's famed "Desert Rats." Enjoying a continuous supply of fuel and other necessities, Allied fighters pushed Rommel's army back more than 1,750 miles—one of the longest retreats in military history. By December 1942, the Germans and Italians held only Tunisia, though firmly and tenaciously, on the African continent.

More than 10,000 black troops were stationed in rear-guard and near frontline positions in Africa by the end of 1942. Assigned to bases in Sierra Leone, Liberia, Morocco, Algeria, Libya, Egypt, Kenya, Chad, and Khartoum, they constructed barracks and hospitals for troops injured in the North African campaign. Along with their white counterparts, they transported fuel, munitions, and supplies, and constructed and maintained roads and airfields.

FDR to Africa

[1943]

FDR PROMISES BAD NEWS FOR GERMANY, ITALY, AND JAPAN IN 1943

JANUARY 1, 1943 (ASSOCIATED PRESS)

President Roosevelt began the New Year with a confident forecast—despite the fact that the mainlands of its chief adversaries, Germany and Japan, were still well out of reach of Allied infantries. Bombers flown from airfields in England were hitting industrial targets in Germany, yet the Wehrmacht continued its massive production of military hardware. But the island-hopping movement of American forces creeping steadily closer to Japan boosted Allied confidence, as did the victorious 1942 campaign in North Africa. In January 1943 the arrival of more American troops to England and North Africa marked a dramatic transition toward American dominance in the European war.

On January 22, 1943, President Roosevelt traveled to Morocco for the Casablanca Conference with Prime Minister Churchill. Though invited, Soviet leader Stalin passed up the meeting. Poised to finally defeat the German advance at Stalingrad, Stalin himself remained suspicious of the Allied strategy of engaging Germany in North Africa first, before launching an invasion on Germany's Western Front, in France. "When are you going to start fighting?" asked Stalin, who was convinced that his two major "Allies" were only too willing to let the Russians bear the brunt of Hitler's military strength.

But Stalin did have some good reasons to trust the alliance. By January 1943, America had sent more than 80,000 trucks to the Soviet Union and more than 50,000 tons of rubber. About half of the U.S. military personnel working to supply the Soviet Union with badly needed supplies were African American. In the North Atlantic, Hugh Mulzac, the first black captain of a merchant marine vessel, piloted the *Booker T. Washington* through the dangerous waters. On voyages to Murmansk, above the Arctic Circle across the Barents Sea, the U.S. Merchant Marine supplied the Soviet Union with over 15,000 aircraft, 7,000 tanks, 350,000 tons of ammunition, and 15,000,000 pairs of boots—worn by Soviet soldiers during the harsh winters on the Eastern Front.

Rubber was a precious commodity in the war, and with the Japanese control of rubber plantations in the South Pacific, the Allies relied most upon Liberia for its supply. After Casablanca, President Roosevelt flew south to Liberia. This was the first time a U.S. president had gone to black Africa.

Liberia was the only black African nation with even minimal leverage with the Allies. Liberia had the ability to produce rubber, but its

Defense industry worker Bertha Stallworth, age twenty-one, inspects an artillery cartridge case at the Frankford Arsenal in Philadelphia.

A company of African-American army nurses line up for review at the 25th Station Hospital in Liberia.

lease arrangement with the Firestone Rubber Company, which controlled 90 percent of its tillable soil, threatened the country's sovereignty. President Roosevelt had four key issues to discuss with Liberian leaders: (1) finalize plans to establish U.S. military bases in Liberia, which were to be used as a springboard for transporting American soldiers, military hardware, and supplies to North Africa; (2) to reaffirm Liberia's commitment to continue supplying the United States with natural rubber; (3) to expel all German citizens, as they posed a security threat to the United States and its allies; and (4) for Liberia to end its neutrality and declare war on Germany and the Axis Powers.

In General Eisenhower's memoir, *Crusade in Europe,* he admitted that he seriously considered using Liberian territory as the initial staging ground for the invasion of North Africa and Europe. American and British military personnel almost came to blows over Liberia, because the U.S. military refused to let the British fly their military supplies through Roberts Field. The situation became so tense that the matter had to be settled personally by FDR and Prime Minister Winston Churchill at their meeting in Casablanca. With Liberia fully on board, the Allies were ready to strike at Hitler's hold on North Africa.

In February 1942, only six months after Ralph Bunche left a teaching position at Howard University to join the State Department, he was assigned as head of the African section of the Office of Strategic Services (OSS). (A new federal agency created by FDR, the OSS think-tank amassed defense information on foreign locations where the U.S. military might be involved in projects of public information, propaganda, or psychological warfare. The OSS later evolved into the Central Intelligence Agency.) Of Africa's strategic importance in the war Bunche wrote that in view of "revelations of Nazi foresight and efficiency in their 'blueprint' for Africa, it is more important than ever to anticipate all possible needs there." On the issue of race, he prepped the Roosevelt administration, noting: "The elite African especially is even more sensitive on racial matters than is the American Negro." Throughout the war, Bunche advised the president and the Pentagon on army policies concerning black troops. His strongest recommendation was for the military to photograph black combat and service units in their posts around the world, as documentation and evidence of the contribution and patriotism of African Americans during the war.

In January 1943 the American public knew virtually nothing of the crucial role of the more than 100,000 black troops in the war zones. With a mind-set fixed on the image of the "real soldier"—meaning the air pilot, the ship captain, or the bayonet-charging infantryman—black and white Americans alike overlooked the importance of the engineering and general-service units to the war cause. Assisted by military information conduits who either limited press releases about the deployment of black units or deliberately devalued their contributions, even black leaders and the black press continued to clamor for "real" African-American soldiers to enter the battle.

On January 5, 1943, William H. Hastie resigned his post as civilian aide to the secretary of war. For two years he had served as the official voice for black American interests in the military. Reporting on the status of blacks in the service, Hastie issued a report criticizing the U.S. military for adhering to Jim Crow social policy. "The traditional mores of the South," he wrote, "have been widely accepted and adopted by the Army as the basis of policy and practice affecting the Negro soldier."

Hastie's report had circulated for a year, garnering rancorous comments from numerous military officials. Lt. Col. James W. Boyer, Jr., who provided military information regularly to Hastie and members of the black press, called Hastie a troublemaker whose allegiance was to the NAACP first "and to the War Department second."

General Marshall rejected Hastie's proposal as so unadvisable and impractical it "would be tantamount to solving a social problem which has perplexed the American people throughout the history of this nation." Hastie later explained that he chose to resign in order to maximize public awareness of the problem.

GERMAN AND ITALIAN ARMIES: OUT OF AFRICA

Two weeks after the Casablanca meeting, the Allies were still wrestling with the basic problem of creating an efficient fighting force. Welding black and white American units together in the North African campaign proved less problematic than blending American, British, and French forces. Language and national pride led to problems in communications and effectiveness. To the embarrassment of the American command, U.S. troops were judged to be in overall poor condition and the least prepared for the war.

On St. Valentine's Day 1943, Rommel tested the newly formed "United Nations" force. Responding to a badly coordinated Allied advance into Tunisia, Rommel sent the German tank corps directly ahead, routing the Allies. At Kasserine Pass, Rommel's men drove into the Allied line, giving the Americans their first real taste of German tank and 88-mm firepower. The tremendous force of the attack caught the Allies by surprise. Hundreds of tanks and trucks were destroyed (some by friendly fire), and the Americans suffered 3,300 casualties. The enemy's losses were less than one thousand but the Germans had insufficient fuel to press ahead, and thus could not further demoralize the Americans. Many American soldiers ran from the battlefield, and some 2,300 GIs surrendered at Kasserine Pass—a humiliating combat statistic and an embarrassment to the American command, but one that the War Department purposely kept out of the American press. Eisenhower, recognizing that American troops were clearly not ready to battle the German Afrika Corps, replaced commanders and brought new units to the front, including black antitank and antiaircraft battalions.

In April of 1943, correspondent Ollie Stewart of the *Baltimore Afro-American* was covering the North African campaign. Stewart's reports were the first ever to describe African-American field artillery in action against Hitler's army:

> This is a story I have wanted to write since I left America . . . the story of colored troops in actual combat, exchanging lead with the enemy. I covered many miles to be on the spot when they began writing a glorious page in the history of the North African campaign. But now that I have seen our lads in action on the Tunisian front, I am both proud and humble. I am proud because they covered themselves with glory as well as with mud—and humble because I cannot tell the story as it should be told. A correspondent can have only a bird's-eye view of a battle front such as this one, and when I found a field artillery unit blasting the Germans out of the mountains just before we took Gabès (on the Gulf of Gabès) on the Tunisian front, I took a front-row seat for an hour without actually knowing the full importance of the action.
>
> It was early one morning that I sat on a ridge behind big guns manned by colored troops in a wooded area. Every time the lads cut loose with a barrage, the earth trembled and my ears roared. . . . The

FEBRUARY 13, 1943 The Women's Marine Corps was formed and became the only U.S. military women's auxiliary that did not admit any African Americans throughout the war.

show was not one-sided. The enemy found our range with his heavy stuff, and I learned what it means to be close to bursting shell fire. It was murderous. Time after time, both sides sounded off simultaneously and the whole mountain vibrated. Interspersed was the roar of tanks charging down a highway with their guns blazing. Machine guns chattered off to one side, and all hell seemed to break in trip-hammer spurts. During a lull, I lit a cigarette and wondered who was winning. There was no way of knowing. These colored soldiers firing away throughout the morning never saw their target. They had to wait for reports, as I did, until late that day. An officer coming back after the advance told me that colored artillerymen did a marvelous job of blasting the Germans out of their mountain strong-hold, making it possible for tanks and infantry to gain considerable mileage. . . . Near the front line I encountered an aviation quartermaster outfit with four colored officers. . . . I must emphasize that every unit near the front is a combat unit. All our quartermasters, engineers, and truck drivers are subject to encounters with the enemy day and night, and all are prepared to fight their way out of a crack. . . . Unshaven and looking like bearded Arabs, living in caves, dirty and tough as leather, our boys are helping every time the Allies gain mileage in this push, which we all hope will last in this theatre of operations.

Black American soldiers are seated at a radar station used by the 90th Coast Artillery in Casablanca, French Morocco, in June 1943.

April 30, 1943
MTO [Mediterranean Theater of Operations]
from: S/Sgt. Cleveland H. Watts

This is written from somewhere in Africa—I get around almost as fast as you. The crossing was good, and at times, very interesting. So far, I like it, even the mosquitos, scorpions, snakes and the million and one other pests. . . . You should hear my attempt at speaking the language that is spoken by the people here. It didn't take very long to learn how to ask for drinks. The scenery is very beautiful, an artists' paradise, even the people are picturesque. Please answer soon.

Sincerely,
Cleveland
[S. Sgt. Cleveland H. Watts
April 30, 1943]

By May 1, 1943, Allied forces pushing out of Tunisia, Libya, and Chad created a three-front bulldozer that the enemy could not stop. On May 7, the final line of the Axis retreat was severed and only a few hun-

Judo instruction is a required course for Marine recruits at Montford Point Camp, North. An instructor shows a recruit how to make the enemy's bayonet useless.

dred Germans escaped out of Africa. Some 275,000 German and Italian soldiers surrendered. Even Eisenhower complained that he had not learned at West Point how to handle so many prisoners. Prison camps were set up in Tunisia and Libya, and many of the POW camps were supervised by black American MPs. The North African victory was America's first in the European war, but to the anger of most GIs, the enemy seemed to be the lucky ones, as thousands of German and Italian POWs were shipped to the United States.

FREDI'S ARMY

On February 14, 1943, Hollywood stars Frederick March, Dorothy Maynor, Canada Lee, and Fredi Washington headed the cast of "Beyond the Call of Duty," a Valentine's Day afternoon radio drama designed to showcase black soldiers in the war effort. Fredi, whose given name was Fredericka, was one of the first black actresses to gain recognition for her work in film. Her best-known performance was as the young mixed-race woman who passes for white in the 1934 movie *Imitation of Life*. Her performance in that film had been so believable that she was accused by some of denying her heritage in her private life.

She did pass for white when it suited her, as when she traveled in the

Posing for the lonely soldier: young women at a dance in Seattle, Washington, take a moment to smile for the camera and for the GIs' insatiable need for "pinup" girls.

South with Duke Ellington and his band. "They could not go into ice cream parlors, so she would go in and buy the ice cream, then go outside and give it to Ellington and the band," a friend recalled. "Whites screamed at her, 'Nigger lover.' "

Far from her glamorous image, Fredi worked for equal rights for blacks on stage and in the movie industry and was a founder of the Negro Actors Guild. She wrote a column for *The People's Voice,* a weekly newspaper published by Adam Clayton Powell, her sister Isabella's husband. Foremost, said Fredi, she wanted black soldiers abroad to know they were appreciated back home.

Pinups were unofficial morale-boosters for black and white soldiers alike. Although the typical white soldier may have kept a picture of a girlfriend, or a surrogate like Betty Grable or Eva Gardner over his bunk or in his backpack, it was more likely for a black GI to have a photo of Lena Horne or another black femme. Actress Fredi Washington wrote to over one thousand black GIs during the war. Most often she received requests for pinups—sexy but modest pictures of herself or other glamorous black stars.

Seated at a typewriter, actress and columnist Fredi Washington wrote to soldiers almost daily during the war.

September 15, 1944

SOUTH PACIFIC
FROM: FREDI WASHINGTON
TO: PVT. LAWRENCE HENDERSON
BATTERY C, 76 AAA GUN BN.
Dear Henderson:

Here are the pictures you requested. Sorry I can't send them all. I do not have them all. The demand has been terrific for photographs and I am having increasing difficulty in getting a hold of them. I hope

SEPTEMBER
15th   1
              9
              4
              4

Pvt. Lawrence Henderson
Battery C, 76 AAA Gun Bn. (3m)
APO 717, c/o Postmaster
San Francisco, California

Dear Henderson:

Here are the pictures you requested. Sorry I can't send
them all, I do not have them all. The demand has been
terrific for photographs and I am having increasing difficulty in getting a hold of them. I hope this will help
to cheer things up a bit for you. I am glad to know that
you will share them with your tent mates since it is
impossible for me to send them to each of you.

Keep right on giving the Japs hell and know that our
prayers are with you.

                    Yours for PV - People's Victory,

                        Fredi Washington,
                        Theatrical Editor

F
WASHINGTON
M
L
enc.

Letter from Fredi Washington to Pvt. Lawrence Henderson, September 15, 1944.

this will help to cheer things up a bit for you. I am glad to know that you will share them with your tent mates since it is impossible for me to send them to each of you.

Keep right on giving the Japs hell and know that our prayers are with you.

Yours for PV—People's Victory,
Fredi Washington
Theatrical Editor

By February of 1943, African Americans made up about 2 percent of the navy's enlisted force. Of 26,000 black sailors, about 18,000 were messmen, 6,000 were in the general service, and 2,000 served in naval construction battalions as Seabees. Angered that the navy had failed to reach a target of 10 percent black recruitment, President Roosevelt insisted the navy quit dragging its feet. The president's orders were heeded, as more than 10 percent of sailors drafted during 1943 were blacks, some 78,000 out of 740,000.

An airman cadet shown on a cot in his barracks studying, gazing fondly at his collection of photos of his girlfriends.

BATTLE OF BISMARCK SEA

On March 3 and 4, 1943, Allied land-based bombers destroyed a Japanese convoy in the Bismarck Sea. American pilots were celebrated back home for the victory, but barely a word made it to American newspapers about the role played by American construction battalions in the Pacific strategy. By the time of the Bismarck Sea battle, more than 10,000 black soldiers, in construction-related units, were deployed in the region, building the very bases from which the American bombers took off and landed. At an inspection of the 96th Engineer Battalion on its one-year anniversary in the South Pacific, Brig. Gen. Hanford MacNider offered his personal commendation. On that proud occasion, General Mac-Nider did not fail to make the connection between the work of America's black soldiers and American success in the Pacific War:

> Fellow soldiers, a year ago today, when you stepped ashore as the first American troop unit in New Guinea, you were making history. You've been making it ever since. You've had a part in the building and upkeep of all our airfields; and thus you've helped make possible the destruction of the convoy in the Bismarck Sea, the flying of the infantry over the mountains, against a hundred enemy actions. You've

Messmen's dreams: opportunities for black enlisted men in the navy were few during the first two years of the war. In this painting navy crew members inspect a fighter plane aboard the USS Ranger. *Artist: Paul Sample.*

contributed your share to every crack we've taken at the Japs. You've carried important works projects, even unloaded ships so we could eat and fight. You've built roads and the mains which give us power and light. You're one of the workingest outfits in this man's Army. All of us here are proud of you. All America will be proud of you when your record gets into the histories. Some of you have been to war with the tanks. You all know about bombs from hanging them on planes and having them hung on you. You've been good soldiers and you're going to be good soldiers. The harder we work and the better we do our jobs, the quicker you and I are going to get back where we belong—to the United States of America, which is all wrapped up in that flag which you are saluting today.

10

THE FIGHTING 99TH

[1943]

Yes, we were black—but that wasn't a negative to us. That just meant we had to be just as good and probably better than the white guys or they would find some way to wash us out of the program—which gave us a great deal of confidence. Sure, we were colored, but yes, we were qualified. We were negroes and Americans, too.

LT. ROSCOE C. BROWN, MEMBER OF THE FIGHTING 99TH

In June 1943, the 99th Fighter Squadron received combat orders for its first mission in the Mediterranean Sea. Assigned to the Twelfth Air Force's 33rd Fighter Group, the pilots of the 99th discovered quickly that their battle was not only against the Germans and Italians. On June 2nd, the day of the 99th's first mission, Lt. Spann Watson learned that black pilots could not always rely on their white commanders:

We were to fly over to the 33rd Fighter Group base and be loaded, briefed, and checked out for the mission to Pantellaria. The briefing was almost over when we got there, and I remember this obviously bigoted redneck was talking in this long southern drawl, and he looked up at us and said, "Y'all boys keep up." That was all the briefing I got before I went to war. So, brother, I kept up.

Pilots learn their "target for today" during a briefing at a base in Italy. From June 1943 through the war's end, African-American airmen of the 99th Fighter Squadron, and later the 332nd Fighter Group, were among the most distinguished units of the Allied forces.

On July 10, 1943—D-Day for the Sicilian invasion—the Allied forces (the U.S. Seventh Army and the British Eighth Army) stormed the beaches and met stiff German resistance. Fighter and bomber squadrons were used heavily in the campaign that successfully pushed the enemy to Messina—and off Sicily to the Italian peninsula. In the Sicily invasion, the 99th flew over 175 dive-bombing and strafing missions. One 99th pilot, Lt. Richard Bolling of Virginia, was shot down and parachuted from his burning plane. He remained adrift in the Mediterranean for over twenty-four hours before he was rescued and sent back to the North African base. Three pilots from the 99th were killed in the offensive that led to the total collapse of the Italian army and the downfall of the Italian leader Mussolini.

Abandoned by his army, Mussolini was deposed on July 25 and imprisoned. In August, U.S. forces firmed up their position on Sicily to await their next move—to the Italian mainland. With "one down and two to go," the American public responded joyfully when General Eisenhower announced Italy's unconditional surrender on September 8.

In America accolades were heaped upon the brave American soldiers who had brought Mussolini to his knees, yet the bravery of the 99th Fighter Squadron was publicly questioned. In September of 1943, *Time* magazine reported that the Tuskegee experiment had not gone well. The source of the negative comments was Col. William Momyer, commander of the 33rd and an opponent of the 99th Fighter Squadron. Momyer suggested that cowardice kept the squadron from responding aggressively when threatened by enemy fire. The 99th had not scored enough "kills," according to Momyer, to warrant keeping them in combat. With more opinion than evidence, Momyer concluded that the black pilots were a failure.

In reality, the 99th had scored fewer kills because their participation in the invasion force was limited, and they were often assigned support service far from the battlefront. Members of the 99th said that Momyer himself had excluded them from briefing sessions for missions they were expected to fly with the 33rd. Momyer's prejudice against the 99th held dangerous and life-threatening implications for the black airmen as they flew missions without knowing Momyer's full strategy.

Just days before the next invasion, onto the Italian mainland, the reputation and fate of the 99th were judged by the military command. The squadron's known support from the White House kept the slanderous charge from carrying the day, and Momyer's desire for the black squadron's removal from combat came to naught. The Allied command had a "cowardice" issue far bigger than the accusations made against the 99th. The invasion of Sicily was marked by incidents of friendly fire, uncoordinated air support, lost troops, and miscommunications. Nevertheless, by mid-August the island fell, and 10,000 German and Italian troops fled over the Straits of Messina, unmolested. (Another thorny courage issue faced Gen. George Patton, who had slapped a soldier in a field hospital, accusing the crying and shaking soldier of cowardice—only to find that the soldier was suffering from malaria with a 104-degree fever.)

September 9 was D-Day for the Italy invasion. The new phase of the war marked the first time Germany would stand alone and head-to-head against the Allies. That morning the U.S. Fifth Army launched its landing assault on Salerno. The 99th provided air support for the ground

A signal corps company has set up its office at the ancient Temple of Neptune in Campania, Italy, which was built about 700 B.C.

mission. The Germans responded with massive resistance, forcing the Allies to retreat.

To meet the German counterattack, an advance team of ten members of the 99th was sent to a newly captured airport near Salerno on the Italian peninsula. From that forward base, the 99th provided air cover for the Allied amphibious advance upon the coast. Because of the urgency of the battle, the courage controversy was put aside. The remainder of the 99th squadron stayed at the base in Termini, Sicily, monitoring enemy and friendly shipping operations and providing escort.

In October the 99th was assigned to fly with the 79th Fighter Group, commanded by Col. Earl Bates. Unlike the bigoted Momyer, Bates fully involved the pilots of the 99th in combat missions. Under the new commander, the pilots of the 79th and 99th pounded at the German army in its slow retreat northward. Flying five or more sorties per day, they flew missions against railroad targets, bridges, and enemy communication links.

THE 24TH CHEMICAL DECONTAMINATION COMPANY

The assault at Salerno was the first Mediterranean invasion to use smoke screens extensively. A detachment of the all-black 24th Chemical Decontamination Company, equipped with generators and smoke pots mounted on boats, screened the beaches where boats were being unloaded. The men laid a smoke haze daily at twilight to conceal anchorage and unloading areas from enemy bombers and screened the beaches during alerts. Covering an area of more than twenty square miles, not a single ship in the smoke cloud was hit by enemy bombs. The 24th, along with other smoke companies, later moved to Naples to maintain the smoke screen there.

BUILDUP IN THE PACIFIC

On the Pacific front in mid-1943, the airfields, docks, and port facilities built by white and black construction battalions in Australia, New Guinea, Guadalcanal, Midway, and the Gilbert Islands began to receive fighter planes, bombers, and navy ships for the next phase of the war: to move another two or three thousand miles closer to the enemy, close enough to be within bombing range of Japan.

Units of African-American soldiers, primarily quartermaster, truck, and general service battalions assigned to move, unload, and store war materials, met up with the construction and aviation battalions that had arrived earlier. Ordnance battalions, most comprised of black soldiers, were assigned to all military and naval stations in the Pacific. Accompanying virtually every landing of the army and Marines, ordnance companies were always nearby. By June 1943, more than 100,000 black

I won the bronze star medal under fire unloading a ship. At the time I was only thinking of one thing and that was getting the ship unloaded.

Things happened so fast I wasn't afraid until the booming was over & I was almost through unloading the ship.

Thank you

James D. McKinney

Letter from Pvt. James D. McKinney to Lawrence Reddick, September 1946. McKinney received a Bronze Star for unloading a ship in New Guinea during an enemy attack.

Dusty road in New Guinea: black soldiers were the first American military contingent to arrive in New Guinea in 1942. Constructing airfields and building and maintaining roads were among their assignments. Artist: Barse Miller.

American soldiers were distributed throughout the base stations in the Pacific.

MEDAL OF HONOR

On March 8, 1943, Pvt. George Watson of the 29th Quartermaster Regiment was aboard a ship nearing the coast of New Guinea when it was attacked and hit by Japanese bombers. The ship was abandoned, but Private Watson, without regard for his own safety, remained in the water, assisting several soldiers who could not swim to reach the safety of life rafts. This heroic action, which subsequently cost him his life, resulted in the saving of several of his comrades. In January 1997, President William J. Clinton bestowed the Medal of Honor posthumously on Private Watson—one of seven African Americans honored forty-four years later, and the only one to earn the medal in the Pacific Theater and in a noncombat unit. "Over and over and over again," noted the president in his remarks at the belated ceremony, Private Watson continued saving others, "until he himself was so exhausted, he was pulled down by the tow of the sinking ship." The seven belated Medals of Honor were the first granted to African-American soldiers since the Spanish-American War.

A Navy recruiter lied to me right to my face. He said there were lots of good jobs and skills for me to learn if I signed the enlistment form, and so I signed it. I told him I didn't want to work in anybody's kitchen, not for the Navy or anybody else. But then I found out they were going to put me in the kitchen, and I wanted out. They said I signed and I had to stay or I'd be AWOL. I told them I signed alright, but I signed for what the lying recruiter promised me and not for work they had for me on a piece of paper. I told them they would have to throw me in jail to get me to wash a single dish. They let me go, and I went and joined the Marines.

Pfc. Robert Fields
U.S. Marines, 1943–45

Citation: Elbert H. Oliver

Steward's Mate First Class, U.S. Navy

For conspicuous gallantry and intrepidness while serving aboard a United States warship during a raid upon that vessel by approximately twenty-five Japanese torpedo planes in the vicinity of the Solomon Islands on June 30, 1943. When members of his 22-mm gun crew were severely wounded by a bursting projectile, Oliver quickly took over the station of the injured gunner and although he himself was bleeding profusely, maintained accurate fire against the attacking planes until eventually compelled to give way to a relief gunner. His aggressive fighting spirit and grim determination to carry on in the face of danger despite acute pain and waning strength were in keeping with the highest traditions of the United States naval service.

From: Pvt. Laurence W. Harris
  356 Av. Sqdn. S.P.A.A.T.
  Lubbock, Texas
  November 4, 1943
To: The Pittsburgh Courier
Dear Gentlemen:

I am writing to you in regards to my classification in the army. I have been in the army air corp for the past ten months. Gentlemen I do not feel, and in fact I know I am not doing the best I could to help win this war. I realize the army has a tough job trying to place each man where they think he is best fitted or will do the best of service for the armed forces.

In my civil life I was a small tool maker. I worked for Silling and Spences Co. in Hartford, Conn. Then I was doing much for the war effort, and was in hopes I could continue in the service. In the past ten months I feel as though I have been a complete failure to myself, and to the helping to win this war. Beside that my morale is very low because of the fact I have given the army ten months to reclassify me to something I could do much [more] than what I am doing.

I was in hopes I could become an airplane mechanic, but the field doesn't seem to be open to negro soldiers.

I only hope and pray that I will hear from you soon to what I could do, to get into some part of the service where I could use my trade.

Thanking you in advance.

Yours Very Truly,

Pvt. Laurence W. Harris

From: A noncom in the 92nd Division
November 23, 1943
To: Mr. C. A. Scott
General Manager
Atlanta Daily World
Dear Sir,

May I extend my heartfelt congratulations to you and your paper for the article printed awhile back concerning the 92nd Division. It really pictured quite a few existing evils that the Negro soldiers and officers are forced to come in contact with. A thousand congratulations to you.

May I add that the conditions are really appalling. This outfit is the most rotten outfit in the World. We have no program—we only walk, walk, walk. These daily hikes are made only to keep us away from the garrisons, because the program made out by Colonel Bailer's, Chief of Staff, is really unfit for an inductee.

The colored officers are fed up with it. They know that they are not being treated fairly, but there is nothing they can do. Whenever they go over bounds, they are simply reclassified. Though we have some brilliant Negro officers they are never promoted. Some of these officers hold degrees from the nation's outstanding universities, while white officers come from Ft. Benning, ignorant as the days are long. In a few months they are captains. The poor colored officer who is his superior in service, tact and etc. is still a Second Lt.

General [Edward M.] Almond is rotten. Possibly the news never reached you but there are several rumors that he has been fired at by soldiers who despise him. Whenever he is introduced, there is the usual "Boo."

When General [Benjamin O.] Davis inspects the P.T.U. [physical training uniform], our cripples are hidden. These are men who are walked "to death" and are physically unfit to carry on. They are really sapping the life out of the fellows. The morale is at as low an ebb as in a whore-house. Nobody gives a d—— about what happens. Unless something is done there will be an internal revolution. They are afraid for us to have our rifles after we leave the field. They search daily for ammunition. I swear to God it is pathetic.

It is true that I am a non-commissioned officer in the outfit, but I shall withhold my name because it will only get me "busted" and a term in the guard house. I ask that you even destroy this letter after reading it. The name on the envelope may or may not be mine.

[Signed] One who desires you to know

Diary Entry of Lt. Hyman Samuelson, a White Lieutenant in Charge of the 96th Engineer Aviation Battalion, in New Guinea; October 11, 1943

Before I die I must help stamp out this crazy idea that the white man has about his superiority over the colored man. In no concrete way has he ever demonstrated it. Here we fight the Germans because they declare themselves a superior race. Individually they have demonstrated their boast. Their medicine, science, manufacturers are, or at least were, superior to that of any other nation. Yet this did not give them the right to declare that they were superior to all other men and to be able to dictate to others. Yet we Americans, the ones who are trying to thrash out Germany's idiotic ideas, feel the same way about negroes. It's wrong—damn wrong! The negro is our equal physically. He is superior to us spiritually. He has the same intelligence as a white man. What he lacks is opportunity, opportunity to get an education, a decent job, decent living conditions. And these are the things which we white men deprive him of. And they are smart enough to know that we are wrong, but being in the minority they can do nothing about it.

> Sometimes I would like to be able to tell them just how I feel, but it would do more harm than a thousand bomber raids in our camp area. And they are inclined to believe that I am just the opposite of what I am. I am harsh and firm and tell a subordinate to do things, not ask him to do it—and do it right. And if he doesn't, he catches hell. But I'm that way because I accomplish more—for myself and my country. But the men think I treat them that way because my color is different from theirs. That hurts, really hurts. I wish there were something I could do about it. I will—some day. Yes, some day I will. But now is not the time. I must keep doing what I think is right, even if it means a knife in my back some night.

ON SCREEN: HOLLYWOOD AND THE BLACK SOLDIER

Bataan, Hollywood's quickly made movie of the last stand of thirteen American soldiers in the Philippines, seemed to mark a new era for black Americans in film when it opened June 3, 1943. Critically acclaimed and a box-office hit, the movie included Kenneth Spencer as Wesley Eeps (pronounced Epps), a black engineer who mastered a machine gun and fought heroically until his death. The NAACP presented Warner Brothers with an award in recognition of the film's interracial casting.

Sahara, an epic about warfare in the Libyan desert, followed, starring Humphrey Bogart and Rex Ingram as a black French-African soldier. Schomburg Center director Lawrence Reddick declared the war films two of Hollywood's best ever:

> He [Ingram] is perhaps the first Negro on the screen who has been permitted to have a white man as his personal servant—a captured Italian soldier. The Negro soldier is allowed to be brave and intelligent. He uses his hands as a cup for the dripping water which quenches the thirst of the whole group. As a climax this Negro, in the face of gun-fire, overtakes a fleeing Nazi, physically overcomes him and pushes his blonde head down into the desert sand. This may be the first time ever that any Negro—even a foreign Negro—has been permitted by Hollywood to assume a heroic role while killing a white man, even an enemy.

11

The Long, Hot Summer
[1943]

Looky here, America,
What you done done—
Let things drift
Until the riots come.

Now your policemen
Let the mobs run free.
I reckon you don't care
Nothing about me.

You tell me that hitler
Is a mighty bad man.
I guess he took lessons
From the ku klux klan.

You tell me mussolini's
Got an evil heart.
Well, it mus-a been in Beaumont
That he had his start—

Cause everything that hitler
And mussolini do
Negroes get the same
Treatment from you. . . .

Excerpt from
"Beaumont to Detroit: 1943"
by Langston Hughes

On May 25, 1943, riots started just before midnight when twelve black welders tried to go to their jobs at the Alabama Dry Dock and Shipbuilding Company in Mobile. More than one hundred black workers were injured in the racial violence that halted work on vital transport-ship production. The violence ended only when an Alabama National Guard unit stationed nearby intervened.

"The whites who were in employment there desired that blacks would hold the most menial jobs," said an NAACP official. "Despite the fact that black boys were fighting, bleeding, and dying on foreign battlefields, this made no impression on the whites who were workers at ADDSCO." Whites resentful over working next to blacks staged many work stoppages and slowdowns throughout the country.

One week after the Mobile uprising, 25,000 white workers in Detroit stopped production on engines for bombers and PT boats at the Packard Motor Company. Work halted in protest of the promotion of three black workers. One striker reportedly shouted, "I'd rather see Hitler and Hirohito win than work beside a nigger on the assembly line." Despite pleas by the National War Labor Board "to resume production of vitally needed war material at once," the workers stayed off the job. United Auto Workers president R. J. Thomas called the action "one of the most shameful exhibitions of this war," and he blamed the local Ku Klux Klan for inciting the plant shutdown. On the fourth day of the stoppage (a Saturday), Thomas made an urgent, and successful, demand that full production resume on Monday, with the return of all workers.

"I delivered the strongest ultimatum I have ever made in asking those Packard workers to go back, but I'm going to make it even stronger, even if it requires that large numbers of the white workers lose their jobs," asserted Thomas.

Days later in Beaumont, Texas, white shipyard workers who had long opposed integration reacted violently to a rumor of a black man raping a white woman. More than 3,000 workers marched to the city jail. Even though the woman could not identify the suspect among the blacks held in the city jail, the workers began terrorizing black neighborhoods. More than one hundred stores were ransacked. Fifty people were injured, and two blacks and one white were killed in the violence.

MAY 27, 1943 The federal government barred all war contractors from discriminating in hiring on the basis of race.

Racial tensions erupted most violently on June 20, again in Detroit. On that ninety-degree Sunday evening at Belle Isle, minor skirmishes broke out between blacks and whites, later escalating when police started searching the cars of blacks entering Belle Isle, although they did not search cars driven by whites. Fighting spread to several areas of the city, with rocks and bottles thrown, cars burned, homes vandalized, and stores looted. More than 1,800 were arrested and 200 injured; thirty-four people were killed that night, twenty-five of them black.

NAACP attorney Thurgood Marshall assailed the city's police department for its handling of the riot. Marshall charged that the police aggressively targeted blacks with a shoot-to-kill policy, while turning their backs on white-initiated violence. "This weak-kneed policy of the police commissioner coupled with the anti-Negro attitude of many members of the force helped to make a riot inevitable," said Marshall. According to Marshall, 85 percent of those arrested were black while whites overturned and burned cars with impunity as police watched.

Throughout the summer of 1943 racial violence ignited in more than twenty cities, including Chester, Pennsylvania, where one black shipworker was killed by guards and four others were wounded at the Sun Shipbuilding Company. In Harlem, more than 185 people were injured and six people killed in racial fighting. The disturbance was caused when a white policeman attempted to arrest a black woman in the company of a black soldier.

From a Letter to the Philadelphia *Afro American*

April 19, 1943
Dear Sirs:

I am writing you this letter in response to [my] subscription of the Afro American *of which I have not been receiving. I hope you will take the matter in consideration because without this paper I have no means of knowing what is happening in my home town which is Philly.*

Few civilians never have the idea of what we boys are really going through down here in Texas, one of the worst states in this country. I've been in the Army for sixteen months and I know what the young boys are facing that are being drafted each and every day. I have been stationed in Mississippi and also in Southern California. Maybe you have heard of the Desert Training Center located at Indio, California. Yes I was there for seven months where the heat was 150 and some days even hotter. But the boys took everything they could dish out and more too; white boys killing their buddies and even killing themselves. I've saw equipment burned up; boys roasted in them and they tell you to be a good soldier.

And now, way down in Texas, where we're not even as good as dogs, much less soldiers, even our General on the post hates the sight of a colored soldier. Why I ask you, do we have to fight on the home front for our lives then go across seas and fight again? Sure I'm giving you the real facts about Ft. Clark, Texas. Everything is true and my buddies can tell you the same thing.

There is a town down here called Bracketville and let me tell you it couldn't be any worse than hell itself. When you go to the movies you are jim crowed; whites on one side and you on the other. And that's right on the post. Sure we're fighting a war, but who starts these wars? Do the colored boys or do the white race who think they can master the world?

If you're a man and you think a whole lot of your paper then print this because three times to one I've got a lot more to tell that would make your head swim. The only thing you can do is sit down and write a letter home. Otherwise you would go crazy and I know, because I almost blew my top.

It's not that we boys don't want to fight but what are we really fighting for? Is it to free America or throw us back ten years? Ask any real Army man and he'll tell you that the colored soldier is the best, can do anything better than a white boy. That why there are some many colored boys in the Engineer and Quartermaster Corps doing the hard jobs.

I've got a wife home, a mother, father and sister and brothers. Some day I'm going back there.

General Davis was down here this week to see what makes Ft. Clark tick. I and every other soldier on this post knows what this report will be.

It will read something like this: "Boys at Ft. Clark are having time of their life."

Yes, we're having a fine time in hell. But to you and all the colored civilians that are still out there, turn this bit of news loose. Let the colored public know what their boys are really going through. That's my story so let's hear about it. Every boy down here is waiting for your answer. About my subscription, being to my change of station, I don't think you knew my right address, it is as follows:

WAR GAMES IN LOUISIANA: WHITE INFANTRY VS. BLACK INFANTRY

In April 1943, the 93rd Infantry Division (the "Blue Helmets") shook the Arizona dust from their boots and boarded seventy-two railroad cars headed east for maneuvers. The maneuvers were war games, designed to train soldiers, in the bayous and backwoods of Louisiana, for jungle warfare. The historic occasion saw a white division (the 85th Infantry) pitted against a black division (the 93rd Infantry).

But the Blue Helmets were dealt a setback even before the games began. Ordinarily in war game maneuvers, competing divisions exchanged officers to act as umpires. In this case, however, both division commanders agreed that black officers serving as umpires of white troops was a bad idea: "Utilization of colored and white officers acting respectively as umpires of colored and white divisions operating against each other may result in the creation of undesirable situations. It is believed highly desirable that all umpires be white," the commanders concluded. Black officers would be used to rate only black units. Consequently, units within divisions, but not the divisions themselves, exchanged umpires.

Judged by their own officers in the war games hardly constituted "an edge" for the 93rd, who overwhelming believed they were not getting adequate support or training from their officers, 70 percent of whom were white. A few weeks before the games, a white officer visiting Huachuca (in Arizona) observed: "Among the white officers the outstanding question [is] as to whether the division will ever be able to perform combat service. The feeling is that it will not and that nobody on the staff would dream of sending it to combat." Absent confidence or comaraderie with their own officers, some war game observers were of the opinion that the 93rd entered the games "expecting to lose." Given the unusual umpiring situation, the idea of winning or losing was downplayed, and the emphasis put on performance in battle conditions.

Under conditions of heat and rain the Red Force (93rd Division) competed in six weeks of competition against the Blue Force (85th Division). Enacting many elements of warfare, including amphibious landings, moving troops into positions through swamps and heavy brush, the two teams were judged also on speed and quality in construction of airfields, bridges, and roads. Both squads transported ammunition and rounded up prisoners of war—all while "enemy" planes dropped sacks of flour "bombs" and umpires jumped from behind bushes to throw blue or red flags, thus "killing" or "capturing" soldiers. At the end of the war games, the white 85th received a very satisfactory report; the black 93rd was rated unsatisfactory. Most strikingly the observer reports indicated that the soldiers worked best following noncommissioned officers, but under their white officers, the 93rd "fell apart." Two of the four observers disagreed with these low ratings.

Some observers concluded that the 93rd did poorly because "this was not their war." Meanwhile, one local mayor (of De Ridder, Louisiana) commended the 93rd for its exemplary behavior during the war games. In a letter dated June 29, 1943, the mayor wrote to Secretary Stimson

> . . . to express my thanks and appreciation of the splendid deportment of the officers and men of the 93rd Inf. Div. (colored) during their stay in this area.
>
> We anticipated no trouble before they came our way, and have given every effort to make their stay pleasant, cooperating with the officers to give the men every possible entertainment and recreation. The troops have been very orderly and well disciplined, causing no trouble or apprehension that could encourage criticism—for which we are thankful.

Complaints were many, however, among the ranks of the 93rd. The major gripe among the men was that their training was deficient and that they were not being taken seriously. White senior officers took the grievances as mutinous. Fearing repercussions, on November 22, 1943, members of two squadrons sent a joint unsigned letter to Secretary of War Stimson:

Letter to the Richmond *Afro-American*

from: 328th Aviation Squadron
Pampa Army Air Field
Pampa, Texas
to: Richmond Afro-American
503 N. 3rd St.
Richmond, Va.
November 22, 1943
Dear Sirs:

I am writing this letter to acquaint you with the horrible and Unamerican treatment of the Negro Personnel of this field and beseeching you to please come to our rescue. Every Negro man on this post is absolutely fed up and disappointed with the bad treatment and discrimination, segregation and injustice imposed upon us. You must please understand that we do not resent serving our country (we are proud to serve), but we would like and want very much to serve it in a more important capacity than we are at this time. We can and would fight if trained to do so, but as yet we hardly know what a gun, or tank, combat plans, a hand grenade, machine gun look like. We haven't had any drilling to speak of that could be classified as drilling. We had three (3) weeks for basic training. It takes that long to learn to do the manual of arms (arms are something we haven't even seen except a 45 on the M.P.'s side, ready to blow your brains out if you resent being treated like a dog or being called a nigger or a Black son of a b———.), much less call it Basic Training.

Here are a few of our handicaps (yes only a few). We hardly know how to enclose in this letter all the information on the matter, please print this in your paper. Please help us.

1st: We are a group of permanent K.P.'s [kitchen police]. We are allowed no other advancement whatsoever. It is true that K.P. pushers (Head K.P.) are made Cpl. and Sgt. But the K.P.'s themselves are a miserable group that will be worked like slaves without any ratings to speak of. We are confined to this job not because we are not fit for anything else but because we are dark. We are referred to on this post as "that nigger squadron at the end of the field."

2nd: We are discriminated against in everything we do or take part in. The post theatre is divided off for the 328th (that's our squadron). Government buildings also. In the hospital when we are improving from our ailments, we are used as K.P.'s there until released. In the Gym we are segregated even for a Colored U.S.O. show. We are allowed (they think it's a privilege) the great privilege of serving the Aviation Cadets at their social functions as waiters and flunkies of all descriptions. Some times we are allowed nights to play games in the Gym and they take these nights away from us to give dances for the Cadets and officers or white enlisted men. At these functions we are subject to all kinds of abusive languages. Such as Nigger, darkie, son of a b———, and everything mentionable. (I won't censor this letter because I want you to get the true picture).

3rd: The 908th Quartermaster Group (colored) which was formerly men of the 328th [were] transferred, but still sleep and eat with us, and share all the hardships and abusive treatments as usual. So everything I mentioned in this letter is pertaining to them too. They are just truck drivers and are called the 908th Quartermaster Company.

4th: There are men in our squadron that have passed the test for O.C.S. and Aviation Cadet, but have not been sent away for training as they requested. The majority of us are well educated, are fit for something other than K.P.'s for the white cadets [and] officers and driving trucks.

5th: Some of us have special trades that we were working on before induction, more important to the war effort than K.P.'s in the army. Some of the men here have gone to Baking and Cooking Schools, finished and [are] back here doing K.P., now for the whites. Some have gone to mechanic school and come back here to be truck drivers. They just drive the trucks not given the opportunity to work on them. We are sick of this treatment and disgusted with the K.P. duty day in and day out. Then there are so many, many dirty jobs around here that falls to our lot.

6th: We get no consideration from our commanding officers at all. He never stands up for us when any racial clashes occur, although he is an Eastern man (Boston, Mass.). He never thinks of trying to get us out of here, or allowing us to quit the mess hall, or allow any request for transfers from here to go through to headquarters. We have been here for ten months (the 10th day of February) and have been laborers and K.P.'s ever sence. Why can't we be given transfers closer home and given better jobs or a[t] least remain here and treated like citizens of the U.S. of America. Instead we are still slaves, laborers and flunkies for the white personnel here.

7th: The bus that comes from town has a contract with this post to carry and bring the soldiers to town. There again we are segregated and discriminated against. Four seats (eight men) for Negroes if we are lucky enough to get on first. The remainder stands regardless if the bus is completely loaded. If we don't get on first, all stand and like it, no protests for the seats allowed, take that and like it or have one of these Texas M.P.'s crack your skull with a 45 or a stick.

8th: The white civilians hate us and we in return despise them because they abuse us in anyway they see fit. The city police have mistreated our boys on many occasions and the military authorities never go to bat for us.

9th: The city police have pulled our men out of Government cars and beat them up. One of our boys locked himself inside the car and they broke the glass and took him out forcibly and beat him unmercifully. He got 30 days in the guard house and 15 days were solitary confinement, while he was sick with bruises from the terrible beating. Our commanding officer asked him about it and before he could tell his side of the story he (the officer) said "That's not the way I heard it." So the boy just shut up then and waited for his trial. The adjutant of our squadron wanted to beat him up again because the boy resented the attitude that they took toward his case.

10th: The main thing we resent about this place is the work we have to do without ratings, the segregation and discrimination for Negroes. The lack of opportunity for advancement. So gentlemen if you will please see fit to help us in some way we the whole squadron and the 908th Quartermaster Company (negro) will greatly appreciate it and will cooperate 100% if investigated.

Copies of this letter are being sent to Colonel B. O. Davis, the N.A.A.C.P. and the War Dept. at Washington.

Thanking You Very Much,
328th Aviation Squadron and 908th Quartermaster Company

By the end of 1943, the number of black officers assigned to the 93rd increased dramatically, more than doubling from 250 to 575. Most of the division's white officers were reassigned, reducing their ranks from 634 to 279.

Six months later Maj. Gen. Virgil L. Peterson declared that the 93rd was ready to be committed to combat duty overseas. "The men have confidence in their officers, in their training, and in their ability to defeat the enemy." By late December 1943, the 93rd were aboard four troop transport ships—*General John Pope, Lurline, Torrens,* and *West Point*—heading for the South Pacific. Still, there were some soldiers who were surprised by the new turn of events: "There were those of us who held tenaciously to the belief that we would never see action or go overseas; however that fallacy has been dispelled. Time took care of that. When all of the men finally awoke to the fact that we were definitely going over, they, as the slang goes, 'straightened up and flew right.' "

By June 1944, the 92nd Infantry Division had completed its training at Fort Huachuca, before traveling east by rail to Virginia, where they were to board transport ships headed for northern Italy.

The all-black 92nd Division followed the 93rd into Fort Huachuca, and participated in the Sixth Louisiana Maneuvers, from February to April 1944. The 92nd received a satisfactory rating. Division commander Maj. Gen. Edward M. Almond congratulated the men: "This is a unit that the Colored race should be proud of, and they will be before we are through; and not only the Colored race, but every American who knows enough to read about his war. . . . You must take great satisfaction that you are now about to actually prove your worth."

The 92nd Division was also judged combat ready and prepared to ship out to the Pacific.

JUNE 15, 1943: Dorie Miller, heroic seaman at Pearl Harbor, was one of a crew of 700 men who were killed when a Japanese submarine torpedoed and sank the aircraft carrier USS *Liscombe Bay.*

Truman K. Gibson, Jr.
Civilian Aide to the Secretary of War
Washington, D.C.
November 5, 1943
Dear Mr. Gibson:

. . . I prayed that I'd be sent to a camp in my home state or that I'd be sent to some camp in a Northern State. My prayers weren't answered and I find myself at this outpost of civilization. I never wanted to be within twenty hundred miles of Alexandria, Louisiana. I am here and I can do nothing to improve my condition. Nevertheless, I prepare to fight for a country where I am denied the rights of being a full-fledged citizen.

A few weeks after my arrival, at this camp, I went to a post-exchange on my regimental area. I knew that each area has an exchange but I thought that I could make my purchase at any of them. Upon entering I could feel the place grow cold. All conversation ceased. It was then that I noticed that all the soldiers and the saleswomen were white. Not to be outdone I approached the counter and was told (even before asking for the article) that, "Negroes are not served here. This post-exchange is for white soldiers. You have one near your regiment. Buy what you want there."

My answer to these abrupt and rudely made statements was in the form of a question—"I thought that post exchanges are for soldiers regardless of color, am I right?" I left this post-exchange and returned to my regimental area. I know that these saleswomen knew not the way of a true democracy.

As long as I am a soldier I fight for a mock Democracy. . . .

A Loyal Negro Soldier

BLACK JOURNALISTS ABROAD

Toward the end of 1943, fourteen black newspapers formed a war correspondents' "pool"—according to their agreement, each paper paid a quarterly amount for the services of all the pooled correspondents. The first two journalists selected were Fletcher Martin and Frank Bolden.

A U.S. Army truck climbs the Ledo supply road that winds from India to Burma and China. Sixty percent of the American troops assigned to rebuild, maintain, and drive supplies along the route were African Americans.

Their stories were wired to the Office of War Information and forwarded to the members by the two black members of the OWI press section. The newspapers participating included the *Afro American Group* (Baltimore), *Atlanta Daily World, Chicago Bee, Chicago Defender, Cleveland Call Post, Detroit Tribune, Houston Informer, Kansas City Call* (Missouri), *Louisville Defender, Michigan Chronicle* (Detroit), *New York Amsterdam News, Norfolk Journal and Guide, Philadelphia Tribune,* and *Pittsburgh Courier.*

Stories filed by black journalists generally profiled black combat units, and, to a lesser extent, black service troops, in all the war theaters. Typically, black journalists emphasized the normalcy of black American soldiers working and fighting for their country.

12

FIGHTERS OVER ANZIO

[1944]

On January 24, 1944, the 99th Fighter Squadron broke out in a big way over Anzio, where recently arrived American troops were reeling from the bombardment of German artillery and planes. In a morning confrontation, fifteen of the 99ths' P-40 planes went after sixteen or more enemy aircraft that were pulling out of a bombing and strafing run over Anzio. The 99th destroyed five, possibly six, German planes and damaged four more. In the afternoon, the 99th planes returned to the skies over the beach and downed three more German planes.

The following day American planes knocked out twenty-one enemy planes, with the 99th credited with four e/a (enemy aircraft) destroyed. "It's a grand show. You're doing a magnificent job," declared Maj. Gen. John Cannon about the 99th and the 79th Fighter Group.

Flying missions over Anzio and Nettuno, the 99th scored impressively for several days. Another German plane fell to the 99th on February 5, and two days later the squadron brought down three more enemy planes. The *Atlanta Journal* editorialized: "The success of the 99th U.S. Fighter Squadron in the air battles over the Nettuno beachhead Thursday will be gratifying to all Americans whatever their race or position. It should be cause for special pride among our Negroes. The fine perfor-mance of the 99th in its first desperate adventure will give its members a confidence in themselves that will make the 99th a unit to be feared by the enemy." For its stunning success in the winter of 1944, the squadron received an official commendation from Gen. Hap Arnold.

After the capture of Salerno, the 99th was sent to Paestum, Italy, where their mission was to patrol the areas surrounding Salerno. Mean-while, Col. Benjamin O. Davis, Jr., was transferred back to the United States to organize another contingent of black fighter pilots, the 332nd Fighter Group.

In April, the 99th was reassigned from the 79th Fighter Group to partner with the 324th Fighter Group. Together they participated in Op-eration Strangle, a joint British and American aerial campaign designed to cut off the enemy from its food, ammunition, and fuel supplies. Op-eration Strangle marked the last operation of the 99th Fighter Squadron as an independent outfit.

THE 332ND

On July 4, 1944, the 99th was reassigned, along with three new all-black squadrons, all trained at Tuskegee. Thus the 99th, the 100th, the 301st, and the 302nd were joined to form the 332nd Fighter Group. Following the lead of the veteran 99th, the new group transitioned to new planes, Mustangs, decorating them with bright red spinners and tails, thus earn-ing them the nickname "Redtails."

Operating as bomber escorts on one of its first missions—a bombing run against Austrian railyards—Capt. Joseph Elsberry, a 332nd pilot, shot down three German planes. A few days later, on July 18, the black pilots scored big, shooting down eleven e/a, Lt. Clarence "Lucky" Lester top-ping the effort with three "kills."

October was a tough month for the 332nd, seeing the loss of fifteen pilots. The group flew twenty-two missions in December, running its total to sixty-two confirmed air-to-air victories by year's end. Bad weather in January 1945 limited the group to eleven missions, the num-ber rising to thirty-nine in February.

BENJAMIN O. DAVIS, JR.

The son of America's first black general, Benjamin Oliver Davis, Jr., spent his childhood on military bases, and at age fourteen he had an experience that made him aspire to become a pilot. His father had arranged for him to fly in an open-cockpit plane. A good student, Davis attended a predominantly white Cleveland high school, where he was elected senior class president. In 1932 he entered West Point Military Academy.

Davis's presence as an African American was immediately opposed by his fellow cadets. For his entire four years at West Point he was subjected to the "silent treatment"—no one would room with him, eat with him, listen to him, or talk to him, except to issue an order. Nevertheless, Davis graduated in the top 15 percent of his class, the academy's fourth African-American graduate, and the first to be commissioned in the twentieth century.

Thanks to his high class rank, Davis was allowed to choose his service area; but when he picked the Air Corps (then a branch of the army), he was rejected. He was told that there were no black squadrons and he would not be allowed in a white squadron. Second Lieutenant Davis reported to Fort Benning to join the 24th Infantry Regiment, which served primarily as a labor pool.

When an experimental training program to train black pilots was started in 1941, Davis was ordered to command the first class, which became the celebrated Tuskegee Airmen. Like his father, who was the army's first black general, Davis became the air force's first black general in 1954.

BACK ON THE HOME FRONT

On the home front, African Americans supported the war effort "like the good Americans that we were and we are," emphasized Elsie Gibbs, then a nineteen-year-old secretary and USO performer at the "colored YWCA" in Montclair, New Jersey. Living with rations was not easy, said Elsie: "But my father, John Gibbs, owned an ice house in Perth Amboy and he had a contract with the army to deliver ice to Camp Kilmer. We

"Be Ready to Jump into Their Shoes": Victory Corps recruitment poster for African-American youngsters encourages them to contribute, volunteer, or help raise money for the war effort. Artist: Charles Alston.

used to get more butter and sugar than we could use from the colored kitchen workers and my father would share it all with our neighbors."

Many products were rationed during the war, including meat, butter, coffee, shoes, gasoline, and motor oil. Black volunteers served as air-raid wardens, fire watchers, airplane spotters, nurses' aides, motor transport corps members, emergency medical workers, and auxiliary firemen and policemen. Helping as block captains, war-bond and -stamp salesmen, selective service and rationing board clerks, African Americans supported Conservation, Salvage, and Victory Garden campaigns. Black youth played its part through membership in the high school Victory Corps and the Youth Participation Division of local defense councils. Many black schools raised money to purchase jeeps for the army. In 1944, children of the South-Central District of Chicago raised $263,148.83 in war bonds and stamps, representing enough money to buy 125 jeeps and two pursuit planes.

Victory gardens were planted by many Americans during World War II. A victory garden was typically a backyard patch of fruits and vegetables. Americans planted these gardens to keep the nation out of a food shortage. Urban neighborhoods used empty lots to plant victory gardens. "Everybody on the block took care of the garden," recalls a

Harlem senior who was then a nine-year-old girl. "And just because you had a coupon didn't mean you got the ration. You had to wait in line, and that's what I did mostly for my mother and aunts. I would hold the place in line."

Children like fifteen-year-old Eugene Redd listened to the radio nightly for information about the war. Redd listened intently for word about his father, who was serving in Italy. "Every night at nine-thirty I turned on the radio to hear Gabriel Heater on WOR. He started every program with either 'There is good news tonight' or 'There is bad news tonight.' I would always get a little frightened if he said it was bad news."

Women played an important role in the war effort. With men enlisted in the armed forces, factories needed skilled workers and turned to women. Producing weapons, tanks, ships, and bombs, women, who usually stayed at home, went to work in the factories. Though discrimination in the defense industry continued in many parts of the country, more than two million African-American men and women went to work for defense plants, and another two million joined the federal civil-service and volunteer groups.

July 1943

Hello Ma,

I got a nice letter from [my son] Scotty. It seems that he is interested in mechanics now. He said he was thinking of taking up Diesel Engineering after he finishes High School two years from now. I think that was a good idea for him to think up by himself. I am going to write and encourage him, also advise him to start on the gas engine first to get the ground work, then he can go to diesel, jet, electric, steam and maybe Atomic energy. After all, he didn't used to like to go to school at all.

> T5 Elliott Brown
> 95th Engineer Regiment
> Camp Claiborne, Louisiana

T5 Brown's fifteen-year-old son, David Scott Brown, eventually gravitated away from any interest in mechanics to become a staff artist for *The New York Times.*

June 2, 1944

To: The Reverend Dr. Adam Clayton Powell, Jr. (New York, N.Y.)

The following is a small list of incidents which have occurred within the past few months, in California Maneuver Area which may draw to your attention the deplorable plight of the Negro soldier and Officer in the Army of the United States.

a. On August 31st 1943, a white private told a Negro Officer who had reprimanded him for not observing the ordinary military courtesy of a salute, if you would take your clothes off and lay them on the ground I would salute them but I wouldn't salute anything that looks like you. The Officer called a Captain and told him of the incident. In the presence of the private, the Captain said, "Well Lieutenant, what do you want me to do about it?" The Officer reported the matter to the major under whom he was serving immediately. The Major advised "I wouldn't make an issue of the incident if I were you." The Officer insisted on preferring a charge against the soldier. He was transferred from the post three days later. He was never notified that the soldier would be tried on any charge. Three weeks later he requested the Commanding Officer of the Post to investigate and received the information that the soldier had been tried by Summary Court and fined $18.00 and restricted to the area for 30 days. . . .

b. In contrast with the above is this case. A Negro soldier on a post in this area committed a minor violation by driving five men in a jeep for a distance of about three quarters of a mile. A colonel saw him load up the vehicle and sent a white corporal in a vehicle to chase him and get his name. When the driver reached his company motor pool, the white soldier drew up and proceeded to get the information asked by the colonel. In the meantime, a Negro Corporal witnessing the proceedings asked the white Corporal, Why don't you mind your own business. You are not an M.P. The Corporal reported the incident to the Colonel who demanded disciplinary action against the Negro Corp. He was tried by Summary Court, reduced to the grade of Private, fined $12.00 per month for two months and restricted to the area of thirty days. He was more severely dealt with for arguing with a Corporal (white) than a white boy was dealt with for insulting a Negro Officer. A Negro Officer on the post protested and within 24 hours, an attempt was made to trump up a charge against the Officer, on which to Court Martial him.

c. At another post, three Negro Soldiers have recently been Court Martialed and sent to prison for Five years, for telling a Major that they were not physically fit for a heavy laboring detail to which they had been assigned. Yet, these men had all before been recommended by the Medical Authorities for discharges because of their physical conditions.

d. On or about January 20 five other men who are in the same category as the above three were told by a Major when they protested that they could not do pick and shovel work, "If I had you Niggers in my section of the country, I'd make you work." Then about ten minutes later he threatened to Court Martial a Negro Officer because the Officer protested his statement.

e. On January 31, this same Major told the Commanding Officer of that company of all very physically broken up men, "If any person is too sick to work he is too sick to eat, so if any man here can't work, don't feed him. Give him half rations; give him quarter rations. Feed them nothing but soup." He added that he'd come by at mealtime from time to time to see that his order was being carried out.

f. Four Negro Officers were assigned to work with this group of "Cripples" in December. When they arrived on the post they found signs on the latrines of the post "COLORED TROOPS NOT ALLOWED." These officers photographed these signs the following day. That afternoon the Commanding Officer of the post removed the signs. Later that evening he called in these Officers and told them that the post was a "Keg of Dynamite" and he wanted us to tell our boys to over-look the little insults and incidents, and not start any disturbance. They couldn't win anyway, and after all only northern Negroes are insulted by the use of the term Nigger. A Southern boy understands that the white man means no harm when he uses that term. It is needless to say that the Negroes told him that they would not carry any such message to the boys and it is needless to say that they didn't.

g. Throughout the area, military authorities have intervened to see that business places, such as beer gardens serve either white or Negro soldiers, and have used their "Off Limits" rule to enforce the Edict. The result? In each town one might find one or two Negro owned "joints" where Negro soldiers and officers must go after hours for recreation. In every other place if a Negro goes in he's told, "We don't serve colored." Throughout the large town of San

Bernadino, California, up to a few weeks ago, signs were posted on the window of many business places "WE CATER TO WHITE TRADE ONLY." Those signs were removed at the request of a Priest, a Rabbi and a Negro clergyman. The army never once attempted to remove this public insult.

[Signed] A Negro Soldier

The NAACP investigated many complaints, and when soldiers' rights were found in violation of the law, the organization filed suit. Many black soldiers, mostly those from northern states who were not accustomed to in-your-face southern prejudice, made their way around the Jim Crow system:

I had a good time ignoring the "jim crow" signs in busses along with my fellow soldiers, going into the forbidden places and demanding that we be served and we were. . . . We made it embarrassing for the white officers and they gave us lectures about our actions . . . The Negro officers didn't have much to say but seemed to be very anxious because of our "rashness." However, the boys were banded together which made us strong and as a result, we never had any real trouble with the Law. We saw to it that we always outnumbered the complainants. The town was overrun with white sailors as it was a seaport town. These sailors were from the North and they were on our side. A white soldier would sit in the bus up front and call to a negro soldier in the back, saying, "Hey, Mac, sit up here with me!" The town people were very hostile to the white sailors because of their attitude toward the colored sailors.

SGT. WILBUR YOUNG, 533RD TRUCK COMPANY,
BEFORE LEAVING NORFOLK, VIRGINIA,
BOUND FOR ENGLAND, IN DECEMBER 1943

SEPTEMBER 15, 1943 The 761st "Black Panther" Tank Battalion moved to Fort Hood, Texas, for advanced armored training.

Landing in England

[1944]

The existence of the drug MARIJUANA (a form of Hasheesh) has been found in possession of coloured troops. This drug is grown chiefly in Mexico as rye grass. Its growth in the US is illegal and taken in large quantities can prove fatal. Usually smoked as a cigarette: if given to women, may excite their sexual desires either as a cigarette or ground up in food. Its detection is not easy though when smoked the smell is quite different from that of ordinary tobacco. There is as yet no proof that this drug has been given to women in this country.

LETTER FROM DUKE OF MARLBOROUGH TO WINSTON CHURCHILL, NOVEMBER 18, 1943

It is difficult to go anywhere in London without having the feeling that Britain is now Occupied Territory. The general consensus of opinion seems to be that the only American soldiers with decent manners are the Negroes.

GEORGE ORWELL, *TRIBUNE* (LONDON), DECEMBER 3, 1943

By January 1944, more than one million American soldiers were stationed in Great Britain, and about 80,000 of them were African Americans. "We felt more welcome in England than we ever felt in the United States—at least I did," said a veteran who had spent four months in Liverpool. "Some GIs were bigots, but I don't think most of the GIs were.

Lots of them just did their jobs just like we did. Mostly we wanted to win a war and go home."

The pleasant English countryside had become a huge military camp, cluttered with Army barracks and vehicles. Ports filled up with transport ships; airfields became packed with fighters and bombers—all waiting to go to the Continent. The buildup of men and equipment in the United Kingdom was so great that people joked that the barrage balloons were necessary to keep Britain afloat. Of American and British design, the barrage balloons were aloft across the country to prevent German planes from strafing civilian or military targets.

THE BALLOON CURTAIN

So effective and fearsome was the barrage balloon defense that prior to December 7, 1941, Japanese intelligence placed a day-by-day watch for balloon formations at Pearl Harbor. On Saturday, December 6, Takeo Yoshikawa, a Japanese spy based in Honolulu, issued his final report. "At the present time there are no signs of barrage balloon equipment," he reported, concluding that American naval sites and airfields were unprotected from strafing and dive-bomber attack. With no balloons in the skies above Pearl Harbor, "there is considerable opportunity left to take advantage of surprise attack," he stated, giving the go-ahead for the assault. Manning the American balloons that flew above the most sensitive and protected American military sites in England were the all-black 320th Barrage Balloon Brigade.

In the memoir of Sgt. Wilbur Young (533rd Port Battalion), arriving in Glasgow, Scotland, in April 1944 was his most pleasant memory of the war:

> We passed beautiful scenery on Easter Sunday. Everybody was dressed up and people yelled and screamed on the shores. The boys on the boat threw cigarettes and candy to the people. Before entering, the English officers welcomed us to England and told us in no uncertain terms that England "was open" to them. "The girls are attractive and you will be very welcome." There were innuendoes in their speeches, hinting that England was quite different from America on that score. The boys

were welcome to fraternize with the women. . . . We found the Scotch people very friendly and they seemed to take to us. . . . The second night we went to Greene's Playhouse which featured Felix Mendelssohn and his Hawaiian orchestra of 20 pieces. There were a white and colored singer. The colored one looked like a good looking Harlem girl but was supposed to be Hawaiian. It was quite a contrast as the white singer was blonde and of course, our Hawaiian had dark hair. We met the fellows in the band plus the singers, especially the colored girl. The place was enormous and reminded me a bit of the Savoy Ballroom except that there were two on either side of the hall and a huge balcony. Found ten women to every man. (Sounds like D.C. in War time!) The place was mobbed. Had all these gorgeous girls smiling and beaming at us. I asked a girl to dance and she almost knocked me down to do so. There were all jitterbugs, thanks to the preceding troops. The white M.P.'s weren't happy about the colored boys having a good time and went around trying to find fault with our uniforms—to no avail. Then they gave the white girls nasty looks. Met the elderly people of Scotland. They were very interested in us. Got curious about the colored men's backgrounds and why white soldiers didn't like colored men and why they told lies about us. They accepted us quite readily and invited us to come back. We left Scotland one week later. On the trip down to Liverpool we rode 3rd class. There were just two classes, 1st and 3rd class. Officers and civilians (wealthy) rode 1st class and enlisted men and the middle class civilians rode 3rd class.

The trip was interesting. Another soldier and I were in a compartment with a middle-aged woman and child and an attractive young woman, a British soldier and two British sailors. Everybody was congenial. We gabbed and talked. Had a stop and the two sailors dashed out and got tea for everybody. When they all found out that it was our first trip there, the occupants in the compartment explained points of interest to us in England. There was no hostility.

MARCH 1944 The U.S. Navy commissioned thirteen African Americans (twelve ensigns and one warrant officer) as its first black officers. Dubbed the "Golden 13" because of the hurdles they cleared in order to integrate the navy, fifty-eight African Americans received navy commissions during WWII.

The African Americans weren't the only black soldiers in England. Several thousand soldiers from the West Indies and Africa manned the many ports. The Allies relied on colonial workers from the West Indies, Africa, and Asia. On many occasions the colonials and black soldiers worked side-by-side. Sergeant Young felt privileged to work with men from all over the globe:

> There was a huge ship in the dock called the *Empress of India*. It had all Indian help. I talked with quite a number of them. They were paid a very miserable wage. Their wages were about four pounds a month—exploited to the hilt. Ran into a very young and good-looking East Indian with a red cap and shabby-looking uniform. Reminded me of the Red Caps in Pennsylvania Station. The majority of them were thin, little and narrow-looking men. They didn't organize or fight their victimization and accepted it. They were only interested in eating and sleeping. They begged for food scraps and for anything. When they saw us there was an immediate kinship. I had a detail of men working and all I had to do was to stand around and look and ask questions. . . . I called them "Ghandi" and asked them what ship did they come on. They pointed to the big ship. I asked how he liked England. "No likee." I asked why they said that and they replied, "Look at it and see." I gave them cigarettes and they salaamed and backed away. . . . They saw friends in us. We would give them whatever we could to help them out. They realized the kinship, one of epidermis. They probably didn't trust the English because of their skins.

The surprising goodwill that black soldiers were met with during their time in Britain was overshadowed by the angry backlash of some white troops. The freedom and acceptance that black soldiers were feeling met head-on with outrage.

"I've seen nice-looking English girls out with American Negro soldiers as black as the ace of spades," said a white lieutenant. "I have not only seen the Negro boys dancing with white girls, but we have actually seen them standing in doorways kissing the girls goodnight."

After some newspapers ran pictures of African-American GIs dancing with English women, the army hastily ordered censors to stop all photographs showing blacks mixing socially with white women. (A 1943 War Department censorship regulation prohibited the mailing or distribution of amateur photographs showing black soldiers "in poses of intimacy with white women or conveying 'boyfriend-girlfriend' implications.") The Red Cross aided the separation of the races by creating black-staffed clubs that came to be known as "colored clubs." The MPs followed the lead by preventing blacks from entering white-staffed clubs and steering white soldiers and white women away from the colored clubs.

NAACP executive secretary Walter White, who visited England in early 1944 at the start of his worldwide fact-finding mission on the condition of black soldiers abroad, registered it as a positive sign when he saw this sign posted by a pub keeper: THIS PLACE FOR THE EXCLUSIVE USE OF ENGLISHMEN AND AMERICAN NEGRO SOLDIERS.

"I must say, he [the black soldier] conducts himself very well. When there has been friction, it is invariably started by the white soldier," noted a British reviewer of the racial climate. Maj. Gen. Ira C. Eaker, commander of the U.S. Eighth Air Force agreed, reporting that where disturbances occurred white troops were responsible for the trouble 90 percent of the time. But a memo from a white female officer (dated May 29, 1944) perhaps best measured the racial animosity barometer. After

Loading supplies for D-Day: at a supply depot in England, black soldiers load and unload supplies in preparation for the invasion of Europe. Artist: Olin Dows.

analyzing negative racial comments made by white officers and enlisted men found in censored mail over a period of several weeks, she concluded: "If the invasion doesn't occur soon, trouble will."

By June 1, 1944, some 134,000 of the 1.5 million American soldiers, sailors, and airmen in Great Britain were black Americans. More than 60 percent of all general service regiments, dump truck companies, truck drivers, and ordnance units were black.

D-DAY

[1944]

"D-Day" was the designation for every Allied invasion of the war in Europe and the Pacific. (The "D" had no meaning beyond signifying the start-up date—as a way of referring to the upcoming event without mentioning the date itself.) But June 6, 1944, became monumentally special because it was the biggest amphibious landing ever undertaken and it was the tide-turning battle of the European war.

The invasion was long in coming. For two years the Soviet Union had been demanding that its allies attack Germany from the West. Stalin suspected that the United States and Great Britain were secretly delaying an invasion in hopes that the Soviets and Germany would cripple each other. Although there may have been some justification to Stalin's complaint, he was never willing to acknowledge the full power and scope of Hitler's army, which owned the entire western coast of Europe from Denmark to Spain, including the region of northern France known as Normandy.

Hitler was aware of the massive buildup in England, and he had long expected an Allied attempt to land on the Continent; but he was not overly concerned about an invasion force landing at Normandy. Hitler was convinced that Normandy, lined as it was with an "Atlantic Wall" of giant concrete pillboxes and heavily mined beaches, was not a likely landing spot. Accepting that someday an Allied invasion would occur, he was certain the effort could not be supplied for very long. Hitler confidently predicted that any assault at Normandy would be pushed back into the sea.

The element of surprise was crucial to the invasion plan. Because neither Hitler nor his military advisers knew for certain where or when the attack would take place, Allied counterintelligence went to elaborate lengths to deceive the Germans. Drawing on the talents of military artists and stage craftsmen from Hollywood and the British film industry, the Allies produced more than one thousand cardboard airplanes, tanks, trucks, and landing craft and put them in menacing-looking positions at Dover, to convince the Germans that Dover, across the Channel from the Pas de Calais, was where the invasion force would strike from.

The ruse worked, and the Germans kept several armored divisions in the Calais region, far east from Normandy. For several days black and white soldiers waited for word to set sail across the English Channel. By Saturday evening, June 3, more than 5,000 black soldiers and sailors in the army, navy, and Coast Guard were aboard the invasion vessels. More than 1,800 African-American soldiers from engineer, port, dump truck, and barrage balloon battalions received orders they would "sail and land" in the secret mission of historic proportions. "We had trained for a big job, but we did not know how big this invasion would be," said Cpl. Fred Marian of the 226th Port Company.

The men of the all-black 582nd Dump Truck Company knew they were in line to land early in the assault. They were scattered in small groups among the 238th Engineer Combat Regiment. Lt. George Worth, a white officer of the 582nd, observed his men outwardly calm and poised. Most of his soldiers were relaxed or entertained themselves playing cards or talking. The white lieutenant watched as company barber T/5 Clarence O. Johnson cut the hair of S. Sgt. Herman Crawley. "These colored boys are good soldiers and do a good job with their trucks," wrote Lt. Worth in his D-Day diary. The 582nd and the 320th Barrage Balloon Brigade were among the select few units in the invasion that would be distributed at both Omaha and Utah.

The 490th Port Battalion with its four black Port companies, the

226th, 227th, 228th, and 229th, were poised to land in the early morning at Omaha. The men of the 3,275th and 385th Quartermaster Truck Company drifted toward the salvo and firestorm that greeted all who landed on the first morning of the assault. The drivers would have to get not only themselves but their trucks ashore.

Late in the evening of June 5, the Allied armada of more than one thousand ships departed from eleven ports on England's southern coast and headed across the Channel for landing targets on the Normandy coast—its mission to liberate Europe. Operation Overlord had begun. On June 6, some 200,000 Allied soldiers met the enemy on rugged French beaches, code-named Omaha, Utah, Gold, Juno, and Sword.

OMAHA BEACH

Allied planes and naval guns bombarded Omaha Beach but the firepower did little damage to the enemy. The bombing that was to have knocked out German pillboxes and beach defenses was not accurate: bombs were dropped too far inland to do any serious damage. Rocky cliffs protected the German cannons, heavy artillery, and machine-gun nests that loomed over the shore. With the poor preinvasion results, the gunfire that met Allied troops at Omaha was murderous. Initial losses were appalling; in some assault companies the casualties were at 90 percent within minutes of landing.

Many soldiers drowned when they were sent out of their landing craft too soon. Earlier amphibious invasions had proven that soldiers, even the best, could not travel for long distances on boats and be expected to hit the shore fighting effectively. Still, no one expected that so many men would become seasick from the six-hour journey across the Channel. Throughout the morning hours, American losses at Omaha were severe.

"If I couldn't swim, I would have drowned," said Corporal Marian. "The rat-tat-tat-tat-tat sounded like it was in my head, and I just prayed to God over and over to help me make it to the shore. And when I got to the beach I prayed to stay alive."

Once ashore the Port companies began unloading supplies of ammunition, food, and equipment under a barrage of fire. To keep the waves of invasion moving, supplies were unloaded continuously. Work shifts were abandoned as the men volunteered to unload ships under machine-gun and artillery fire.

"We were in holes dug in on the beach when artillery fire from the bluffs started giving us hell," said Cpl. Joseph McLeod. "That was about ten in the morning. After it slackened, we got up and went to our LCT and unloaded 105 mm shells."

D-Day was "a day of ducking bullets and anything that would kill a man," said Sgt. George A. Davison of the 320th Barrage Balloon Brigade—the American unit whose signature "balloon curtain" became one of the war's most powerful images. The Allied command had elevated the brigade to a central defensive position in the Normandy campaign. Originally organized as a noncombat unit to protect American cities, the 320th was redesignated a combat unit in accordance with the tactical decision that the best defense against low-flying Luftwaffe planes was a "balloon curtain" over Normandy beaches.

The balloons were designed to keep enemy planes from dive-bombing the invasion force. Planes flew above or away so as not to become entangled in the balloons or the wires from which they were suspended. Operating the system required carrying the equipment into the battle zone, judging wind and atmospheric conditions, inflating, and—as happened on D-Day—deploying the balloons under ferocious fire.

The balloons "confounded skeptics in keeping enemy raiders above effective strafing altitude," reported *Stars and Stripes.* With the defense in place, German planes did not dare fly anywhere near the invasion—one German plane that tested the "balloon umbrella" was brought down in a fiery crash.

Medics with the 320th "covered themselves with glory on D-Day by landing in the face of heavy fire to set up a first aid station on the beach," *Stars and Stripes* also reported. Bodies were floating in the water. Vehicles brought ashore were destroyed in the barrage. Six of the black medics received Purple Hearts and Bronze Stars for aiding wounded soldiers.

Feeling nauseous from the waves and "scared to death" from the bullets whizzing past his head, Cpl. Waverly B. Woodson never thought the day would end with him as a hero. "I thought it was all over from the start. I was neck-deep in water when our LST [landing ship tank] hit a German mine. The shrapnel got me but I kept making my way to shore with bullets hitting the water and men floating dead in the water."

Despite a leg injury, Woodson swam and waded to the beach, then set up a medical aid station on the shore. Under savage fire he retrieved and treated other badly wounded men, and saved three others from drowning. For the next eighteen hours, Woodson worked continuously before receiving treatment for his own wound.

Hollywood director John Ford landed on Omaha Beach with a Coast Guard camera crew to document the historic landing, but he was unable to record the heroism of the black soldiers at Omaha:

> I remember watching one colored man in a DUKW loaded with supplies. He dropped them on the beach, unloaded, went back for more. I watched, fascinated. Shells landed around him. The Germans were really after him. He avoided every obstacle and just kept going back

A medic administers first aid to a wounded soldier on Omaha Beach. Medic teams were among the 1,800 African-American soldiers who landed at Normandy on D-Day, June 6, 1944.

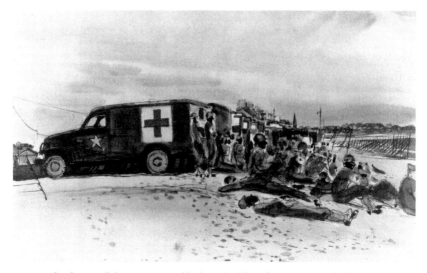

Waiting for the wounded on D-Day: a black medical battalion waits to unload casualties from the Normandy invasion. Artist: Harrison Standley.

and forth, back and forth, completely calm. I thought, "By God, if anybody deserves a medal that man does." I wanted to photograph him, but I was in a relatively safe place at the time so I figured, "The hell with it." I was willing to admit he was braver than I was.

UTAH BEACH

The landing force at Utah Beach came ashore 2,000 yards farther south than planned, but there were far fewer fatalities and casualties in the Utah landing than at Omaha. By midmorning, the soldiers, including the 582nd Dump Truck Company, were working to secure the beach. Units of the 320th sent their balloons aloft, and medics attached to the 320th aided the wounded. During the first day, the 582nd participated in the demolition of mines and beach obstacles and helped open the roads along the shore. The 582nd also worked on the construction of a treadway bridge over the Douve River, linking the beachheads of Utah and Omaha. By afternoon, Utah was swarming with soldiers, tanks, trucks, and amphibious supply carriers.

That night, over national radio, President Roosevelt led the American people in prayer: "Almighty God: Our sons, pride of our Nation,

Antiaircraft balloons manned by the all-black 320th Barrage Balloon Brigade hover above Normandy, as African-American medics evacuate wounded soldiers from Omaha and Utah beaches. Artist: Lawrence Beale Smith.

this day have set out upon a mighty endeavor, a struggle to preserve our Republic, our religion, and our civilization and to set free a suffering humanity."

SIGNAL CORPS

Following D-Day, black American signal corps units were setting up communications lines. Black signal corps laid wire from the hedgerows of Normandy, across France, Luxembourg, and Belgium and deep into Germany. In the face of enemy snipers, mines, and artillery fire, the 29th Signal Construction Battalion repaired railroad pole lines. The units set up over 200 miles of open-wire pole lines and forty miles of underground lead-covered cable.

An all-black signal corps battalion assisted in the installation of communications for the Supreme Headquarters Continental Command Post, the office of General Eisenhower. A special commendation for the 41st Signal Corps battalion came from Maj. Gen. W. S. Rumbough, chief signal officer of the European theater of operations (ETO): "The work was done at high speed, and the men worked far in excess of their normal working schedule to accomplish their job."

SUPPLIES AT NORMANDY

The biggest surprise to the Germans was not D–Day itself but the ability of the Allied forces to disembark huge quantities of trucks, guns, tanks, and other supplies continuously during the first few days of the invasion. Because Hitler was certain the liberators would simply run out of the critical equipment needed to punch through the German defense, the führer was astonished to learn of ports, docks, cranes, and protected harbors being set up by Allied construction battalions.

Seeing the Allies had made a huge leap toward Germany, on the night of June 13, 1944, Hitler ordered the use of the V-1 rockets—the *Vergeltungswaffen* ("vengeance weapons"). Choosing civilian targets rather than Allied troops or supply concentrations, Hitler terrorized London. During the summer, 2,000 V-1s were launched from northern France and Belgium. In the fall, Germany introduced the more powerful V-2, aiming those at civilian targets in England and Holland.

SAINT-LÔ

In July, the Allies reached Saint-Lô in France after battling through hedgerow country. In pursuit of the enemy, white and black truck and troop transport units had frequent contacts with the enemy and often joined in the fighting. Brig. Gen. Charles Lanham, CO of the 22nd Infantry, recalled the black servicemen as brothers in arms while attacking German positions south of Saint-Lô:

> As daylight neared, confusion mounted. Our columns clogged in endless traffic jams, bogged down in bomb craters, crawled through detours over broken fields, struggled across improvised stream crossings. All around us the night erupted with flaming towns. German artillery

and bombs added to the confusion. Every once in a while a huge German tank would pound out of the darkness and cut into our column, thinking it his. Running fights ebbed and flowed about us. As daylight broke, we were literally cheek by jowl with the Germans—in the same villages, in the same fields, in the same hedgerows, in the same farmyards. A hundred sporadic fights broke out—to the front, to the flanks, to the rear, within the columns, everywhere.

It was early that morning that I first became aware of the fact that our Negro truck drivers were leaving their trucks and whooping it up after German soldiers all over the landscape. This, I might add, is not hearsay. I personally saw it over and over again in the early hours of that wild morning. But in addition to my own personal observation, many reports reached me throughout the day of the voluntary participation of these troops in battle and their gallant conduct.

WHOSE WAR IS IT ANYWAY?

The seesaw of black soldiers fighting for America and simultaneously being rejected by their white countrymen was an unfortunate and continuous blemish on the American cause throughout the entire war. Cpl. Rupert Trimmingham, who had emigrated to the United States from Trinidad, joined the army to fight for his country, only to find the enemy getting treated like the winners.

April 28, 1944

Dear *Yank:*

Here is a question that each Negro soldier is asking. What is the Negro soldier fighting for? On whose team are we playing? Myself and eight other soldiers were on our way from Camp Claiborne, La., to the hospital here at Fort Huachuca. We had to lay over until the next day for our train. On the next day we could not purchase a cup of coffee at any of the lunchrooms around there. As you know, Old Man Jim Crow rules. The only place where we could be served was at the lunchroom at the railroad station but, of course, we had to go into the kitchen (JC rules). But, that's not all; 11:30 A.M. about two dozen German prisoners of war, with two American guards, came into the station. They entered the lunchroom, sat at the tables, had their meals served, talked, smoked, in fact had quite a swell time. I stood on the outside looking on, and I couldn't help but ask myself these questions: Are these men sworn enemies of this country? Are they not taught to hate and destroy . . . all democratic governments? Are we not American soldiers, sworn to fight for and die if need be for this our country? Then why are they treated better than we are? Why are we pushed around like cattle? If we are fighting for the same thing, if we are to die for our country, then why does the government allow such things to go on? Some of the boys are saying that you will not print this letter. I'm saying that you will.

Cpl. Rupert Trimmingham

Fort Huachuca, Arizona

June 9, 1944

Dear *Yank:*

I am writing to you in regard to the incident told in a letter to you by Cpl. Trimmingham (Negro) describing the way he was forced to eat in the kitchen of a station restaurant while a group of German prisoners were fed with the rest of the white civilians in the restaurant. Gentlemen, I am a Southern rebel, but this incident makes me none too proud of my Southern heritage! Frankly, I think that this incident is a disgrace to a democratic nation such as ours is supposed to be. Are we fighting for such a thing as this? Certainly not.

If this incident is democracy, I don't want any part of it! . . . I wonder what the "Aryan supermen" think when they get a first-hand glimpse of our racial discrimination. Are we not waging a war, in part, for this fundamental of democracy? In closing, let me say that a lot of us, especially in the South, should cast the beam out of our own eyes before we try to do so in others, across the seas.

Cpl. Henry S. Wootton, Jr.

Fairfield—Suisun AAF, Calif.

Also signed by S. Sgt. A. S. Tepper and Pfc. Jose Rosenzweig

June 9, 1944

Dear *Yank:*

Just read Cpl. Rupert Trimmingham's letter titled "Democracy?" in a May edition of *Yank.* We are white soldiers in the Burma jungles, and there are many Negro outfits working with us. They are doing more than their part to win this war. We are proud of the colored men here. When we are away from camp working in the jungles, we can go to any colored camp and be treated like one of their own. I think it is a disgrace that, while we are away from home doing our part to help win the war, some people back home are knocking down everything that we are fighting for.

We are among many Allied Nations' soldiers that are fighting here, and they marvel at how the American Army, which is composed of so many nationalities and different races, gets along so well. We are ashamed to read that the German Soldier, who is the sworn enemy of our country, is treated better than the soldier of our country, because of race.

Cpl. Trimmingham asked: What is the Negro fighting for? If this sort of thing continues, we the white soldiers will begin to wonder: What are we fighting for?

Pvt. Joseph Poscucci (Italian)
Also signed by Cpl. Edward A. Krentller (French), Pfc. Maurice E. Wenson (Swedish), and Pvt. James F. Malloy (Irish)

July 28, 1944

Dear *Yank:*

Allow me to thank you for publishing my letter. Although there was some doubt about it being published, yet somehow I felt that *Yank* was too great a paper not to. . . . Each day brings three, four or five letters to me in answer to my letter. I just returned from my furlough and found 25 letters awaiting me. To date I've received 287 letters, and strange as it may seem, 183 are from white men and women in the armed service. Another strange feature about these letters is that the most of these people are from the Deep South. They are all proud of the fact that they are of the South but ashamed to learn that there are so many of their own people who by their actions and manner toward the Negro are playing Hitler's game. Nevertheless, it gives me new hope to realize that there are doubtless thousands of whites who are willing to fight this Frankenstein that so many white people are keeping alive. All that the Negro is asking for is to be given half a chance and he will demonstrate his worth to his country. Should these white people who realized that the Negro is a man who is loyal—one who would gladly give his life for this wonderful country—would stand up, join with us and help us to prove to their white friends that we are worthy, I'm sure that we would bury race hate and unfair treatment. Thanks again.

Cpl. Rupert Trimmingham
Fort Huachuca, Arizona

RED BALL EXPRESS

[1944]

"The Red Ball was designed to save the United States Army," asserted John Houston, former quartermaster sergeant. "And we did! We just never got the credit." Arguably the most elaborate and best executed makeshift plan of World War II, the Red Ball Express solved the problem of supplying an army that had advanced swiftly—and dangerously— a long way from its supply source.

FROM THE BEACH TO THE FRONT LINE

Even during the ferocious battle at Normandy on D-Day, white and black soldiers had begun unloading supplies for the eventual push toward the enemy's homeland. In the first weeks of the invasion, and often under intense enemy fire, they built supply dumps for ammunition, food, and fuel. As the battle moved away from the coast, they constructed larger depots and unloaded shiploads of war materials around the clock. Within sixty days, more than 90 percent of all the Allied supplies on the continent were at Omaha Beach.

By August, the Allies were sweeping eastward—successfully but perhaps too quickly. Believing victory to be close at hand, the U.S. First and

An MP of the 783rd Military Police Battalion waves on a Red Ball Express convoy trans-porting much-needed fuel and supplies to the advancing Allied armies. The Express got its name from a railroad term for a fast freight train. Thousands of truck drivers—75 percent of them African Americans—hauled cargo through France nonstop from August to November 1944.

Third Armies advanced several miles per day. Never thinking that they were possibly being drawn in by the enemy, the fast-moving Allied armies were about to outrun their supply lines. By mid-August, General Patton and his Third Army came to a halt, caused by critical shortages of "beans, bullets, and gas." Deliveries to forward divisions—which were now 300 miles from the supply depots at Omaha Beach—slowed to a trickle.

"On both fronts an acute shortage of supplies—that dull subject again!—governed all our operations," Gen. Omar Bradley wrote in his autobiography, *A General's Life*. "Some twenty-eight divisions were advancing across France and Belgium. Each division ordinarily required 700–750 tons a day—a total daily consumption of about 20,000 tons." If the Germans were to strike the vulnerable front, the results would have been disastrous for the Allies.

A thirty-six-hour brainstorming session among American commanders created the Red Ball project. A petroleum pipeline was considered, but it would have taken too long to construct, and the French railroad system had been rendered useless by German bombs. The only way to supply the endangered army was by truck. An earlier Red Ball–type operation had worked in June to rush supplies to English ports prior to D-Day. The truckers and quartermasters—most of them all-black companies that had handled the Normandy supply wagon superbly—should be able to carry out the Red Ball Express, reasoned the commanders. (The name "Red Ball" came from an old railroad term meaning "priority freight.")

"We got orders to get our trucks loaded and line up outside Saint-Lô, headed to Chartres [south of Paris]," said Sgt. Willard Moore of the 3,438th Quartermaster Corps. On August 25, about 3,000 trucks in convoys of sixty-seven truck companies were the first to start rolling. Ordered to stay sixty yards apart and to travel at twenty-five miles per hour, at about thirty trucks per mile, the convoy appeared endless. Within four days, 132 companies with more than 6,000 trucks were operating on the Red Ball, and more than 75 percent of the drivers were African Americans.

AUGUST 23, 1944 Lasting world peace can be achieved if "the four of us" stick together, says President FDR. If the four nations [United States, Great Britain, China, and the Soviet Union] can maintain their new and close friendship, said FDR, "we may have a peaceful period for our grandchildren to grow up in."

"We knew we were making a big haul but I remember thinking too that we must look like a row of ducks to the German planes which would come peep on our line from time to time," recalled Sergeant Moore. "Governors [regulator gears] were on our engines to keep us from going faster than twenty-five—but I am already thinking the first thing I'm going to do is take the governor off, because when we get shot at, I want to make damn sure I am running faster than twenty-five miles per hour."

By September most drivers knew how to make the governors inoperable and were cutting the time of each run in half. "We were risking court-martial because we were defying orders," said Sergeant Houston. "But I don't think we would have been a successful operation any other way. Our officers knew we were saving more lives with our own initiative, breaking the law, than if we had sat back and said, 'Yas, suh.'" Intent on improving delivery times, most officers cared little about how fast the men drove. Besides, disarming the governors helped the vehicles on steep grades. "If we came upon a sector where some joker wanted us to slow down, I would have my men slow down," said Houston. "Otherwise we would gun it all the way." For inspections, the drivers regularly reconnected the governors.

At night, vehicles drove with "blackout lights," their truck head- and taillights taped into glowing "cat-eyes," to allow drivers to keep one another in sight yet prevent the enemy from spotting the convoy. Rest-stop areas were available, though many two-man teams simply improvised their own two-or-four-hour driving and sleeping shifts. Drivers learned to use their motors as a kitchen aid—heating C-rations, making coffee, and boiling eggs on the engine manifold. Some could cook potatoes, apples, and corn, which they purchased from French farmers.

Two parallel one-way highways—one for inbound, one for outbound traffic—were established between the Normandy beachhead and the frontline sectors east and southeast of Paris. The two-and-a-half-ton trucks carried jerry cans of gasoline, motor oil, artillery shells, and cases of C-rations. Signs and markers along the way kept drivers from getting lost, and also publicized daily goals and achievements. Disabled vehicles were moved to the side of the road, where they were either repaired on the spot by roving mechanic units or towed to repair depots.

Red Ball drivers were constantly on the lookout for mines, snipers, ambushes, and strafing by enemy planes. Many trucks were mounted with .50-caliber machine guns, and some were credited with bringing down German planes. According to one account, a convoy of trucks loaded with gasoline barreled through a burning French village to get the fuel to the front, ignoring the possibility that their cargoes might explode. Drivers often sandbagged the floor of their cabs to absorb mine blasts.

Temporary drivers were also enlisted from the infantry divisions bivouacked in the Normandy region. Most were white soldiers with civilian experience operating trucks. "Some of the white fellas were very good drivers," recalled a black driver. "But some must have claimed they had experience because they thought we had an easy job. Those guys would grind gears like coffee." A few drivers, falling to the temptation of the black market, were known to sell whole truckloads of gas or rations.

After the first week of operation, General Eisenhower directed most of the Red Ball's petroleum supplies to the U.S. First Army and the British 21st Army, effectively putting the brakes on Patton's Third Army, which was moving too swiftly forward. By September 2, the Third Army's daily allotment of gasoline was cut from 400,000 to 31,000 gallons. "My men can eat their belts," General Patton pleaded, "but my tanks gotta have gas." By September 5, the Red Ball drivers were supplying the two American armies daily with over one million gallons of gasoline.

Simultaneously, a pipeline that would eventually replace the Red Ball was being constructed by engineers. Tank trucks received the gasoline at the pipeline's endpoint, then rushed the fuel forward to the battlefront. Airplanes, too, were enlisted in the petroleum transport. Runways were built to handle C-47 transport planes carrying precious fuel to the front.

ON THE RETURN TRIP

Red Ball trucks rarely returned empty. From forward areas they carried empty jerry cans, artillery casings, injured soldiers, and captured German POWs. Transporting the dead bodies of American soldiers was the

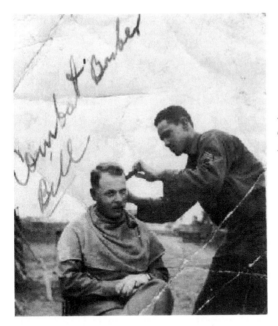

S. Sgt. Willard Moore cuts an officer's hair at a bivouac area somewhere in France.

grimmest and saddest return assignment. One Red Ball veteran remembered the "hearse detail" as a gruesome but honorable job.

"Some guys were queasy about carrying the dead. They would complain about the smell or having to hose down the truck afterwards. But I thought it was the greatest honor I had in the war," said the former driver. "I was carrying guys who had given everything for their country. I would put in my mind that I was driving for a prince or a king or a president."

From August 25, 1944, until November 16, 1944, when its mission was officially ended, the Red Ball Express delivered massive amounts of fuel, ammunition, and food to the frontline armies. Moving 20,000 tons of supplies per day, on runs of up to 400 miles, the Red Ball transported nearly 500,000 tons of supplies breaking all military speed records for transportation of war supplies. Its success spawned other express lines, including the White Ball Express, which connected Rouen and Le Havre to Paris in October 1944.

Many years later, Col. John S. D. Eisenhower, a WWII veteran and son of the Supreme Allied Commander in Europe, wrote: "The spectacular nature of the advance [through France] was due in as great a measure to the men who drove the Red Ball trucks as to those who drove the tanks." The colonel concluded, "Without it [the Red Ball] the advance across France could not have been made."

From *Time* Magazine, July 24, 1944

Cool in Combat

Negro Marines, under fire for the first time, have rated a universal 4.0 (Annapolis mark of perfection) on Saipan. Some landed with the assault waves. All in the four service companies have been under fire at one time or another during the battle. Some have been wounded, several of them have been killed in action. Primarily they were used as ammunition carriers and beachhead unloading parties, but on Saipan some were used for combat.

When Japs counterattacked the 4th Marine Division near Charan Kanoa, twelve Negroes were thrown into the line. Their white officers said they accounted for about 15 Japs. Said Lt. Joc Grimes, a white Texan: "I watched those Negro boys carefully. They were under intense mortar fire and artillery fire as well as rifle and machine-gun fire. They kept advancing until the counterattack was stopped." Negro Marines were at their best while performing their normal duties. Credited with being the workingest men on Saipan, they performed prodigious feats of labor both while under fire and after beachheads were well secured. Some unloaded boats for three days with little or no sleep, working in water waist deep. Some in floating dump details were the first men to pile off their ship toward the beach. On an open transport, where a detachment of Negroes was left to load small boats, they volunteered to unload and tend the wounded who were brought to the transport. They handled stretchers, washed the wounded and even wrote letters for them.

Commendation

"To the 18th, 19th, and 20th Depot Companies and the 3rd Ammunition Company, congratulations from their Commanding Officer. Well Done."

Col. Earl H. Phillips

SOUND OFF!

[1944]

Though firearms were frequently kept away from black soldiers at many military bases, black units often excelled at rifle-handling drills and the maneuvers known as the "Manual of Arms." A white newspaper correspondent who traveled to several camps before filing a story titled "Negro GI's Set War to Swing Tempo" was mystified at the proficiency displayed by the African-American troops. After watching separate brigades of white and black soldiers parade, journalist Minna Lederman noted striking differences between the two drill patterns:

> The Army gives officers a thorough training in how to sound out its Hut-tup-thrup-four, in all variations, as a scientific principle. But a good Negro non-com is more apt to make an easy art of cadence-counting. He can weave a stately pattern of accents, speed them up, slow down again, and yet, by well-shaped, resonant commands, maintain a basic quick-time of a hundred and twenty beats to the minute. With Negro troops the result is that smooth, forward-surging, lilting motion.

"And what a sense of theater!" observed a white officer while scrutinizing two marching regiments, black and white. "When a well-trained Negro presents arms, you reel. His salute is like a blow."

More than in any other military procedure in the U.S. Army, black soldiers, including noncoms, recruits, and enlisted men, were allowed to bend the rules and practices of marching and drilling. Allowing drill leaders to transform the staid army language of "Parade rest!" and "Attention!" into such uptown, or down-home, expressions as "Get off it!" and "Get on it!" just may have been the army's biggest concession to the "new" culture in its midst. Even in the view of many base commanders, altering the sacrosanct commands "Port arms!" and "Present arms!" to a more fast-stepping "He's gone!" and "He's back again!" was simply good policy for training and morale purposes.

It is with spirituals, however, that black troops "really go to town," enthused Lederman, who first heard spirituals put to martial use at Camp Croft, in South Carolina. "A regiment of dark, helmeted men, encouraged by their colonel, marched forward singing, en masse, 'Like a tree by the water. I will not be moved.' "

"On marches, if they are not tactical and therefore silent," commented Lt. William Wheeler at a marching demonstration at Fort McClellan, Alabama—

> Negro soldiers, like everyone else, will try out the songs of the last war. Or maybe a little Stephen Foster. But on bivouac, when fires are burning down and all the tired men have gone to bed, the musical ones—which means most of the rest—will gather around to sing spirituals.
>
> They sing them straight or swing them. Sometimes a quartet gets together and the rest join in the chorus. Or one man alone chants the words and everyone else just hums. If allowed they will stay up long after tattoo [evening bugle] and go through the works in a big way.

At Fort McClellan, Lederman listened intently as a group of men from a black medical unit sang "The History of Pearl Harbor," a spiritual written by Pvt. John Frazier (to the tune of "O What a Time").

> In nineteen hundred and forty-one, when
>   The Second World War had just begun.
> Old Hitler from Berlin stretched out his paw, and brought
>   The European countries into war.

Old Hitler himself wrote out the plans:
   A dreadful place called No-Man's Land.
He told his people that they need not fear,
   Because he, himself, will be the engineer.

O what a time, my Lord; yes, what a time, my Lord.
Great God Almighty, what a time!

Now listen right closely, I'll tell you the news.
   The first thing he did, he put out the Jews.
The next thing he did in the European land, he brought
   All the little nations under his command.
He and France began to fight; they took
   Bee-youtiful Paris late one night.
Old Great Britain, she got troubled in mind,
   Went to forcing men on the firing line.

CHORUS (O what a time . . . etc.)

Now Old Japan, with his old sharp eyes,
   Pretended he wasn't on either side.
When he came to the United States,
   So he and Roosevelt could communicate;
He acted like a man who would not argue.
   [pause and humming pleasantly]
He sneaked right around and bombed Pearl Harbor!

CHORUS

The Japs bombed ships right under their belly,
   The first hero was Captain Kelly.
When his mother got the news I know she cried,
   But he won his medal before he died.
There is one hero, an enemy-killer.
   You've heard his name. It's Dorie Miller.
He was a soldier from his heart.
   Those planes found right from the start.

CHORUS

"Hut, two, three, four," didn't have much snap to it, so American troops began to march to a new cadence created by a black soldier, Pfc.

Willie Lee Duckworth. On a cold spring night in March 1944, Duckworth was one of 200 weary soldiers trudging home to Fort Slocum, New York, on a thirteen-mile hike. On orders from his sergeant, Duckworth was told to take over the count, and he improvised his own drill for the men.

"Sound off," commanded the private, at first softly, and then he began to make up words as the men moved in step. He started his chant:

"The captain rides in a jeep! The sergeant rides in a truck!"

He continued the cadence.

"The general rides in a limousine—but we just out of luck!"

Then, continuing his invention and adding a swinging end-line worthy of Ellington or Calloway, the private from Sandersville, Georgia, created the U.S. Army's most famous call and response:

"SOUND OFF! One, two, three, four; one, two—three four."

Duckworth's cadence caught the attention of Fort Slocum's commander, Col. Bernard Lentz, an authority on the army's cadence system. Astonished to see work squads and drill teams energized by the chant, Colonel Lentz had Duckworth teach the cadence to drill sergeants, and it became known throughout the army as the Duckworth Chant. Colonel Lentz incorporated the chant into the daily drill at Slocum; he even went so far as to publish Duckworth's creation in an official army drill manual.

For more than thirty years he had been trying to perfect a method to eliminate drudgery from infantry drills, explained Lentz. And Duckworth's chant allowed the army to "inject precision" into the procedure. Versions of Duckworth's Chant included: "Your mother was home when you left! You're right! Your sister was home when you left! You're right!"—which was both lively and allowed for the precision that Lentz desired.

As the chant spread from base to base, soldiers, black and white, improvised on the chant, which became known as the "Jody Call"—"Jody" being a country expression "for any man or white man whose name you didn't know," explained Duckworth. The improvised lyrics were sometimes outrageous and unprintable:

Ain't no use in goin' home.
Jody got your girl and gone.

Got a gal, she six feet tall.
Jody got her 'gainst the wall.
Got a gal in Alabam,
Hair is soft, and butt like ham.
Ain't no use in feelin' blue,
Jody got yo' sister, too!
Sound off!

The popularity of "Sound Off" among GIs was noted at the War Department and before V-J Day copies of the chant were distributed to military posts throughout the world. Duckworth obtained a copyright for his invention—and a partner in Colonel Lentz, whose name also appears on the copyright.

The song remained within the army until civilian moviegoers heard it used as a background marching song in the 1949 movie, *Battleground*. Singer Vaughn Monroe recorded the tune, "Sound Off!" in 1951, and Mickey Rooney starred in a 1952 movie of the same name.

From a *Baltimore Afro-American* Report on Black Soldiers in the Pacific

When the first colored USO attraction in the Pacific reached New Caledonia, so many men sought glimpses of "the women" that a special detail of MP's had to be dispatched to the area to clear the roads. Next day work for Tan Yank troops was almost stopped because 8,000 soldiers either on pass or AWOL from work turned up in the camp area of a port unit to see the show. Cpl. Henry White of Cleveland stepped to the microphone, signaled Cpl. Saul Van Kirk of Philadelphia to turn on the juice, and announced the band's opening set of numbers, "Take the A Train," and "Jeep Blues." Soldiers in the front, middle, and back rows of the port unit's theater clapped their hands in rhythm with the music. Soldiers seated on the ground stamped their feet in the dust. One soldier

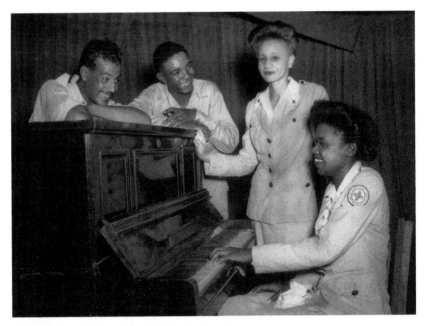

USO performers in Assam, India. Left to right: *Cpl. Robert Barttow, Pvt. James Montgomery, Jeannette C. Dorsey, and Willie Lee Johnson.*

squealed "Ooooo-oo-eee. Send me!" And everybody roared with delight. The hot midday sun beamed down mercilessly on the backs of the audience. In the middle of the saxophone solo a soldier sitting on the ground rolled over on his stomach and beat the ground. "Lawd, just wait 'til I get home."

Vincent Tubbs, correspondent, Baltimore Afro American, *August 1944*

Port Chicago Mutiny

[1944]

When I heard that more than 200 black guys died in the States, it made me wonder why did they always have us doing the most dangerous jobs—and then swear that what we were doing wasn't really important. Doing the most dangerous job sounded pretty important to me.

SGT. CALVIN BASS, U.S. ARMY, 1943–45

On Monday, July 17, the night crew of sailors at the Port Chicago Naval Munitions base, forty miles northeast of San Francisco, carried ammunition aboard two ships, the *E.A. Bryan* and *Quinault Victory,* the latter on its maiden voyage to the Pacific. Mostly black enlisted men working as stevedores, the sailors transported the 500- and 1,000-pound bombs, and gingerly rolled the 2,000-pound blockbusters. Some officers made bets with each other about the amount of explosives that could be loaded in a day, and they pushed their men to meet unrealistic quotas.

The bombs, even clanging against each other, could not explode, the crews were told. Detonators were removed from all bombs, and so explosions were not possible. Still problematic, however, were the 600-

pound incendiary bombs, which, containing activated fuses, were considered "live"—and handled most carefully.

At 10:19 P.M. the first ship blew up, and the other ignited only seconds later. Fire and billowing smoke rose several thousand feet above Port Chicago. A naval aviator flying overhead at 5,000 feet climbed to 8,000 feet to avoid the flames. Large pieces of burning metal weighing hundreds of pounds rained down upon the Port Chicago community, along with undetonated bombs and other debris, damaging over 300 buildings and injuring almost 400 people, some more than a mile from the exploding vessels. The force of the blast was estimated at over five kilotons of dynamite, one-third of the explosive power of the atomic bomb dropped on Hiroshima.

The blast marked the largest Stateside military disaster of WWII, killing 320 naval personnel and civilians, including 202 black ammunition loaders and nine white officers who were overseeing the operation. Throughout the night and the next few days, surviving ammunition workers moved ammunition dumps away from the burning and smoldering ruins, and searched through the debris for survivors.

"I am gratified to learn that, as was to be expected, Negro personnel attached to the Naval Magazine Port Chicago performed bravely and efficiently in the emergency at that station last Monday night," said Rear Adm. Carleton H. Wright, commandant of the Twelfth Naval District, in commending the workers. "These men, in the months that they served at that command, did excellent work in an important segment of the district's overseas combat supply system. As real navy men, they simply carried on in the crisis attendant on the explosion in accordance with our Service's highest traditions."

Three weeks later, on August 9, the navy attempted to resume the loading at a newly constructed pier at Vallejo, three miles north of the ravaged naval base. Of the 328 men ordered to resume loading, 258 refused. All were arrested and sent to the brig.

The navy sent chaplains, teachers, and psychologists in to talk to the men; a month later many still refused to return to the highly dangerous job. On September 14, fifty sailors were charged with mutiny.

Seaman Second Class Freddie Meeks was among those sailors facing court-martial. Meeks, who had escaped death only because he was off on a three-day pass to Oakland, returned to find most of the men in his unit were dead. For several days he helped retrieve body parts, a task that confirmed his decision never to carry ammunition again.

"To see the wreckage and all the people that were killed, the way it blew them all to pieces," said Meeks. "You see, there weren't any bodies, there were just pieces of flesh they shoveled up, put them in those baskets and brought them into the warehouse." The decision by the fifty men to stand firm on the issue of safety was clear and simple; said Meeks, "You didn't want to go and fool with it anymore."

Their six-week trial before a navy panel ended on October 24 with a guilty verdict for all. Sentences ranged from five to fifteen years' imprisonment at hard labor, with dishonorable discharges.

Protests arose over the U.S. military's use of black soldiers to handle explosive materials, and the NAACP Legal Defense Fund took up the case. Arguing before the judge advocate general of the navy in 1945, attorney Thurgood Marshall introduced evidence of rampant discrimination in the field of munitions transportation. The black laborers at Port Chicago were assigned the most dangerous work, given no special training in ammunition loading, forced into competition by officers, and denied promotions. Marshall noted that 90 percent of U.S. explosive munitions were handled by black service personnel. Despite Marshall's efforts, the convictions were upheld. In a cost-cutting move led by Sen. Theodore Bilbo, full death benefits for the families of the survivors were reduced from $5,000 to $3,000. In July 1945, the components for two atomic bombs were loaded aboard ships at the rebuilt port for transfer to the South Pacific.

In January 1946, Marshall was able to get the sentences of the sailors significantly reduced. The fifty mutineers were released from prison but were still held on navy ships for several months as a "probationary period" before release with dishonorable discharges. The discharges were later changed to honorable, but the convictions were not overturned. In December 1999, President Bill Clinton pardoned the three known survivors of the fifty convicted sailors. Upon receiving his pardon, Meeks said he had never lost hope of vindication. "I knew God was keeping me around for something to see," he said. "But I am sorry so many of the others are not around to see it."

AUGUST 7, 1944 Five thousand army soldiers enter Philadelphia to end a weeklong city-bus strike. The workers walked off their jobs to protest the hiring of eight black drivers. The employees returned to their jobs by order of the U.S. War Department.

August 16, 1944

To: Cleveland Call & Post

Dear Editor:

I am writing you about a very delicate matter and that is about the conditions of Camp Claiborne. The conditions for a Negro soldier down here is unbearable the morale of the boys is very low. Now right at this moment the woods surrounding the camp are swarming with Louisiana hoogies armed with rifles and shot guns even the little kids have 22 cal. rifles and BB guns filled with anxiety to shoot a Negro soldier. All of this allegedly is supposed to have started because of two white women who are supposed to have been raped within the last week on the camp grounds which I doubt very much. Now this is the setup last week previous to this last raping that was supposed to have been committed. One of our boys caught one of the white mgrs who operates one of the P.X.'s where the fellows buy the necessities of life down here having sexual relations with one of the colored girls employed there. Being enraged over the indignities we suffer he took a shot at him but missed wounding one of the Negroes guarding him. After this incident around 11 o'clock they blew us out and the officers in charge of the neighboring companys came and had rifle inspection smelling the barrels of our guns to see if they had been recently fired to locate the individual who fired the shot at their white brother. Then our rifles were confiscated. Prior to this 2 or 3 Negroes have been shot but they [have] never taken any steps like that then. So now we are at the mercy of their enraged and prejudice whites who are patrolling the neighboring woods. This camp isn't run by government regulations its controlled by the state of Louisiana and white civilians.

I have heard a rumor that they have found 3 Negro soldiers dead between Glenmore La. and Camp. I don't know just how authentic it is because they try to keep us in the dark but I wouldn't doubt it a bit. They have fellows down here in the worse of condition bent over dragging their legs, and when investigators from Washington come down they distribute the disable around where they could not be seen. If a fellow has a complaint to his well-being and wants to go to sick call they make him wear a full field pack or else put him on extra detail as punishment. Transportation from camp to town is very poor when they have every convenience possible for white soldiers. We used to have dances twice a week but some of the uncle Tom's on guard duty broke that up by slapping the soldiers around. There's quite a few down here who wouldn't hesitate a minute to kill you for their big white chief. Most of the noncommission officers down here are white mouths they cut your throat with their tongue for a stripe. So you see Editor as I am taken it upon myself to be an advocate for the boys from upstate. This place is a living hell I am a Northern boy and we feel that we can't tolerate these conditions any longer. I hope there's some way the Negro people of Cleveland Detroit Chicago & New York the individuals who understand a better Way of life would instigate an investigation of this place because I see things brewing down and I am afraid that we colored soldiers are going to be the goats or victims of a one sided affair. Editor due to circumstances I wish to remain incognito. So we are looking forward to the Negro Public as a hold to make a move to counteract this injustice we are suffering and they say fight for democracy in foreign lands and islands we have never heard of before when it doesn't exist here. So long until time brings on a change for hundreds of Negro soldiers who feel as I do.

Yours sincerely,
A disgusted Negro Trooper
1331 Engr. Gen. Sec. Rgt.
Camp Claiborne, La.

November 23, 1944
Somewhere in Germany
From: Cpl. Thomas Boleware
To: Mary

. . . *All any of us can speak about is the present. We know what goes on this minute, but anything can happen the next, for so much goes on. All we can do is strive for survival today and hope we can do the same tomorrow. You know people get killed every day, and you never know when your time is next. However, all of us have hopes of returning, and find you little girls still on the waiting list. But, dear, here's one thing I want to tell you. I can't promise you I'll be back or that I'll be suitable for you, for no one knows what's coming of him. So Darling, I'm not going to tell you to wait for me, for you may be disappointed after having waited and then find that I didn't get back or was lost of a leg or arm. You couldn't appreciate a man like that could you? Dear, if you have someone you can trust that is good evidence of a good future for you, I advise you to go ahead and plan your future now. I hate like Hell to lose you baby, but I really love you too much to have you wait and then I never return. . . .*

December 22, 1944
Somewhere in France
From: Sgt. Jimmy W. Kelly
To: Verletta
Dearest Verletta:

Your very interesting letter was received today and I enjoyed reading it so much. To me it seemed as if I had entered into space—back to the swell days '40 and '41, when I too graduated from High School and entered college, the poor benighted Freshman. And then came 7 Dec '41. I was hip but Uncle Sam had me shipped. So here I am. A&T in Greensboro, N.C. is my alma mater.

About six weeks ago I visited Paris and the city really is a beauty. It has everything. After having spent a short time in England it was like being home again, only my time was limited. Perhaps I shall return someday when all the world is free and gay.

When we were in England I used to attend the hops on the weekend

> I   Somewhere In France
> 22 December 1944
>
> Dearest Verletta:
>   It has been my pleasure to spend
> and celebrate two special days since I
> last correspond with you. They were
> Thanksgiving and my Birthday. Your very
> interesting letter was received today and
> I enjoyed reading it so much. To me
> it seemed as if I had entered into
> space – back to the swell days of '40
> and '41, when I too graduated from
> High School and entered College, the poor
> benighted Freshman. And then came 7 Dec '41.
> I was hip but Uncle Sam had me shipped.
>   I

Letter from Sgt. Jimmy W. Kelly to "Verletta," from somewhere in France, December 22, 1944.

and their dances are a mixture of Jitterbugging, waltzing, Fox trot and the likes. Southampton Red Cross Club was really solid! It had a mixed G.I. and Civilian band giving out everything from the "Count" to "Tommy D." The "cats" and "chics" were as frantic as the squares at the Savoy in Manhattan. Over here the girls don't know how to dance and the language keeps the chatter to a minimum. . . . When time permits I will send a photo of myself (Hitler's nightmare). Remember I want yours also.

Must go—Jimmy

"TRIPLE NICKEL":
555TH PARACHUTE INFANTRY BATTALION

In December 1943, the all-black "555th Parachute Infantry Battalion (Colored)" arrived at Fort Benning for airborne training. The first troops in the unit were volunteers from the all-black 92nd Infantry Division stationed at Fort Huachuca, Arizona. The "Triple Nickel," as the battalion was called, waited anxiously to be deployed overseas; however, they were sent in a different direction—to the West Coast of the United States, to defend the nation against an odd but dangerous Japanese weapon, bomb-carrying balloons.

Assigned to "Operation Firefly," the black paratroopers were dropped in the Pacific Northwest to fight forest fires set by Japanese incendiary balloons. During this mission, the 555th earned the nickname the "Smoke Jumpers." The Triple Nickel worked secretly, because both the War and Navy Departments did not want the Japanese to know that their long-range balloon bombs were actually working. Not until May 22, 1945, did the departments admit that many fires in the northwestern United States were caused by the balloons. The joint Army-Navy statement urged the public to keep tight-lipped about the balloons.

"What would aid the enemy greatly would be exact information as

Trainees of the 555th Parachute Infantry Battalion go through exercises in a C-47 transport plane at Fort Benning, Georgia. Each prepares to make one of the required five qualifying jumps.

to the time, locality and effect of any specific incident or the number of balloons which land or are sighted. Such information would permit him to evaluate the results of his fantastic effort and possibly correct his methods. This specific information the War and Navy Departments will still seek to keep from the enemy."

Newspaper and radio stations were aware of the successful attacks and the deployment of the specialized 555th PIB and other army personnel to put out more than one hundred fires in the Pacific Northwest. But in the interest of national security, neither the fire bombs nor the heroism of the Triple Nickel could be reported in the news, in obedience to military authorities, who warned "that civilians themselves take the same patriotic course and refrain from spreading news of any specific balloon incident of which they may hear."

TWO TRIALS
AND TWO GENERALS
[1944]

A week before D-Day, two trials involving black soldiers were under way at opposite ends of the world war. One received a modicum of attention from the American public, the other was shrouded in darkness for more than fifty years.

Shortly before midnight on Friday, May 5, 1944, a white woman was lying in bed next to her sleeping husband at their home in a suburb of Bath, England. She heard a tapping sound below in the street, and with her husband still asleep, she rose to see Cpl. Leroy Henry, a black American soldier standing outside her front door—or so stated the prosecution in the rape trial of Corporal Henry.

Henry said he was lost and would she please help him find his way back to Bristol, testified the alleged victim, a thirty-three-year-old Englishwoman. She said she then dressed and went downstairs to let him in the house. "I thought I could explain it better inside," she said, and to be further helpful, she walked with him down the dark road to assist him in finding his way back to the U.S. Army base.

Twenty minutes later, her husband awoke to find her gone. He went outside to look for her and came upon his wife on the road, looking disheveled and distressed. A black soldier had made her climb over a wall into the bushes and raped her, she told her husband. On their way to the local police station to report the alleged crime, she saw Corporal Henry and pointed him out to the police, who arrested him and transferred the soldier to the custody of the U.S. Army. Within four days, Henry stood before a military court-martial, charged with rape.

Insisting on his innocence, Henry offered a completely different explanation of his relationship with the woman. He said he knew the woman, and they had had sex twice before and she had told him to come by her home after dark, and to tap on the window if he wanted her to come outside. On the prior occasions, Henry testified, he had given her money, one English pound; but this time she had demanded two pounds, and he had refused to pay.

English newspapers, to the surprise of many American observers, rallied to Henry's defense. Most were put off that an American, black or white, could be tried by an American court under American law and sentenced to death for a crime that was not a capital offense in Britain. In England, rape had not been a capital offense since 1861.

Some editorials ridiculed the woman's charge and behavior that evening. Even the U.S. Army's prosecuting attorney was hard-pressed to explain her unusual behavior, which he characterized as an example of English politeness: "The action of the woman in getting out of bed and walking off with a dark stranger is rather odd, but in our relations with the English they do things that we don't do. . . ."

At the trial's conclusion, Corporal Henry stood as the court issued its verdict: "We find you guilty and sentence you by the unanimous vote of every member present to be hanged by the neck till dead." The court-martial panel was composed of seven white and one black officer.

Many courtroom observers charged that Henry had been "railroaded" on flimsy evidence that would have been dismissed if directed against white soldiers. Between 1942 and June 1944, six American servicemen (five blacks and one Latino) were executed for rape in England. No white soldiers were executed for the crime.

One day after the Henry verdict, Cecil H. King, editor of the *Daily Mirror* (London), wrote in his personal diary about the inequity in the judgment and sentencing of black and white soldiers:

This feeling is fairly common—that the negroes are nicer and better behaved than the ordinary Yank. So there is some indignation when negro soldiers are condemned to death for raping English girls. In the most recent case the evidence would certainly have resulted in an acquittal in an English court. In the far more numerous cases of rape or murder by white American soldiers, the punishment, if any, is of a wholly different order of severity.

Local people who spoke of their awareness of a relationship between Henry and the woman were inclined to believe his story. Over 33,000 Brits signed a petition calling for Leroy Henry to be reprieved.

The NAACP cabled General Eisenhower on June 3, 1944, requesting a stay of execution. Citing a military study that black GIs, who constituted 8 percent of the military personnel in Europe, accounted for 21 percent of convicted servicemen—and 42 percent of those convicted of sex crimes—the NAACP asked for an opportunity to review the court-martial record of Leroy Henry.

NAACP Secretary Walter White observed that far too often black soldiers were the victims of sexual paranoia by white males:

Not all the relations between American Negro soldiers and English, Scottish, and Welsh white women are on a sexual basis. But many of the white soldiers, particularly officers, so bitterly resented the sight of a Negro soldier walking on the street or sitting in a café or restaurant with a white woman that they were unable to restrain their fury. Many if not most of the racial clashes in England were the results of such incidents.

On June 17, General Eisenhower made a surprising and stunning reversal in the Henry case. First, he tossed out Henry's death sentence, stating there was "insufficient" evidence to justify the death penalty. Then, three days later, Eisenhower finalized his dissatisfaction with the case by exonerating Henry of all charges and ordering the soldier returned to duty. In his unprecedented intervention on behalf of a black soldier charged with a sexual crime, Eisenhower said there was not enough evidence to warrant a retrial.

American newspapers, which followed strict military censorship rules about stories pertaining to black and white relations, had avoided the story altogether or provided only the vaguest details about the case. Those that did report the outcome were critical of General Eisenhower for letting the "culprit" off. The *New York Times* correspondent suggested Eisenhower had reversed the verdict because "British Liberal and Leftist weeklies had been building [it] into an Anglicized version of the Scottsboro case." Despite a brief editorial backlash, the trial was soon forgotten.

Meanwhile, a much bigger sexual assault trial with race at its core was under way at the same time as the English trial of Corporal Henry. Half a world away, six black soldiers were accused of raping a white U.S. Army nurse at Milne Bay, New Guinea.

Transcripts obtained through the Freedom of Information Act and historical documents relating to the military tribunal in New Guinea indicate that no press representatives were invited, no editorials were ever written, and no petitions or inquiries were ever made by the NAACP or other civil rights groups. Almost sixty years later, the chief of the prison facility that held the six defendants termed the trial "gross negligence."

ON THE NIGHT of Wednesday, March 15, 1944, five black soldiers were walking along a road near the shore at Milne Bay, New Guinea. It was 10:15 P.M. when they came upon two white couples—a male sergeant and lieutenant and two U.S. Army nurses, both second lieutenants—in a secluded area close to the beach.

Huddled on separate blankets in front and behind their jeep, the sergeant said to his date, "Take this blanket and put it over your shoulders," according to the testimony of one of the nurses, as the black soldiers approached the couples.

"We made no threatening gestures. We didn't make any verbal threats," said Arthur T. Brown, a nineteen-year-old private, in a pretrial statement. But, Brown continued, they did laugh and teased the sergeant and lieutenant about their romantic rendezvous with the two women. One man allegedly suggested that if the sergeant and lieutenant could have sex with the two women, they all could. Pvt. Brown insisted that the two white men were willing to listen and helped devise a "plan" that would give the black soldiers an opportunity to woo either woman.

"We all went away from the jeep while the officer and the sergeant was discussing the plan," said Brown. One nurse, described as "the slim one," concurred with Brown's testimony. Sergeant Flanagan explained the plan to her and to the other woman—who was called "the stout one."

"He said they wanted to play around with us girls and then that it would be up to us. It was our decision whether we would or not," said the slim nurse, who added, "and if they [the two white males] would make any resistance towards them they had threatened to kill them." During discussion of the plan, two U.S. Army trucks stopped on the nearby road, but no attempt was made to contact either for help.

By the nurse's testimony, in the chronology of what then occurred, four of the five men had contact with her—and two penetrated her sexually. None of the men had sex with the other nurse, because she was menstruating, although in pretrial statements the defendants described her as inviting and willing to have sex, stating at one point, "Who wants me?" After the alleged rapes, the black soldiers then left and the sergeant ran off, not to return again that evening.

The two nurses were seated in the jeep, when moments later two more black soldiers came upon the site. Pvt. Lloyd White, Jr., said he and a friend went to the spot because they had heard that "a man with two women was down there."

"This lieutenant was standing outside the jeep. Two women were inside," said the twenty-year-old private in a pretrial statement. Private White said neither woman resisted his advances.

"She didn't resist. She put her arms around my shoulder. I started asking her for something. I told her I had been overseas twenty-two months and asked her for some. . . . I went around to the other side and talked to the slim one. The officer said that the girls had gone through an ordeal. He didn't say anything when I kissed them. I asked the lieutenant if he could make arrangements with the skinny one. She got out of the jeep."

According to White's testimony, he fondled the nurse sexually but did not penetrate her. "She pulled up her pants and we went back to the jeep. The jeep wouldn't start. The officer asked me if I knew how to start it without a key. I said, 'No.' We looked for the key and couldn't find it.

Before I got ready to go, he came up and put his arm on my shoulder and told me not to tell anyone. His hand was trembling. I told him that he didn't have to be scared. He said that if I didn't tell anyone, he wouldn't tell anyone."

Private White made certain to exonerate his friend, whom he said "did not at any time bother the girls." The nurse agreed that the other man did not participate in the sexual activity, but she disputed White's claim that he had not penetrated her. She testified he had "held a knife in his right hand" during the assault.

Defended by a single attorney, who advised the defendants not to make any statements on their own behalf, the trial of the six men started on May 11 and lasted three days. On May 13, the court found Brown, White, and the others—Pvt. Andrew Gibson, Pvt. Leroy E. Greene, Pvt. Charles A. Horn, and Pvt. Eugene A. Washington, Jr. (none older than twenty-two, and all members of the 808th Quartermaster Amphibious Truck Company) guilty and sentenced each man "to be hanged by the neck until he is dead." For almost four months, the six held out hope that their cases would be reviewed and they would be granted a new trial.

On September 10, 1944, Gen. Douglas MacArthur reviewed the charges and affirmed the lower court's ruling. MacArthur issued death sentences for the six defendants and directed that the men not be returned to the United States for execution but be hanged in New Guinea. Without the influence of newspapers, civil rights groups, or any other public commentary—which would likely have found some or all of the men guilty of disgraceful and immoral behavior but not rape— MacArthur found no mitigating circumstances in the case. No appeal was granted. October 2, 1944, was set as the execution date.

All six maintained their innocence. On October 1, the day before the hanging, Leroy Greene wrote home to his parents:

Dearest Mother and Daddy:
   How are you? How have you been since I last heard from you? Well, Mother and Dad this is going to hurt you. I'm in serious trouble and I have to pay the penalty with my life. I'm sorry that it had to happen this way. Listen Mother and Daddy, don't think for once your teachings and advice was in vain, injustice was given to me.

Please pray and trust that Edward [his brother] won't be overtaken by misfortune as I was. I saw it coming Mother but I could not tell you about it. It is too bad Mother and Dad. I've got to die in a foreign land. I wanted so bad to see you and daddy and Edward again. I wanted especially to see Edward again. When he departed for the Army, I didn't once think we wouldn't see each other again. I love you Mother and Dad and I hate so much to leave you; but they say there is no hope for me, and I must die. Weep not for me Mother for I have found Jesus. Please read Psalm 55 always, for remembrance of me. I am going to read it up until my death.

I wanted so much to buy you a new home but fate wouldn't allow me a Chance. I hope by some means you will get it though.

Please give the Williams, Alexanders, Holmes and Mr. and Mrs. Gordon my one and last regards. I'm sending to the office for your picture to see it for the last time.

Listen! Mother, I'm sending what money I have to you. I'm also returning both money orders, which I didn't get a chance to use. I'm sending my class ring also. I hope these as the last gift from me to you will do you some good.

By the time this letter reaches you I will have entered the great unknown. I won't say good-bye, I'll only say so-long because I hope to meet you in heaven.

One who thought there was no one like you,

Leroy

Keep this letter always.

The day before his execution, Eugene Washington, Jr., wrote to his father:

Dear Dad:

Life for me is at an end. Don't grieve my misfortune. Take care of Mom. I'm sorry I can't help any more. All the plans we made together, you must do alone. Don't think of me in terms of this incident, try to think of me as you did prior to my entering the Army. I go now to seek our Maker, The Lord. I am in his hands. You, Mom, and I may still have our home together in our Father's land. I have seen the light.

Your Son,
Eugene

P.S. I hope someday you'll be able to learn the truth about this. You won't see me any more.

All six men were hanged on October 2, 1944.

To Walter A. Luszki, who witnessed the trial and hangings, and chronicled them nearly fifty years later in his 1991 book, *A Rape of Justice: MacArthur and the New Guinea Hangings,* MacArthur's order represented "a reflection of the racist attitudes of the military and of American culture that prevailed in the era of the Second World War." Of the twenty-one soldiers who were executed by MacArthur's orders during the war, eighteen were blacks.

"What do you want to know about him for?" said a relative of one defendant who was contacted sixty years later. "Nobody has talked about him for a long time. But I sometimes remember." She said she did not know that five other men had been executed for the alleged crimes. She said the pain of his death would never leave her, and she requested that her name and relationship not be made public.

ANOTHER SEXUAL ASSAULT case occurred in Italy in June 1944, following the Allied takeover of Rome. Twenty-two-year-old Pvt. Louis Till, father of three-year-old Emmett Louis Till of Chicago, was charged with raping two Italian women and killing a third. Pleading not guilty, Private Till was convicted and hanged at Aversa, Italy, July 2, 1945.

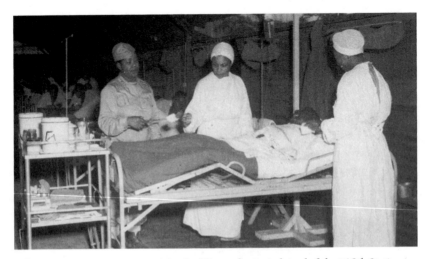

African-American nurses treat an injured soldier at the surgical ward of the 268th Station Hospital, Base A, Milne Bay, New Guinea.

Requiem at a New Guinea graveyard.
Artist: Sidney Simon.

(During the 1955 trial of two white men for Emmett Till's murder, Mississippi's two U.S. senators provided the defense with sealed military information concerning Louis Till's execution. Emmett's mother, Mamie Bradley, said the army had never told her the cause of her former husband's death. The information was used in the trial to support the defense's "like father like son" theory.)

SUFFERING INDIGNITIES

Even celebrities, such as boxing greats Joe Louis and Sugar Ray Robinson, suffered indignities. In his autobiography, legendary boxer Robinson wrote about how he and Joe Louis were arrested by military police for standing in the wrong section of an Alabama bus terminal.

"Soldier, your color belongs in the other bus station," the white MP told Joe Louis. When Louis asked what his color had to do with which bus he boarded, seeing as "I'm wearing the same uniform just like you," the MP replied, "Down here, you do as you're told."

The Court-Martial of Jackie Robinson

On July 6, 1944, Lt. John Roosevelt Robinson, a black officer with the 761st Tank Battalion, was riding a civilian bus from Camp Hood, Texas, to the nearby town of Belton. He refused to move to the back of the bus when told to do so by the driver. Allegedly, the driver pulled a gun on Robinson, who in response hit the driver with his fist, breaking several of his teeth. Court-martial charges were lodged, but the case could not proceed because the battalion commander, Lt. Col. Paul L. Bates, would not consent to the charges. Bates's superior officer, the commander at Camp Hood, then transferred Robinson to the 758th Tank Battalion, whose supervisor immediately signed the court-martial consent.

Lieutenant Robinson's trial opened on August 2 and lasted for seventeen days, during which time the 761st departed from Camp Hood. Robinson was charged with disobeying orders of military police. The charges specified that "Lieutenant Robinson behaved with disrespect toward Captain Gerald M. Bear, Corps Military Police, by contemptuously bowing to him and giving several sloppy salutes . . . in an insolent, impertinent and rude manner." A second charge stated that Lieutenant Robinson had disobeyed a lawful command by the white captain to remain in a receiving room at the MP station. Robinson was eventually acquitted because the order was a violation of War Department policy prohibiting racial discrimination in recreational and transportation facilities on all U.S. Army posts, and he was not charged for his actions on the civilian bus. Likely because he tenaciously insisted on his civil rights and, in part, because he was already a well-known amateur athlete, Robinson received an honorable discharge in November 1944. "For the good of the service" as the military review panel put it, Lieutenant Robinson's turbulent military career came to an end.

"I had learned that I was in two wars, one against a foreign enemy, the other against prejudice at home," wrote former army lieutenant Jackie Robinson about his wartime experience.

In 1941, Jackie Robinson had graduated as UCLA's first four-letter man, starring in track, basketball, football, and baseball. He had made his national reputation in football as "Rabbit Robinson" of the UCLA Bruins, a quick and rugged fullback who could score and punch holes for another great UCLA athlete, tailback Kenny Washington. Robinson was quite conservative in his personal life. Neither a smoker nor a drinker, he would play checkers rather than carouse with the other players.

Excelling in many sports, one coach had called him "the best basketball player in the United States." Robinson also won the Pacific Coast intercollegiate golf championship, swimming titles at UCLA, and in tennis he reached the semifinals of the national black tournament. In 1945 he signed a professional contract to play baseball with the Kansas Monarchs of the Negro Leagues.

At Camp Davis, North Carolina, a group of black soldiers convinced their light-skinned buddy, Romare Bearden, to buy sandwiches for the rest of them at the whites-only service club. "He went in the club without any trouble. And every night we put his pale face to work," said Sgt. Hughlon Johnson. "Bearden was a good guy to get us chow, and we laughed about it, but that was one of the ways we learned to get through a bad situation."

19

ISLAND TO ISLAND

[1944]

"More than twenty Japs died in an attempt to annihilate a patrol of 93rd Division troops in three ambushes, Tuesday and Wednesday, but our men shot their way out, losing only three men. The tactical advantages held by the enemy made the encounter one of the worst since the division's arrival on Bougainville," reported journalist Vincent Tubbs.

At Bougainville, Allied forces (American, Fiji, and New Zealand troops) clashed fiercely with the Japanese, and both sides fought an infestation of malarial mosquitoes. In March 1944, several all-black units landed at Bougainville, including the 24th and 25th Infantry Regiments, the 593rd Field Artillery Battalion, the 318th Combat Engineer Battalion, the 318th Medical Battalion, the 793rd Ordnance Company, and the 93rd Reconnaissance Troop. Attached to the Americal Division, they fought the enemy, disease, and jungle existence for the next several months.

On March 30, units of the 25th Infantry joined the assault on Hill 500, site of a Japanese stronghold of machine-gun, artillery, and mortar fire. The next day, Pfc. James O'Banner became the regiment's first enlisted man to kill an enemy soldier. Sent into the jungle to "pursue and destroy," a battalion of the 25th Infantry crossed the Laruma River, then, moving through rugged terrain, lowered men and equipment down a sixty-foot river bluff by rope. On April 3, a patrol spotted an enemy machine-gun nest that was well protected by pillboxes. Pfc. Wade Foggie set up a rocket launcher and fired eight rounds into three enemy pillboxes, destroying them all and killing about ten enemy soldiers—for which Private Foggie was awarded the 93rd Division's first Bronze Star.

"Orders converted the reconnaissance patrol into a combat unit," correspondent Tubbs's field report continued. "And ammunition was dropped by Lt. Derill [sic] Bishop, pilot of an artillery liaison plane, who also directed artillery fire on Jap positions."

One of the most highly decorated liaison pilots of the Pacific war, Lt. Darryl C. Bishop bravely flew his light plane over the jungle forest and behind enemy lines.

LIAISON PILOTS

"Liaison pilots never got the kind of attention we got, because they were not supposed to!" laughed retired Col. Roscoe C. Brown, member of the "Fighting Ninety-ninth" in explaining the hierarchy within the elite and proud pilot community. With aircraft suited more for recreational flying than for warfare, black liaison pilots served in Europe and the Pacific, often in the thick of battle.

"They were in as much danger as any of us," said Colonel Brown. "But those guys have waited a long time to get recognition, and I hope now is their time."

Practically unknown to whites or blacks, liaison pilots were assigned primarily to reconnaissance duty—flying lighter and slower Piper Cub–class planes just over treetops to "spot" or get a quick view behind enemy lines. Liaison pilots were often engaged in fierce encounters.

Ace black pilot Darryl Bishop recalled:

> I was with the air section of the 593rd Field Artillery Bn of the 93rd Infantry Division at Bougainville. Of the two pilots in the section, I was the senior. As soon as our planes were assembled we started on missions in enemy territory. On one of the missions in the Allied drive against the Japs on Hill 500 across the Tonokina River, a Japanese 15-centimeter artillery piece was spotted from the air by an observer and

On Oct/12 - 1944 at 4:30. we had left the island
I mona in the Solomons going about 3 miles out to sea
to meet our supply ship from Australia. I had just finished
reading a Western story when out of a cloud came a
jap ship. I had just gave a white soldier a book for the book
said I hadn't seen a book in so long.
   We had been after this japanese ship a long time as we
had nick named him Washing machine charlie, as he
had boasted in his broadcast where they would drop the
next bomb and most times did. he was up to date on
the American plans and everything. when when he would
come on a mission he would brag to us to lay our guns
down and come on their side a we would rule the world,
any way this times we were caught unaware.
   The first bomb that hit the ship killed one soldier
and knocked another into the sea. We were given orders
not to get him but I just couldnt see my comrade drown
helpless orders were given to move on, one soldier was
thrown a line and was got out right away, but I just
couldnt leave and know there was those soldier yet in the sea helpless
so I dived to find him. he was hung under a barge and
had been knocked unconscious by the swerving of the ship
I am sorry to say that he died afterwards, from the
jar from being knocked from the ship.
   His name was Eddie Bradley from memphis tenn
he couldnt swim, we gave him artificial respiration
and pumped about 5 gals of water out of him, he never regain
consciousness.
   on the next Day, Oct 13. Gen. M.c Arthur sent his
staff and I was decorated with the medal of bravery & promoted
to Corporal.
   The enclosed picture was made at French Haven New Guinea

Letter from Cpl. William Murray to Lawrence Reddick. Murray relates his experience in receiving a Bronze Star during an October 1944 battle with the enemy in the Solomon Islands.

me. We immediately radioed to headquarters and the artillery fire was brought on the area. Not only was this one of the weapons which had been harassing the American forces, but rifle and small arms fire were a constant menace. Because of this pilots often had to take over the firing of artillery missions because of the nervousness of observers. Most observers were white officers.

Other missions were those of photographing enemy areas, dropping food and ammunition to Allied troops and relaying radio messages to Headquarters from patrols in dense jungles or relaying directions to them. I was awarded two Air Medals and one Air Medal with an Oak Leaf Cluster.

Sgt. John C. Clark and S. Sgt. Ford M. Shaw (left to right) clean their rifles in a bivouac area alongside the East West Trail in Bougainville. Both are members of the 25th Combat Team of the 93rd Division.

Citation: Award of the Air Medal (Oak Leaf Cluster)

First Lieutenant DARRYL C. BISHOP, (01166437), Field Artillery, United States Army, for meritorious achievement while participating in sustained operational aerial flights in the Northern Solomons (Bougainville) and Bismarck Archipelago, as Liaison Pilot, during the period 1 June 1944 through 30 August 1944. During this period, he participated in aerial flights for a total of more than one hundred and seven hours, although hostile enemy attack was probable and at times expected.

There were other black liaison pilots. Former Lt. Marvin Platz of San Diego remembers a black pilot during flight training in November 1943 at Fort Sill, Oklahoma. "We shared a plane for our daily flying. It was during our artillery pilot training." Instruction included classes in airplane mechanics, aerodynamics, and weather. Liaison pilots were highly skilled, and even with the L-4 Cub's 70-mph cruising speed, compared to the 330-mph Mitsubishi Zero, talented liaison pilots could get their slower craft to maneuver "almost like a helicopter," said Platz. "Don't try this at home, but since the Cub could stay up at about forty miles per hour, if you went into a headwind of forty miles per hour or more, you could hover or move backwards."

My dear, dear Barbs,

Darling, you and the General (that's mother) are the only two ladies that ever says "God bless you darling" in each and everyone of your letters. I always close my eyes on the last line of your letters and say those words then look and there they are. Remember the same goes for me too even if I don't ever say it, hear. I have to stop now—I don't want to—but I must. Did I have you? If so, I shan't again—I promise you.

Lovingly, Robert [Sgt. Robert Mance Edwards]
South Pacific, May 2, 1944

USS Alabama, Thanksgiving Night, South Pacific
To: Evelyn at Prairie View College

This gives me the greatest of pleasure to address you these few lines. Altho I am knot a College Grand. But I guess you can read these few lines. I am writing to you. I received your letter and was very much surprised to hear from you. I have no objection of you writing too me. I am single and hope you one. But I know you have a boy friend somewhere. I had a girl friend once. But you see I am away and some body stole my girl. So I have been looking for one. But don't seem to find her. Maybe it's you. You never can tell what will happen in this world. I haven't seen all of it yet. But I have seen lots more than I could have reading in a book about it. I hope you don't get offended about what I said. Look like I am getting off on the wrong subject too soon Before I describe myself too you. Well I am six feet tall 3 in, your color nigh 180 lbs I like all sports. . . . I am very sorry I have not got a photo of myself at the present. When I get into port I will have some made and send you one: Will you send me one of you please. I will be so happy if you would. . . . I am glad to know that you are in school and doing fine. I read alots thats my hobby. I had a chance to read Strange Fruit *by Lillian Smith. I think it's a swell book. I also am reading* Negro Delimma [sic]. *You should read it I haven't finish it yet but gee I think it's the best book I have ever read so far and I have read a many one. . . . I happen to be on a battleship. The "Mighty A"—the U.S.S. Alabama. Evelyn I hope to know a whole lots about you. I want you to be my pinup girl. Maybe forever. What you say about it (smile) Well I guess I have said enough. I hope you will have a swell Xmas this year and many more too come. This make three Xmas I have not been home. So have a swell time and think of a lonely sailor far away in a distant land. I will be looking for a letter from you in next mail call and a photo. So long until next time.*

M.B. Walker STM 1/c

Letter from George D. Clements to Lawrence Reddick. Clements details his experience in the Coast Guard in the fall of 1944.

. . . I had duty aboard the C.G. Cutter—The Tiger. In Honolulu, I ran into my first bit of "Jim Crowism" it came from the civilians. But their "Jim Crow" was caused more by ignorance than bitterness and deep rooted evilness. The white service man had told them we were animals and that we were destructive and that we had tails like monkeys—that we had a bad smell body and mouth. That caused the native population to shy away from the Negro serviceman but through good manners and intelligent behavior we over came these difficulties. . . .

My next duty was aboard a Landing Ship Tank (in code LST). It was the 71. I made three invasions on her Guam, Leyte and Okinawa. I made runs from the Marshalls to Saipan—we had three air attacks at Saipan a night during the time we were running supplies into it. . . . Of course I felt grand fighting for this country. But this is what bothers me. After risking my life and seeing guys like William Wodhouse, James Johnson and few others I know give their lives so that Rankin and Bilbo can say that they were lousy sailors and soldiers. Yes, this makes me angry. I felt great over there fighting where everyone was equal to come back and receive these insults because my face contains more pigments than a white man and because my hair is wooly instead of straight. It not fair and it takes from the United Nations victory these insults do.

George D. Clements STD 2/c

On September 14, American troops landed in the Moluccas, on Morotai Island, whose strategic location and airfields were necessary for sustained air bombardment of the Philippines and, later, Japan. The same day, American forces landed in the western Carolines, on the Palau Islands. The conquest cost more than 10,000 American lives, and more than 14,000 on the Japanese side.

Black and white construction battalions expanded runways on the islands. Tarmacs were rebuilt and reenforced to accommodate American bombers. The Battle for Leyte Gulf marked the first appearance of kamikaze, or suicide, runs. In October 1944, massive amounts of supplies were shipped to the vicinity of Hollandia (now Djajapura) and Wakde, off the north coast of New Guinea. Meanwhile carriers and battleships approached the Leyte Gulf—the staging area for the assault on the Philippines.

In December 1944, the 24th Infantry shipped from Guadalcanal to Saipan and Tinian. Both islands had been declared secure, but they were still infested with enemy soldiers. The black infantrymen were assigned

A U.S. Army soldier and a Chinese soldier each place the flag of his ally on the front of their jeep just before the first truck convoy crosses the China border en route from Ledo, India, to Kunming, China.

to clear Saipan and Tinian of all Japanese who had not surrendered. For eight months they cleaned out enemy caves and tunnels throughout the islands. The regiment killed or captured 722 enemy soldiers, with a loss within its own ranks of about a dozen killed among thirty casualties. In July 1945, the 24th were redeployed to the Kerama Islands, near Okinawa, to destroy remnants of Japanese forces there.

November 29, 1944; South Pacific
To: Olus
  Thanksgiving Day has come and gone, the day was not far different from any other but the spirit was recognizeable with the presence of turkey, the same being boiled.
  I love you Olus tons and tons and tons more. Do you like repetition? Well, okay then. I love you.

  Your husband, Claude [Lt. Claude Jones]

December 25, 1944; Pacific Islands
Pvt. Eddie Taylor to Miss Flora Lee
My Dearest Darling,
  I can never begin to find words to express my intimate feeling and internal love for you to write this 25th day of Dec. in the Christmas season. I dream of you as time goes on. You must realize Darling these sacrifices, like millions of other boys are making, are not in vain.

To: Army & Navy Screen Magazine
By Request Dept.
New York, N.Y.
August 26, 1944
  I am a "negro soldier" in a combat division and there are more than fifteen thousand "negro soldiers" in the Division, we've been preparing for combat for more than twenty months, now the final test is on.
  We have an "all negro" Division in action, and we have "negro soldiers" on every front wearing "Uncle Sam's Uniform" and fighting for the safety of the country the same as all other "Soldiers" of "America."

Last night, I saw the film "This is America" and there was not a single one of "my people" in the screen, it was film of "Whites only," why don't the armed forces release the "negroes" and fight their own war, for if this is "america" for "whites" only, we, the "negroes" have nothing to fight for.

Will you please give me an explanation on "this America."

I remain,

Obligatingly yours,

Cpl. J.H. Bectin, 34462685

Co. A, 371st Inf. APO 92

Fort Huachuca, Ariz.

Let's Set the Post-War Pattern

About one soldier in every ten in this man's Army is a Negro. Wherever you go from the beaches to the front—you see these lads doing their stuff.

Which leads up to the story of three GIs—white boys—who were caught on the road one night with the gas needle angling toward the zero mark. They made several bids for refill without success—until they pulled into an orchard where a Negro medic outfit was dug in for the night. Piled in a neat stack under a tree were about 30 cans—all empty. Empty, that is, except for the few drops that always stick inside of a GI can.

Well, these Negro GIs came out of their holes and tilted the empties into one can. By the time the 30 cans were wrung dry there was enough gas in the jeep to get to the next dump.

"Don't mention it," was what the Negro sergeant said as the GIs resumed their journey.

The decent things Joes do for each other should be mentioned. They ought to make things a little easier when we go back home.

Editorial from the London edition of Stars and Stripes,

the daily newspaper of the U.S. Armed Forces (September 14, 1944)

In August 1944, the Associated Press reported how black quartermasters had taken a "considerable role" in capturing German troops.

"They have captured many as they speed along secondary roads rushing up supplies. These men on occasion have leaped from trucks with rifles and flushed out hidden Germans. Often they arrived at the front lines with a mixed load of prisoners and supplies," reported the AP.

One black platoon had taken about seventy prisoners while bringing up food, fuel, and ammunition to the front. "But to tell you the truth," said Sgt. Edwin Kelly of Richmond, Virginia, "we'd rather not take them prisoners. We'd rather fight until we get it over with."

By late August, many Germans were seeing Hitler's promised victory slipping away. In the U.S. Third Army's sweep to Argentan, in northwestern France, more than 11,000 German soldiers were killed and 39,000 taken prisoners. "*Führer kaput* [finished]," said a prisoner.

THE BLACK PANTHERS

On October 10, 1944, the 761st Tank Battalion came ashore at Omaha Beach. As they had no war experience, some observers scoffed at the ferocious name that they had bodaciously chosen for themselves, the "Black Panthers." Their M4 tank was less powerful than the menacing German Panzer (Panther), but after two years of intense armored training, the 761st appeared confident that the battalion would live up to its own fearsome name.

The tankers were welcomed by the Third Army commander, Lt. Gen. George S. Patton, Jr. The general had once written to his wife that "a colored soldier cannot think fast enough to fight in armor." In greeting the Black Panthers, whom he had observed conducting training maneuvers in the States, Gen. Patton backed off of his bigotry:

"Men, you're the first Negro tankers to ever fight in the American Army. I would never have asked for you if you weren't good. I have nothing but the best in my Army. I don't care what color you are as long as you go up there and kill those Kraut sons of bitches. Everyone has their eyes on you and is expecting great things from you. Most of all your race is looking forward to you. Don't let them down and damn you, don't let me down!"

On November 8, 1944, the 761st Tank Battalion rolled into the towns of Moyenvic and Vic-sur-Seille. During the attack, SSgt. Ruben

Rivers, in Company A's lead tank, ran into a roadblock obstructing the advancing tank column. Without regard for his personal safety, he climbed out of his tank under direct enemy fire, attached a cable to the roadblock and moved it off the road. His action prevented a serious delay in the offensive and was instrumental in the success of the attack.

Staff Sergeant Rivers's action helped get the Black Panthers back on track after its harrowing and tragic first night encounter with the enemy. The evening before, a French farmer—either a collaborationist or forced by the enemy—led a herd of cattle directly in the path of an advancing column of tanks, tank destroyers, and trucks loaded with infantrymen. When the vehicles stopped, German artillery and infantrymen opened fire with automatic weapons. Several Americans were killed in the ambush, including five men of the 761st, all members of the same tank crew.

On November 9, Company C of the 761st ran into an antitank ditch near Morville. In a storm of snow and freezing rain, German tanks fired at the battalion.

Escaping his burning tank, Sgt. Samuel Turley grabbed a machine gun and, ordering his men to retreat, returned fire. Correspondent Trezzvant Anderson described Turley's heroism this way:

Cpl. Carlton Chapman, a machine gunner in an M-4 tank of the 761st Tank Battalion, takes in the view near Nancy, France, in November 1944.

Standing behind the ditch, straight up, with a machine gun and an ammo belt around his neck, Turley was spraying the enemy with machine-gun shots as fast as they could come out of the muzzle of the red-hot barrel. He stood there covering for his men, and then fell, cut through the middle by German machine-gun bullets that ripped through his body as he stood there firing the M.G. to the last. That's how Turley went down and his body crumpled to the earth, his fingers still gripped that trigger. . . . But we made it!

The Black Panthers pushed onward. From the day it entered combat, the 761st spent 183 days in continuous action, only pausing to move from one assignment to another. Battling through France, Holland, and Luxembourg, the 761st then took part in the American counteroffensive following the Battle of the Bulge. In a major battle at Tillet, in Belgium, the Black Panthers fought for two days straight against German armored and infantry units, which ultimately withdrew in the face of the Black

It might be stated however, that during my six months in the combat zone as Surgeon for the 761st Tank Battalion there were several instances in which we had occasion to observe my comrades in danger, to note their reaction as well as to see many instances of bravery exhibited by them.

On this exciting November afternoon when the Germans shelled our assembly area, using my ambulance to target in upon, we experienced a good example of how we react in danger. It was felt that under such conditions most everyone is full of fear but that the fear of failing ones comrades under similar danger is greater than the fear of being killed any minute. Therefore, from a personal standpoint, the call of one of my wounded men sounded much more compelling to me at the time than the shrieks of the German shells exploding around me. It might be stated that I was slightly injured during this episode.

I might only add further that our Negro Tank comrades fought over Europe with eight white infantry battalions, usually with our men riding upon the tanks and there was little evidence or occasion for the usual prejudices to be seen.

It is hoped this has forwarded the information you requested.

Sincerely yours,

G. Norman Adamson, M. D.

Letter to Lawrence Reddick from Capt. G. Norman Adamson, a surgeon who traveled with the 761st Tank Battalion.

Panthers' attack. The operations of the 761st at the Bulge prevented the resupply of German forces, which had encircled American troops at Bastogne. Pressing forward against fierce German resistance, the 761st worked far in advance of artillery support in March 1945. Battling to break the vaunted Siegfried Line, the 761st inflicted more than 4,000 casualties on the German side.

During its six-month tour of duty, the 761st served as an attachment to the 26th, 71st, 79th, 87th, 95th, and 103rd Infantry Divisions and the 17th Airborne Division. The Black Panthers fought major engagements in six European countries and participated in four major Allied campaigns. The battalion destroyed, captured, or assisted in the liberation of more than thirty towns, several concentration camps, four airfields, and three ammunition supply dumps. Its own overall casualty rate was nearly 50 percent, and the 761st lost seventy-one tanks.

The 761st was also among the first American units to link up with Soviet forces. On May 5, 1945, the Black Panthers reached Steyr, Austria, on the Enns River, where they joined the Russians.

> . . . It might be stated however, that during my six months in the combat zone as Surgeon for the 761st Tank Battalion there were several instances in which we had occasion to observe my comrades in danger, to note their reaction as well as to see many instances of bravery exhibited by them.
>
> On this exciting November afternoon when the Germans shelled our assembly area, using my ambulance to target in upon, we experienced a good example of how we react in danger. It was felt that under such conditions most everyone is full of fear but that the fear of failing one's comrades under similar danger is greater than the fear of being killed any minute. Therefore, from a personal standpoint, the call of one of my wounded men sounded much more compelling to me at the time than the shrieks of the German shells exploding around me. It might be stated that I was slightly injured during this episode.
>
> I might only add further that our Negro Tank comrades fought over Europe with eight white infantry battalions, usually with our men riding upon the tanks and there was little evidence or occasion for the usual prejudices to be seen.
>
> Capt. G. Norman Adamson, M.D.

Medal of Honor to Ruben Rivers

Staff Sergeant Ruben Rivers

Citation: For extraordinary heroism in action during the 15–19 November 1944, toward Guebling, France. Though severely wounded in the leg, Sergeant Rivers refused medical treatment and evacuation, took command of another tank, and advanced with his company in Guebling the next day. Repeatedly refusing evacuation, Sergeant Rivers continued to direct his tank's fire at enemy positions through the morning of 19 November 1944. At dawn, Company A's tanks began to advance towards Bougaktroff, but were stopped by enemy fire. Sergeant Rivers, joined by another tank, opened fire on the enemy tanks, covering company A as they withdrew. While doing so, Sergeant Rivers's tank was hit, killing him and wounding the crew. Staff Sergeant Rivers's fighting spirit and daring leadership were an inspiration to his unit and exemplify the highest traditions of military service. [Originally given a Silver Star, Rivers's award was upgraded to Medal of Honor in 1997.]

Pvt. Jonathan Hoag, of an American chemical smoke generating battalion, is awarded the Croix de Guerre by Gen. Alphonse Juin, commander of the Free French Army in Italy. Hoag was honored for courage shown in treating the wounded, even though he himself was wounded in a battle near Pozzuoli, Italy, in March 1944.

Drivers of the 666th "Hell's Angels" Quartermaster Truck Company, 82nd Airborne Division stand proudly after chalking up 20,000 miles each without an accident since arriving in the European theater of operations. Left to right: T/5 Sherman Hughes, T/5 Hudson Murphy, Pfc. Zacariah Gibbs.

To: Rev. and Mrs. Isaac
V-Mail (ETO)
Somewhere in France
Nov. 7, 1944
Dear Mother and Dad,

As I sit here thinking of you I thought I would write you. I hope both of you are well and happy. I am fine. Please disregard that letter I sent. I am very lucky some times. Maybe I'll be the same over seas. I trust and have faith in God.

I am longing to hear from all of you often. Maybe by the time I get one from you I'll also get one from some one else. I feel much better today. Still sorta unhappy, because I have not got no letters from you. I am hoping to hear from you soon and often.

Your son,
[Pvt.] Verdell Isaac

Medal of Honor to Charles L. Thomas

Captain Charles L. Thomas

Citation: For extraordinary heroism in action on 14 December 1944, near Climbach, France. While riding in the lead vehicle of a task force organized to storm and capture the village of Climbach, France, then First Lieutenant Thomas's armored scout car was subjected to intense enemy artillery, self-propelled gun, and small arms fire. Although wounded by the initial burst of hostile fire, Lieutenant Thomas signaled the remainder of the column to halt and, despite the severity of his wounds, assisted the crew of the wrecked car in dismounting. Upon leaving the scant protection which the vehicle afforded, Lieutenant Thomas was again subjected to a hail of enemy fire which inflicted multiple gunshot wounds in his chest, legs, and left arm. Despite the intense pain caused by these wounds, Lieutenant Thomas ordered and directed the dispersion and emplacement of two antitank guns which in a few moments were promptly and effectively returning the enemy fire. Realizing that he could no longer remain in command of the platoon, he signaled to the platoon commander to join him. Lieutenant Thomas then thoroughly oriented him on enemy gun dispositions and the general situation. Only after he was certain that his junior officer was in full control of the situation did he permit himself to be evacuated. First Lieutenant Thomas's outstanding heroism were an inspiration to his men and exemplify the highest traditions of the Armed Forces. [Thomas's original Silver Star award was upgraded to Medal of Honor in 1997.]

THE SIEGE OF BREST

At France's most northwest point, the seaport of Brest stood as a German naval stronghold. Center of German U-boat and submarine operations, its "boat pens," which were fortified with massive amounts of concrete, had withstood Allied bombs for four years. In August 1944, General Eisenhower's standing order, to "bomb and keep bombing until Brest surrenders," was finally supplemented with ground support.

An armorer checks ammunition belts of the .50-caliber machine guns in the wings of a Mustang fighter plane before it leaves an Italian base for a mission against German military targets.

In the twenty-six-day assault, African-American soldiers trained in artillery were an integral part of the campaign to remove the enemy garrison. Moving with the Ninth Army's 8th Corps, three black artillery battalions—the 333rd and 969th (equipped with 155-mm howitzers) and the 578th (with 8-inch howitzers)—secured the flanks of the American advance, filled gaps in the line, and attacked pillboxes and forts surrounding Brest.

On September 19, Brest and its harbor, considered as "the most spacious anchorage in Europe" came under Allied control. Surrendering at last to the American force, according to an Associated Press report, was the "strutting" and cane-carrying Lt. Gen. Hermann Ramcke, who was apprehended along with the "lieutenant colonel who was his aide, four orderlies and a fine Irish setter on a leash"—and 36,389 German soldiers.

Each of the black artillery battalions received satisfactory to laudable combat reports. One social problem did occur: a group of white soldiers complained about having a black chaplain assigned to their unit. The field command did not respond immediately to their objection, but after the black chaplain had to be hospitalized for injuries sustained in a shell attack, a white chaplain was assigned to his post. After the Brest victory, American service divisions that were delivering supplies throughout the

Pilots of the 99th Fighter Squadron, credited with shooting down eight of the twenty-eight German planes destroyed in dogfights over the new Allied beachheads at Anzio, on January 27, 1944, talk over the day's exploits at a U.S. base somewhere in the Mediterranean theater.

siege began the task of transforming the bomb-devastated harbor into a working port for the influx of more war materials.

On December 18, Eisenhower turned once again to the Red Ball system and drivers to transport reinforcements. In one week, the quartermasters moved 250,000 men and 50,000 vehicles to the battlefront. (Not even in Vietnam or in the Persian Gulf War was the U.S. Army capable of moving so many personnel and so much equipment so quickly.)

December 21, 1944; Somewhere in France
Pvt. Taylor Reed to Miss Gladys
V-Mail
My Dear Darling Wife,
    France would be more better if you were here with your hubby. Darling please keep our letters moving across the waters. Please write me soon darling.

                                        Your hubby [Pvt. Taylor Reed]

20

BATTLE OF THE BULGE: HITLER'S LAST CHARGE

[1944–45]

In early December of 1944, Adolf Hitler devised what would become his last major counteroffensive against the Allies. Undetected by the American and British commands, Germany amassed over 250,000 soldiers along the Ardennes, a low mountainous ridge on its western front with France, Belgium, and Luxembourg. Hitler's plan was to destroy the 80,000 Allied troops in the captured territory. Unprepared for an attack, they were battle-weary infantry veterans, quartermaster and maintainance personnel, and newly arrived artillery crews, including several untested African-American combat units.

Hitler's strategy (for the plan was entirely his own and was opposed by his top military advisers) was to wait for bad weather, in order to keep Allied planes from bombing German positions once they were discovered. With overwhelming manpower and artillery he would crush the fatigued and untested American force. Devising a scheme to take advantage of American diversity, he deployed English-speaking German soldiers behind American lines. Dressed in American uniforms and driving captured American jeeps and trucks, these German commandos infiltrated the Allied line, where they sowed much confusion.

Dining at Bastogne: during the Battle of the Bulge in December 1944, virtually all American servicemen fought as combat soldiers, including kitchen and laundry workers, who were quickly trained to fight as infantrymen. Artist: Aaron Bohrod.

"Three times I was ordered to prove my identity by cautious GIs," Gen. Omar Bradley later recalled. "Passwords and dog tags weren't enough to prove identity. You were an American only if you knew who won the 1944 World Series or the name of Dizzy Dean's brother (Daffy). You were an American only if you knew the capital of New York or the taxicab company in *Amos and Andy.*"

Black soldiers joked that they had their own questions for the German imposters: "What does water from the colored water fountain taste like—chocolate or grape? If they thought they knew, we would have popped them."

However, the infiltration and sabotage worked. On December 18, more than 8,000 American soldiers were captured by the Germans. Next to Bataan, it was the greatest mass surrender of an American military force in history.

By December 21 the German advance had taken a recognizable shape—a giant bulge, headed toward the Atlantic. At Bastogne, in the center and completely surrounded, were a collection of Americans

On Easter morning, March 10, 1945, T/5 William E. Thomas and Pfc. Joseph Jackson pre-pare to "roll specially prepared eggs on Hitler's lawn."

under an acting commander of the 101st Airborne Division, Brig. Gen. Anthony McAuliffe, the division artillery commander. Called upon to surrender by a German envoy, he replied, "Nuts." The one-word response spread throughout the Ardennes and helped raise the spirits of the defenders. The next day, the bad weather broke and C–47s dropped supplies to the encircled men at Bastogne.

One black quartermaster sergeant remembered the Battle of the Bulge feeling like the last days of the earth:

> The German 88s made a screaming sound when they came at us, like giant wildcats coming through the trees. There was no letup in the shelling we took and our job [quartermasters] was every job. We were running supplies, shooting, getting shot at, blown up. I think as many black GIs were killed at the Bulge as anywhere else in the war. Dish-

Soldiers of the 161st Chemical Smoke Generating Company, U.S. Third Army, lay a smoke screen to cover bridge-building activities across the Saar River near Wallerfangen, Germany.

washers and cooks were operating machine guns and antitank weapons. When the 88s let up we would carry the bodies—black and white GIs—back to the trucks, and at times the 88s would start up again. Hitler did not stop the bombs for the white boys—not the Americans, white or black.

In the largest battle ever fought by the U.S. Army, some 600,000 American troops were engaged at the Bulge. Twenty thousand were killed and 40,000 wounded, and 20,000 were taken as prisoners of war. On the German side, 30,000 died, 40,000 were wounded, and 40,000 were taken prisoner. The battle proved climactic for Germany, which now simply had too few resources to fight effectively.

On December 21, the 101st Airborne formed its perimeter defense line around Bastogne, and two black artillery battalions, the 333rd and 969th, protected the perimeter. A third black artillery battalion, the 578th, was under heavy fire but protected the rear. "The steadiness and

The body of an American soldier is carried on a stretcher in the vicinity of Malmedy, Belgium, where on or about December 17, 1944, the Germans committed many atrocities. In Wereth, eleven black American soldiers were slaughtered.

determination of all concerned in this trying movement when a heavy artillery battalion was fighting a rear guard action is worthy of the highest praise," declared the 578th's commander after the battle.

The 590th Ambulance Company, a black unit, was among the first to reach the troops at Bastogne. In the midst of the siege, Tech. 4 Broman Williams set up and maintained an improvised kitchen, feeding one thousand men daily. Other black enlisted men, including kitchen and laundry workers, were given quick training in firearms and fought as infantrymen.

Maj. Gen. Maxwell D. Taylor, commander of the 101st Airborne sent the following message to the 969th: "The Officers and Men of the 101st Airborne Division wish to express to your command their appreciation of the gallant support rendered by the 969th Field Artillery Battalion in the recent defense of Bastogne, Belgium. The success of this defense is attributable to the shoulder to shoulder cooperation of all units involved. This Division is proud to have shared the Battlefield with your command. A recommendation for a unit citation of the 969th Field Artillery Battalion is being forwarded by this Headquarters."

THE ORIGINAL HELL'S ANGELS

Before the motorcycle gangs, "Hell's Angels" referred to the black American drivers of the 666th Quartermaster Truck Company who drove Hell's Highway, a thirty-mile road stretch between Eindhoven and

Soldiers from the Belgian Congo parade in Lebanon. More than one million colonial African soldiers fought and provided labor for the Allies during World War II.

Nijmegen, Holland, that was heavily bombarded but paved the way for the Allied advance. From December 1944 until March 1945, the "Triple Six" were the angels and lifeline to the 101st Airborne Division at the Battle of the Bulge, carrying troops, ammunition, rations, and other vital supplies. Attached to the 82nd Airborne Division, the 666th was hit hard by enemy bombs and artillery near Schmitt, Germany, in February 1945, with losses of infantrymen, drivers, and trucks. Formally commended for "outstanding accomplishments," the 666th carried over 2,000 tons of supplies and more than 17,000 soldiers over icy and snowbound roads in a ninety-day nonstop haul. Bombing and strafing were not the only difficulties confronting the 666th: as warmer weather thawed the roadbed, their truck tires were exposed to shell fragments, glass, and unexploded bombs beneath the surface. (Dutch officials estimate thousands of unexploded bombs and rockets remain undetected in the region, where, as recently as 2003, two people were killed when a WWII bomb exploded accidentally.)

AFRICANS IN WORLD WAR II

Over one million Africans fought for the Allies in World War II. Serving in combat and labor battalions in Asia, Africa, and Europe, African soldiers came as recruits, volunteers, and draftees from almost every African colony. Fighting under the British flag were the Kings African Rifles (KAR), well-trained soldiers from Kenya, Nyasaland (now Malawi), Somaliland (Somalia) and Tanganyika (Tanzania). Considered "hardy and tenacious" were the soldiers of the British 81st and 82nd West African Divisions, comprised of men from Nigeria, Sierra Leone, Gold Coast (Ghana), Gambia, and the British West Indies.

At the outset of the war, the French colonies in Africa were divided into four sectors: North Africa, West Africa, Equatorial Africa, and Madagascar. After the Franco-German armistice in 1940, the collaborators of the pro-German Vichy regime controlled these colonies. This meant that the native troops, commanded by French officers, were not fighting for the anti-Hitler coalition. Only gradually did they follow General de Gaulle's call in 1940 "For a Free France."

The Free French Army relied heavily on its African contingent, which at times swelled to more than half of Gen. Charles DeGaulle's ranks. The French colonies (including Senegal, Togo, Guinea, Benin, Mauritania, Congo, Mali, Bourkina Faso, Chad, Tunisia, Algeria, Gabon, Niger, Cameroon, Madagascar, and Guadeloupe and Martinique in the French West Indies) supplied over 500,000 soldiers to fight in Europe and over 200,000 workers to man its war industries. During the war, Brazzaville, the capital of the French Congo (Republic of Congo) was proclaimed the symbolic "capitol of Free France" and home of its government in exile, by General de Gaulle. Yet on August 26, when General de Gaulle marched triumphantly down the Champs-Élysées, no African soldiers were permitted in the parade. It was most important, claimed De Gaulle, for the people of France to see themselves liberated by Frenchmen. In the Pacific region, more than

50,000 black soldiers of the Netherlands East Indies army fought against Japan.

GOOD SPORTS

Sports competition among soldiers, though sometimes racially sparked contests of whites versus blacks, contributed substantially to breaking the racial barriers in an important sector of postwar American life—professional sports. Games and athletic competition among soldiers were largely spur of the moment and improvised, and thus free from the incessant racial review that accompanied nearly every decision involving more than a dozen black soldiers.

By the winter of 1944–45, large numbers of soldiers were stationed in areas of conquered territory, and recreational activities were part of the daily routine. Soldiers who threw and batted balls in the vicinity of each other could easily see and judge the best athletes. Commonly some white soldiers invited blacks into their informal games. Football, basketball, baseball, and track and field contests were held informally, and on some occasions with great formality.

New Year's Day 1945

Cpl. John (Big Six) Moody, a 230-pound "one-man army," led an integrated Fifth Army football team to a 20–0 victory over the Twelfth Air Force in the New Year's Day "Spaghetti Bowl." More than 20,000 soldiers packed a Florence stadium to see Moody break a scoreless tie in the second period, "ripping around right end from the 50 yard line to the Air Force 36. Then he cracked through to the 9. GIs on the Army side of the stadium began to chant, 'We want a touchdown,' just like back home, and they got it immediately when Moody banged through. He placekicked the extra point."

Playing linebacker, Moody intercepted a pass in the third quarter "and shook off several would be tacklers to speed twenty yards to pay-dirt" and again kicked the extra point, reported *Stars and Stripes*. The most versatile player on the field, Moody's "booming punts kept the [12th Air Force] in the hole all afternoon.

"Only players with genuine football experience were picked, since both starting elevens, without a single exception, are comprised of men who spent at least two seasons on a college gridiron," the *Stars and Stripes* report continued. "You can bet your bottom buck that any football coach in the business—either pro or college—would give a right arm to be able to requisition a batch of these Joes."

Moody, picked from a 92nd Division ordnance company, was a former black college All-American from Morris Brown College. (In 1946, two professional teams ended the prohibition against black players that had existed in the NFL since 1934. Signed to pro contracts one year after the war were four black players: Kenny Washington and Woody Strode of the Los Angeles Rams, and Bill Willis and Marion Motley of the Cleveland Browns.)

But in America, baseball was the sport by which all other sports and athletes were measured. Before the war there were rumblings that major league baseball might someday integrate. Few were the team owners in the major leagues "who [were] not aware of the fact that the time is not far off when colored players will take their places beside those of the other races in the major leagues," said Clark Griffith, owner of the Washington Senators, in 1938.

"White males who were confident in their athletic skills were happy to play sports with us," said one black soldier. "And we all had a great time playing." Other white males who insisted on barring blacks from athletic competition were viewed as cowardly—even by white competitors.

"It's too bad those colored boys don't play in the big league," drawled Jerome "Dizzy" Dean, star pitcher for the St. Louis Cardinals, "because they sure got some great players." In the 1930s, Dean hired Satchel Paige to tour with his winter barnstorming team of white all-stars. Paige won four of six outings against Dean. One survey revealed that in over 150 games between blacks and "all-star" white teams during the 1930s, the black teams won two-thirds of the contests. On the opening day of the 1945 season, pickets outside Yankee Stadium read: IF WE CAN STOP BULLETS, WHY NOT BALLS?

"We played our best against them," said Sgt. Leon Day. "It was our chance to show we were as good as they were—and sometimes we were better." In the army baseball championship of the Mediterranean the-

A field artillery battery fires its 155-mm howitzer at a German position somewhere in France.

ater, the four-hit pitching of Leon Day, formerly of the Newark Eagles, on September 4, 1945, shut down the Third Army, 2–1. The series was the first ever army championship to field black and white players together on the same team.

THE TRIPLE NINE

On January 20, 1945, the all-black 999th Field Artillery Battalion, positioned high in the Vosges Mountains of France (east of the Bulge campaign) received orders to come down the mountain as quickly as possible for a major battle developing against the Germans at Colmar.

Even before Colmar (a battle best known to Americans from the Hollywood movie *To Hell and Back,* which focused on the exploits of Lt. Audie Murphy—without showing a single black soldier) the 999 had

distinguished itself in several combat situations, including its first assignment in August 1944 with the U.S. Third Army in pursuit of the Germans. Facing constant and stiff enemy resistance, the 999 took up posts
in seventeen towns in the nine-day, 180-mile running battle against the
German Seventh Army. Firing one thousand rounds per day, the battalion pummeled German positions and helped establish the bridgehead
over the Seine, cutting off the enemy's escape route.

In September, the 999 had supported the American forces and the
French 2nd Division in expelling the Germans from France. The 2nd
Division was comprised largely of French-African soldiers—members of
the French "colonial infantry," which included Senegalese, Algerians,
and Moroccans. (The Moroccans' taunting chant "Tunisians are women,
Algerians are men, and Moroccans are heroes" was indicative of the

*African-American tank crews stand by awaiting the call to clean out scattered Nazi machine-
gun nests in Coburg, Germany, in April 1945.*

bravado with which they approached battle.) The international force pushed the Germans across the Muerthe and Moselle rivers.

But in January 1945, just prior to Colmar, the 999th was lauded for its extraordinary task of transporting five heavy and bulky 8-inch howitzers up the steep, snow-covered mountain road in the Vosges Mountains. The battalion drew praise, too, for the harder job of bringing the arsenal down the icy trail. With chains, logs, and makeshift plows, the crew brought the weapons and ammo safely down the mountain in an operation that the command acknowledged was highly dangerous.

"Nevertheless you accepted the mission cheerfully," read the commendation from the 3rd Division Artillery Command, "and by an extraordinary display of ingenuity and hard work accomplished the movement in a remarkably short time. The entire matter is a splendid testimony to the efficiency and training of the 999th Field Artillery Battalion."

In two days the 999th descended from its mountain perch and traveled some fifty miles to Colmar. At the battlefront they were joined by the all-black 969th Field Artillery Battallion, which had distinguished itself with the 101st Airborne Division at Bastogne. Together the two African-American units proceeded to Colmar, France, attached to the French army. On January 23, the first day of the assault, the 969th fired an astonishing 912 rounds. For the next two weeks, both battalions supported French and American divisions, circling and firing upon the enemy until Colmar was liberated on February 8. During ten months of combat, the 969th supported all four of the American armies in the European theater [U.S. First, Third, Seventh, and Ninth Armies] and fired a total of 42,489 rounds from its howitzers.

THE DOUBLE STANDARD

If the 827th Tank Destroyer Battalion were a white unit, Hollywood might have made a movie about them—"a great movie" insists a former battalion member.

For twelve days in January, the 827th Tank Destroyer Battalion was as fearsome as any tank-killing outfit in war. In freezing sleet and snow, the 827th battled a firestorm assault. Strafed by Hitler's best-kept secret,

Soldier of the 12th Armored Division, Seventh U.S. Army, stands guard over a group of Nazi prisoners, captured in the surrounding German forest in April 1945.

jet fighters that "flew faster than anything we had ever seen before," the 827th kept itself occupied with its primary mission: to destroy German tanks.

"Enemy tank destruction was our business, and that's all we wanted to do," remembered former Pfc. Charles Branson, an 827th assistant gunner. For Branson and his comrades, trouble came as much from their officers as from the enemy. Between the officers and enlisted men, there existed no such thing as esprit de corps.

Trained at Camp Hood, the battalion received instruction in its main task, tank destruction, and it was also used extensively to train officers—too many officers, in the opinion of the enlisted men (as well as postwar evaluators of the battalion). In two years, the 827th experienced eight complete turnovers in its command team. An all-black officer team, the seventh such group, was the battalion's favorite, but they were soon replaced by a team of white junior officers—some of whom had previous and unfavorable experiences with black troops. In the view of the 827th, the new officers received just before deployment to combat were "the worst."

"We trained a lot of officers," said Branson. "And we knew the good ones from the bad ones."

Reports filed by their assigned officers indicated a great diversity of opinion regarding the battalion's abilities. More than 70 percent of the men had scored poorly on written aptitude and intelligence tests, the results of which caused them to be classified generally as misfits—unable to read maps, take direction, or follow orders. A more notorious reputation, earned when one of the men killed another soldier with a meat cleaver, remained as part of the battalion's "baggage."

"We had one or two crazy ones—what battalion didn't?" said Branson. "The white officers were mostly southern and they did not like us, and we did not like them. They lied about us, and some of our guys just wouldn't listen to anything they said. Our job was to knock out tanks and that is what we did. We didn't want to be any more popular with them than they wanted to be popular with us."

Failure to obey orders was the most common infraction of the rules by members of the 827th, whose postwar reputation (the opinion of their officers) was dismal. A white officer who told his men to pull an army vehicle out of a burning barn that housed land mines was ignored. When he threatened to shoot the men for not responding, they simply walked away.

"In a pinch some guys are just not going to lay down their life for someone they don't trust. We loved our country, so we fought as best we could. But we did not love our officers."

"Just do the job and don't ask us to do nonsense" was the essential philosophy of the 827th. Regarded as rebels who were known to drink and carouse with women, they never enjoyed the manly reputation of some win-at-all-costs white units. They did, however, produce an astonishing battle record.

On January 11, while guarding the road between two German towns, Rittershoffen and Hatten, Company C of the 827th sighted sixteen German tanks approaching. Taking dead aim across an open snow-covered plain, the company opened fire. Caught completely off-guard by the 827th, the German tanks exploded one by one. Eleven tanks were destroyed, and the remaining five tanks retreated.

The next day, the 827th destroyed four more German tanks in Rittershoffen. Accompanying the 315th Infantry into the two towns, the 827th engaged in street fighting and shelled buildings to drive out the enemy. At Hatten, an 827th crew knocked out two tanks at a range of 1,400 yards. Yet, just as the 827th was proving itself in combat, the long-standing grudge by the unit's white officers against the enlisted men came before an untimely judicial review.

An army inspector arrived, and in the field he conducted four days of interviews. Testimony was taken only from the officers, not the enlisted men. The commander of the 315th had given the 827th an excellent report, but the inspector recommended that the 827th be withdrawn from combat.

The battalion was not fully disbanded, but it was almost completely discredited, and most of the men were reassigned to noncombat duties. A recommendation that the men be assigned housekeeping chores at a regional army headquarters was made, but not acted upon.

"Any white unit that accomplished what we did against the Nazis would have been commended generously. They [the white officers] just had to be in charge," said Branson.

"I don't think some would have minded losing the war outright, just so they could puff up their chests. They just *had* to be in charge."

Gen. George S. Patton, Jr., U.S. Third Army commander, pins the Silver Star on Pvt. Ernest A. Jenkins of New York City for his "conspicuous gallantry" in the liberation of Chateaudun, France.

Medal of Honor to Edward Carter, Jr.

Staff Sergeant Edward A. Carter, Jr.

Citation: For extraordinary heroism in action on 23 March 1945, near Speyer, Germany. When the tank on which he was riding received heavy bazooka and small arms fire, Sergeant Carter voluntarily attempted to lead a three-man group across an open field. Within a short time, two of his men were killed and the third seriously wounded. Continuing on alone, he was wounded five times and finally forced to take cover. As eight enemy riflemen attempted to capture him, Sergeant Carter killed six of them and captured the remaining two. He then crossed the field using as a shield his two prisoners from which he obtained valuable information concerning the disposition of enemy troops. Staff Sergeant Carter's extraordinary heroism was an inspiration to the officers and men of the Seventh Army Infantry Company Number 1 (Provisional) and exemplify the highest traditions of the Armed Forces. [Carter's original Silver Star award was upgraded to Medal of Honor in 1997.]

The Big Three

Roosevelt, Churchill, and Stalin (the Big Three) met at Yalta in the Soviet Union on February 4, 1945, to divide the forthcoming spoils of war. Roosevelt, clearly listening to new voices in the State Department like anticolonialist Ralph Bunche, pushed for an end to European colonialism and sought to create self-governing democracies in eastern Europe. However, Churchill betrayed his own democratic leanings to insist on preserving the British Empire and its many colonies. Joseph Stalin, for his part, agreed to free elections in eastern Europe, though he may have been less than sincere, as he would disavow that position soon after the war.

Pfc. Luther Woodard admires the Bronze Star awarded to him for "his bravery, initiative and battle-cunning." The award was later upgraded to the Silver Star.

Medal of Honor to Willy James, Jr.

Private First Class Willy F. James, Jr.

Citation: For extraordinary heroism in action on 7 April 1945 near Lippoldsberg, Germany. As lead scout during a maneuver to secure and expand a vital bridgehead, Private First Class James was the first to draw enemy fire. He was pinned down for over an hour, during which time he observed enemy positions in detail. Returning to his platoon, he assisted in working out a new plan of maneuver. He then led a squad in the assault, accurately designating targets as he advanced, until he was killed by enemy machine gun fire while going to the aid of his fatally wounded platoon leader. Private First Class James's fearless, self-assigned actions, coupled with his diligent devotion to duty exemplified the finest traditions of the Armed Forces. [James's original Silver Star award was upgraded to Medal of Honor in 1997.]

i rec— your letter and i felt as a
a hero all over again. and i
highly apresate your horner. and
you ask me how i felt while
while doing it. i could not explain
Just how i felt while killing those
Japs. the Bronze Star was awarded
me for my credit of 14 Japs. i was
excited once when my ship was
shelled 8 times and every shell
was a hit. and it was loaded with
all tipes of ammounition + gas all
so. as far as Jim Crow" in the
pacific all was treated about the
same in a way. the cinilions people
there smell.
i was very proud of the Bronze
Star. But to talk about it gines me
a tight feeling in the cheast.

Pfc. Luther Woodard wrote to Reddick a year after the war about his feelings over killing four-teen enemy soldiers.

21

The Forgotten Front: Return of the Buffalo Soldiers

[1944–45]

No war campaign was tougher for the Allies, or for African-American soldiers, than the long battle to take back Italy from Hitler's grasp. Only one day after the Allies captured Rome, on June 5, 1944, the European war shifted dramatically from Italy to France. Bolstered by the Allied conquest at Normandy, French liberation appeared imminent and thus more critical to the Allied war plan than Italian liberation. More than 250,000 soldiers from the Italian front were transferred to France. With troop reductions and a shortage of ammunition owing to the priority war effort in northern Europe, new troops, including the untested all-black 92nd Division, arrived in Italy to confront one of Germany's strongest and most impenetrable lines of defense.

Hitler had drawn a new southern border for Germany, known as the Goten Stellung, or Gothic Line, by which he appropriated some of Italy's prime real estate—the industrial and agricultural region of the Po Valley. Along the Gothic Line, mountainsides and rock cliffs were blasted and shaped into impenetrable defensive positions, and quaint medieval villages were transformed into armed fortresses. Constructing concrete bunkers and underground barracks with slave labor, the Germans destroyed bridges, cratered roads, and scattered the landscape with mines. Also distributed liberally along the Gothic "wall" were hundreds of cannon and machine-gun emplacements.

Along Hitler's monstrous fortified line of defense, which spanned 190 miles, east to west across Italy, from the Ligurian Sea to the Adriatic, German troops were told to hold the line at all costs. By Hitler's personal order, any officer who withdrew from the line would be executed. Against the Gothic Line the Allies deployed what was probably the most ethnically, racially, and religiously diverse military force in history. And were it not for raging battlefronts elsewhere, the Italian campaign from August 1944 to April 1945 would have qualified as one of the bigoted führer's worst nightmares.

In Italy, an African-American combat patrol advances three miles north of Lucca, the furthermost point occupied by American troops, to knock out an enemy machine-gun nest. Here a bazooka fires at a target some three hundred yards away.

Signal Corps Operator on the Gothic Line: communications in the mountainous Italian region required running lines over the rugged terrain, deploying reconnaissance teams that went behind enemy lines, and even using a "pigeon brigade" to get messages back and forth as swiftly as possible. Artist: Ludwig MacTarian.

On July 30, 1944, the first wave of Buffalo Soldiers—the 370th Regimental Combat Team—disembarked at Naples, where they were greeted by a jubilant crowd of fellow black American soldiers from service and technical units, like quartermaster Pvt. Edward Winn. "Most times you would see a black soldier, he was carrying ammunition, cans of fuel, or chow for the food line—anything but a gun," said Winn. "These guys were carrying rifles. A black GI carrying a rifle was not a normal sight to see every day in Europe in 1944."

The rest of the 15,000-man division came in stages until November. Assigned to the U.S. Fifth Army, the Buffalo Soldiers drew immediate attention from the international news media and world leaders. In August, Prime Minister Winston Churchill, while congratulating the British Eighth Army and the American Fifth Army for their progress in Italy, singled out the two "newcomers" to the European war—the black American troops and the American soldiers of Japanese ancestry, known as the Nisei.

THE "RAINBOW" WAR

Nicknamed the "Rainbow Division," the polyglot contingent that battled the Gothic Line were American, French, British, Polish, Greeks,

Brazilian, New Zealand, South African, West Indian, African, Arab, Indian, Italian loyalists, and the Palestine Division (aka the Jewish Brigade), which included refugee European Jews, Sabras (Palestinian-born Jews), Yemenis, and Falashas from Ethiopia. Christians, Buddhists, Hindus, Moslems, and Sikhs all were aligned with the Allied force in Italy. Hitler certainly never dreamed that his army would be beaten by such a decidedly non-Aryan "United Nations" force.

On August 24, the 92nd Infantry Division went into battle, beginning the offensive push against the enemy at the Arno River, just south of the vaunted Gothic Line. At dawn the 598th Field Artillery Battalion fired its cannons at German positions, and over the next few days the 370th Regimental Combat Team moved forward to attack and clear enemy positions and minefields.

Ordered to spearhead the move north, troops from the 1st Armored Division and three battalions of the 370th Regiment crossed the Arno on September 1. Working through the night, the 370th cleared minefields and built a treadway bridge for the tanks and armored infantry as-

A German prisoner wearing civilian clothes sits in a jeep at the south gate of the walled city of Lucca, Italy, awaiting removal to a rear area.

sault to follow. Within twenty-four hours the units accomplished their first objective, the capture of Mount Pisano, then headed toward the enemy-occupied ancient walled city of Lucca.

With the 92nd advancing rapidly, most of the German force withdrew from Lucca, and the 370th, engaging in sporadic machine-gun and rifle fire with the enemy, took control of the city. Waiting for the rest of the Fifth Army to move up, the Buffalo Soldiers cleared enemy resistance along the road from Pisa to Lucca, and patrolled Highway 12, which served as a crucial east–west ammunition and communications route for the Germans. Establishing a perimeter defense around the village, the regiment's engineers set about the task of restoring the town's water supply, which the retreating Germans had sabotaged.

Battling the Germans and the most treacherous terrain in the European war, over the next several months the 92nd earned a reputation among the enemy as tough soldiers, and among the local Italians as gentlemen liberators. German propaganda enticed black soldiers to abandon the fight, firing shells containing leaflets that urged "colored soldiers" to leave the American side and join their German brothers.

Propaganda leaflets such as this one encouraged black American soldiers to defect to the "friendly" German army.

A specially designated sixteen-man 92nd Division Mule Pack Battalion scoured the countryside for pack animals, which they either bought or rented from the local villagers, merchants, and farmers. Rustling up over 370 mules and 170 horses, the battalion was aided by an Italian veterinarian and local blacksmiths who hammered horseshoes from the metal stakes the Germans used to anchor their barbed wire. With more than 500 Italian volunteers, who were given American uniforms with the Buffalo insignia patch, the battalion created a four-legged transportation system that moved thousands of pounds of supplies, slowly but efficiently, over terrain where motor vehicles could not go.

From September to December 1944, the 92nd Division and an attachment of Brazilian troops moved steadily northward along one of the roughest sectors of the Italian campaign. To transmit messages between patrols in mountainous regions and Division Headquarters on the coast, patrols traveled with a pigeon loft, containing four or five carrier pigeons. The fastest way to transmit messages, the pigeon's beat overland vehicles by several hours and even days. Pigeoneers complained that their pigeons were overworked and exhausted. One tired pigeon reportedly carried the message "Send more pigeons!"

Three U.S. Senators

Remarkably, three American soldiers who fought in the Italian campaign later became U.S. senators. Robert Dole, who was shot in the back and lost the use of his right arm, recalled his experience with the Buffalo Soldiers at the 1996 annual GOP Convention:

"The 10th Mountain Division, with whom I served in Italy, and the black troops of the 92nd Division who served nearby, were the proof for me, once again, of the truth I am here trying to convey. The war was fought just a generation after America's greatest and most intense period of immigration. And yet, when the blood of the sons of the immigrants and the grandsons of slaves fell on foreign fields, it was American blood."

For Daniel K. Inouye whose family of Asian ancestry (along with more than 110,000 other Japanese-Americans, including 70,000 who were American citizens) were relocated to detention centers for the duration of the war, the Italian campaign became an opportunity to battle racism at home and abroad:

"I have a special, personal memory of the 92nd. In the hours after I was wounded and doctors were treating me at the field hospital, I remember a nurse showing me a bottle of blood. It had a name on it—Thomas Jefferson Smith, 92nd Division—and while they were rigging it for transfusion into my left arm, I realized that fighting men did more than fight, that they cared enough about each other and the men assigned to their sector to donate their blood for the time when somebody would need it to sustain life. I was to have seventeen transfusions in that first week alone. I am very, very grateful for it, and perhaps this is a fitting time to extend my thanks to every man in the 92nd Division who donated blood that helped save my life."

Edward W. Brooke, a U.S. senator from 1967 to 1979 (and the first African American elected to the Senate since Reconstruction), served as a second lieutenant, later captain, in the 366th Combat Infantry Regiment of the 92nd Division. A graduate of Howard University who had studied political science under Ralph Bunche, Brooke learned Italian and went behind enemy lines as a spy. Using the identity "Carlo," Brooke passed for an Italian to gain information. He also met his future wife, Remigia Ferrari-Scarro, the daughter of a prominent Genoan paper merchant, during his time in Italy.

Brooke was struck by the vast difference between the friendly Italians, "who paid no attention to color, and white Army officers. . . . A black GI who had an orientation lecture in the morning on wiping out Nazi racism was segregated that evening in the 'colored' post exchange." In his book *The Challenge of Change,* Brooke lauded his fellow Buffalo Soldiers for fighting hard and giving their lives for their nation's cause.

On Christmas Eve 1944, a platoon of about sixty Buffalo Soldiers played Saint Nicholas, distributing a truckload of surplus food, chocolate, and cheese to the villagers of Barga. "We had never seen so much food," remembered Irma Biondi, then a seventeen-year-old girl. "They were wonderful, so nice to us," she said. "My little brothers followed them like shadows."

Tullio Bertini, then a twelve-year-old boy, remembers the same Christmas, and the Buffalo Soldiers his family had invited to their home for Christmas Eve dinner. "In general the black soldiers were always welcome in our house, they seemed to think of our home as a home away from their home." Born in America, Tullio and his family, who were visiting Italy from Boston at the time war broke out (and thus unable to return), enjoyed talking with the soldiers from back home. He recalled:

> About five or six black soldiers came to our house for a Christmas eve dinner. My mother, father, and I were present, and two other ladies, Fedra who lived across the street, a former teacher, and Mariuccia, a neighbor that helped out with household chores. My mother and Mariuccia planned a dinner. The soldiers furnished some of the food. The soldiers also brought along a hand operated record player and a few records of American dance music. We had the dinner, the soldiers mellowed by drinking wine, played music, danced with my mother, Fedra and Mariuccia, sang Christmas carols, and had a good time. I thought it seemed the soldiers felt like they were in America, and I also think that my mother and father felt the same way, perhaps thinking that soon we would go back to the United States. The color of their skin did not come into focus. I thought they were Allied soldiers who had come to help get the Italians out of the WWII mess.

Tullio sang "Silent Night" with the Buffalo Soldiers, but none in the house were aware that the Germans had launched a surprise offensive. During the evening revelry, German, Austrian, and Italian Fascist soldiers dressed in civilian clothes had penetrated Barga and neighboring Bottinaccio, Sommocolonia, and other villages. At dawn on Christmas morning, a barrage of German artillery began and uniformed enemy soldiers were swarming through the Tuscany region, directly toward the forward line of the 92nd Division.

In the surprise assault, which was part of a desperate attempt to push through Allied lines and take the port of Livorno, about forty black soldiers were killed and twenty captured. Lt. John Fox died shortly after ordering his own artillery force to fire on his position because it was about to be overrun by advancing enemy soldiers. Lieutenant Fox was posthumously awarded the Medal of Honor in 1997.

The Allies responded with a three-day air assault of 4,000 sorties to stop the advance, then moved an Indian Infantry Division into the region to bolster the 92nd Division. In reality it was headquarters and the senior officers of the 92nd who had failed to see the attack coming; however, division leaders let the Buffalo Soldiers take the fall—and the full brunt of criticism. For many military historians, those few days' setback came to define the 92nd Division. Military press officers who regularly protected individual units from negative reporting, if only for reasons of morale, let loose on the 92nd. Allied Headquarters issued critical press releases to the media without hesitation.

On December 28, UPI reported from the "forgotten front" that the Buffalo Soldiers were unable to hold the German line: "The German radio said that most of the American prisoners taken in the attack were Negroes, and today Allied Headquarters confirmed that the defending troops were of the Negro Ninety-Second Division." News that an all-black division was surprised and overrun by an enemy force was treated by the military and political I-told-you-so's as proof of cowardice and incompetence. Front pages in American newspapers proclaimed that the black troops of the 92nd Division had lost ground to the enemy.

In a postwar assessment, the German general Otto Fretter-Pico summed up the December 25 assault as a situation in which good soldiers were poorly assigned: "Your troops were deployed on a front which was too long for the number of men available and your reserves were too far in the rear areas which prevented their being deployed immediately." He added that the lack of air and naval bombardment also contributed to the temporary German advance.

The same week of December 1944 in which the Allies were fighting in the Battle of the Bulge in northern France, allotments of heavy ammunition reached a new low in Italy. The best artillery weapons for mountain fighting, guns like the 155-mm howitzer, were limited to less than twenty rounds per day in Italy—as compared to the 200 rounds per day sent to the Bulge. Instead, a substandard light-weapon strategy was deployed. The 92nd Division was instructed to respond to heavy German artillery fire with a strenuous routine known as "infantry weapons shoots." With only rifles, machine guns, and 40-mm antiaircraft guns, infantrymen were ordered to shoot "in concentrated fire" for five minutes at heavy enemy artillery, then run to a safe location before the enemy could respond effectively. The "shoot and runs" were conducted every half-hour over a twenty-four-hour period. Though highly touted by the officers who devised the strategy, the plan simply did not work in real battle, and the dubious routine was later reduced to fifteen to twenty "shoot and runs" per twenty-four-hour period.

From January until April 1945, the 92nd Division's general performance was judged exemplary despite bouts of low morale due largely to a pervasive feeling that the Italian war was considered to be of secondary importance by top command. Certainly, the war in Italy was important, if more to keep the German army engaged on its southern front than to win outright. In February the under-supplied piecemeal strategy contributed to one of the great tragedies of the Buffalo Soldiers and the American war effort.

From the limestone cliffs of Punta Bianca (or White Point), huge railroad and coastal guns rained terror on Allied forces. Positioned at the strongest point in the entire Gothic Line, the guns were able to fire 900-pound projectiles for more than thirty-eight miles, and smaller shells a distance of nearly seventy miles. On February 6–10, a regiment of the Buffalo Soldiers was in the "Valley of Death"—in the plains south of Viareggio, and in the shadow and plain sight of the 5,600-foot-high Punta Bianca. Assigned to a sector of the valley, the 366th Infantry found themselves pinned down. The four-day battle was costly to the 92nd Division. A total of 659 enlisted men and forty-seven officers were killed, wounded, or missing in action. About half of the casualties were sustained by the 366th Infantry. Commanding officers later admitted the "main contribution was that they had kept enemy forces pinned down in this sector and served to keep the enemy confused as to future Allied intentions. Further, a considerable amount of information as to hostile strength and disposition was developed. This proved to be of considerable value during the spring offensive.

"When we hit that hill the Germans mowed us down like clay pigeons," recalled Sgt. Willard A. Williams of the 360th Infantry Regiment, who remembered only twelve or thirteen men making it to the top uninjured.

"There was no doubt that we were pretty well mangled. The real horrifying thing was our radio had been hit by shrapnel so we could not direct the artillery. They were zeroing in on us, and the enemy, just below on the other side of the hill, protected by a knoll, were lobbing mortar fire into our midst, so we were catching hell from both sides. We were pinned down there for several hours. I had resigned myself to dying because in the cross-fire the shrapnel sounded like bees around a hive. . . . We were assigned what was tantamount to suicide missions to carry out. One of these missions wiped out an entire company."

His buddies had performed "far above and beyond the call of duty," said Williams, yet they were castigated as cowards. More than half of the men of the 366th had been killed or wounded in action, but the regiment was deactivated as a combat regiment on March 14, 1945, at Bottinaccio, Italy, and converted into two service units (224th and 226th Engineer General Service regiments).

"A more devastating blow could not have been dealt this group of soldiers who were proud of their outfit and their contribution to winning the war," said Brown who watched battle-hardened officers and enlisted men, who had seen their friends killed, cry when they heard of this ultimate humiliation.

"We were completely shattered. As far as I was concerned, this ended the history of the 366th, which had been written in blood across the mountains of northern Italy."

Medal of Honor to Vernon J. Baker

First Lieutenant Vernon J. Baker

Citation: For extraordinary heroism in action on 5 and 6 April 1945, near Viareggio, Italy. Then Second Lieutenant Baker demonstrated outstanding courage and leadership in destroying enemy installations, personnel and equipment during his company's attack against a strongly entrenched enemy in mountainous terrain. When his company was stopped by the concentration of fire from several machine gun emplacements, he crawled to one position and destroyed it, killing three Germans. Continuing forward, he attacked an enemy observation post and killed two occupants. With the aid of one of his men, Lieutenant Baker attacked two more machine gun nests, killing or wounding the four enemy soldiers occupying these positions. He then covered the evacuation of the wounded personnel of his company by occupying an exposed position and drawing the enemy's fire. On the following night Lieutenant Baker voluntarily led a battalion advance through enemy mine fields and heavy fire toward the division objective. Second Lieutenant Baker's fighting spirit and daring leadership were an inspiration to his men and exemplify the highest traditions of the Armed Forces. [Baker's original Silver Star was upgraded to the Medal of Honor in 1997.]

Italy, Undated (1945)
From: Lt. Wm. T. Calvin
Well, I have finally gotten in the thick of battle (smile). If you read the negro papers you can see what a wonderful job our boys are doing. We hope the war will be over soon but we must remember we still have Japan to defeat. Lt. Dailey is really making a hero of himself. I will look for trucks with the 3278th QM mark and if I see one I will enquire about your husband. Italy is a very beautiful place. I have visited Naples, Paris and many interesting sites. Sorry we have to shell so many beautiful buildings. The people are very friendly but hard up for providing food. They are for whoever is in power at that present time. . . .

In April the Buffalo Soldiers confronted the devastating guns at Punta Bianca once again—but this time with a credible arsenal of its own. With Allied successes in France and Germany, ammunition supplies to the Italian campaign were finally restored. On April 14, the all-black 679th Tank Destroyer Battalion moved determinedly and steadily up the mountain to positions within 1,000 yards of the railroad guns. Jockeying to protected points behind rocks and ridges, the thirty-six–gun battalion closed to within 500 yards of the bigger gun.

Destroying the railroad gun would not be an easy task. The gun was not in view until the huge steel doors swung open and the cannon rolled forward. Even then it was impossible to see the weapon because a smoke generator obscured the barrel from sight. Until the sound of its enormous blast traveled down the mountain, soldiers were not aware it was in use. The antitank guns of the 92nd Division needed to follow with split-second accuracy of the instructions of a forward observer who watched for the blast of smoke, fresh from the barrel. Once they fired it, the Germans immediately retracted the gun into its protected cave and closed the steel doors. On April 15, a squad was able to knock out the smoke generator and now the big gun could be seen, just barely, by the forward observer. Finally he could clearly see the smoke from the gun, when fired, and then was able to direct the weapons of the 92nd.

Each time the German gun fired, the thirty-six Hellcat tank destroyers opened fire, directly at the gun ports, hitting the steel doors with nearly 200 rounds of ammunition before the cannon backed into the cave and the doors closed. German tanks and assault vehicles were sent to stop the assault, but the 679th turned its guns and destroyed the assault party. Firing for four days on the weapons that had killed thousands of citizens and soldiers, the 679th finally silenced the Punta Bianca gun on April 19.

Nine days later the 679th was again called upon to take out a German cannon, this one on Mount Moro, overlooking the city of Genoa. Three battalions of 92nd artillery pushed up the mountain on the evening of April 27. By morning, about thirty guns from the 598th and 600th Field Artillery Battalions were within 1,000 yards of the Mount Moro fortification, and twelve tanks of the 679th were within 400 yards. Artillery commander Brig. Gen. William Colbern sent terms to his German counterpart, to surrender by noon or face obliteration. At 11:56 A.M. the German commander surrendered to the 473rd Infantry—the white regiment attached to the 92nd Division.

Within the next forty-eight hours, the 92nd Division captured Genoa, Mussolini was arrested and executed (by Partisans), and the German command in Italy signed terms of surrender, ending the war in Italy officially on May 2. Over 11,000 German POWs were taken by the 92nd Division in April and May. Arrested, too, was Rita Louisa Zucca, a young Italian-American woman who had become infamous among American troops as Italian radio's "Axis Sally." Born in New York City, Zucca, who had studied at a convent school in Florence for five years, had become well-known for sultry radio messages in English encouraging "my American boys" to surrender.

On June 6, the 92nd Division staged the dramatic return of one of Genoa's greatest treasures. Missing from the city's Shrine of Christopher Columbus was a golden urn containing the human remains of the Italian explorer. A platoon from the 92nd had helped recover the urn from its hiding spot in the mountains, where it was placed during the war. Following a horse-drawn caisson, an honor guard of 2,000 Buffalo Soldiers accompanied the urn to the Piazza della Vittoria in Genoa.

Viareggio, Italy
June 26, 1945

. . . Last evening at a demonstration here at Regimental headquarters, one of the Lieutenant Colonels commended the Regiment on its outstanding accomplishments in the recent All-Division competitions. Out of the possible twelve citations, the 371st Infantry won nine of them. The Colonel went on to say that he could not understand why men who could uphold such standards as excellent soldiers could not set a better standard in the control of venereal disease.

At that point the Colonel—and certainly most of his audience—forgot all about the commendations and the citations. The colonel proceeded to lecture on Venereal disease, which in itself was not surprising; but I, and perhaps all the others, shall always remember the essential statements made by the Colonel. . . . Even now I'm not sure exactly why I'm writing you—except that I've got to tell someone about some of the things that go on here and are forever used to our disadvantage.

Pfc. Hoyt W. Fuller
Company D-371st Infantry

SPORTS AT THE FRONT

For the Buffalo Soldiers of the 92nd Division, "payback was sweet" when its best athletes went head-to-head against the 85th Division and the 10th Mountain Division in the Fifth Army's GI Olympics in Milan, Italy. Though all were comrades in the defeat of the German army, and all were equally battle-weary, the 92nd wanted greatly to "shut the loud mouths of the 85th Division who were still talking trash" about defeating the "colored boys" of the 93rd Infantry Division in the Louisiana War Games of 1943.

"After fighting the enemy, and plenty of our own American guys, for two years," said Sgt. Calvin Bass, a sprinter on the winning mile-relay team, "we had plenty of reasons to want to run those guys into the ground," thereby avenging the War Game loss by the black soldiers.

The Buffalo Soldiers won nine of thirteen events, finishing first and second in four events. Pfc. William Dillard zipped to a pair of Mediterranean-theater-of-operations records in taking the 100-meter high hurdles and the 200-meter low hurdles. Other 92nd Division record breakers were Sgt. Thenlo Knowles, who won the 800 meters in 2:02.1; Sgt. Mose Ellerbee, from Tuskegee Institute, who won the 100 meters in 0:11.6; and Pfc. Russell Jones and Sgt. Lloyd Crable, who deadlocked at 6 feet 1 inch in the high jump. The Associated Press noted that all of the contestants wore sneakers instead of spikes.

"That's not entirely true," said Sergeant Bass. "There were not enough sneakers to go around so I was one of the guys who ran in my socks. And my socks and my feet were tore up by the cinders." Sergeant Bass took a blue ribbon on the winning mile relay team, handing off the baton to the foursome's anchor, speedster Roscoe Lee Browne (who later became an acclaimed actor).

On August 11, 1945, Cpl. Charles Edwards was the star performer at the European Theater Track and Field Championships in Nuremberg, Germany. Edwards took first in the 200-meter dash, third in the 100 meters, and ran the anchor legs on the winning 400-meter and 800-meter relay teams. The African-American runner also placed third in the broad jump. Gen. George Patton presented medals to the victors before a crowd of some 50,000 U.S. servicemen and -women.

In Australia, among the returning soldiers from New Guinea was Sgt. Richard Cureton, winning pitcher from the 1942 MacArthur Cup. Cureton resumed playing with an all-black baseball team in the Australian league. Australian baseball historian Brian Vincent Davis remembered sitting, as a boy of twelve, next to Richard Cureton. "His immense black forearms served to remind me of my tender age and the colour of my skin, but mostly of his strength. I'd never sat so close to a black man before. On his wrist was a watch with a flat steel clasp band on which was engraved the war theatres he had served in—Bougainville, Guam, etc. This memory has always remained with me."

On April 12, 1945, President Roosevelt, vacationing at Warm Springs, Georgia, complained of a "terrible headache." Two hours later he died of cerebral hemorrhage. The impact of his death was profound. White and black Americans mourned the president who had served the nation for more than twelve years.

Before the month's end, Europe's two Axis leaders were also dead. On April 27, Mussolini, disguised as a German soldier, was stopped by antifascist Italian Partisans near Milan. The next day Mussolini and his mistress were shot and killed. Their bodies were then strung up by their feet in front of a gasoline station. A day later, Adolf Hitler exchanged marriage vows with Eva Braun, his longtime mistress, as Soviet cannons thundered and enemy troops surrounded Berlin. On April 30, with Braun slumped on a couch, dead from poisoning, Hitler sat down next to his bride and shot himself in the head with a pistol. Their bodies were taken to a rear garden, doused with gasoline, and burned.

In late April, the Allied nations of the world held a conference in San Francisco to create the United Nations. Meeting until June 26, they formed a charter and discussed the future of "human rights" and the "equal rights of men and women" in the postwar period. As the principal author of the American- and British-advocated system of "trusteeships," which had the dual purpose of replacing the League of Nation's mandate system and protecting former colonial interests, American representative Ralph Bunche brilliantly yet quietly structured trusteeships toward eventual independence. As a result of Bunche's clandestine maneuvering, the issues self-government, an end to colonialization, and "independence" were a cornerstone of the new UN Charter. But, in the United States, the change in the status of African Americans seemed microscopic.

"NEGRO TROOPS FAIL," SENATOR EASTLAND ASSERTS

On June 29, 1945, Sen. James Eastland of Mississippi, ranting from the floor of the Senate, assailed black troops as "an utter and abysmal failure." Eastland said that "high-ranking generals" in Europe had confided to him that the soldiers of the 92nd Infantry were cowards.

July 3, 1945 (Associated Press)

Eastland's Charges Hit
SHAEF Has No Knowledge of Offenses Laid to Negroes

Paris, July 2—Supreme Headquarters Allied Expeditionary Force (SHAEF) said today it had "no knowledge" of an alleged incident in Stuttgart to which Senator James O. Eastland, Democrat of Mississippi, referred last Friday in a Senate debate, when he said that French Senegalese troops had locked 5,000 German girls in a subway for five days and criminally assaulted them.

Supreme Headquarters also had no comment on Mr. Eastland's statement that it had been necessary to disarm "a good many Negro soldiers in Normandy" because they had broken into French farmhouses and attacked French women. It was pointed out, however, that there were no Negro combat troops in the Normandy campaign. The only Negroes used there were service troops.

LYNCHING AT FORT LAWTON

On Monday night, August 14, 1944, the body of a man was found hanging from a tree, about 500 yards from the army barracks at Fort Lawton, Washington. MPs removed the rope from the neck of the dead man, an Italian POW.

The same night the POW barracks was pummeled with rocks in an attack allegedly instigated by about fifty black GIs. During the assault twenty-four POWs were injured and Guglielmo Olivotto, a private in the Italian army, was killed and his body left hanging in the forest nearby.

Many of the 4,000 black soldiers stationed at Fort Lawton were said to be resentful of the congenial treatment given to the enemy POWs. In the winter, the black combat battalion had been assigned to assist the POWs in shoveling snow. Among the best-treated prisoners of any known war, the Italian POWs generally performed light labor and enjoyed weekly trips to the movies. They were even allowed visits to local bars and dances, which excluded black soldiers. Even local newspapers and local residents commented on their extraordinary freedom.

"Girls come out to service dances and make a big fuss over the Italians," a local man told the *Seattle Times* in August 1944. "They find 'em romantic. You know, speaking a foreign language and all that."

The army brought charges against forty-three black soldiers and quickly tried them. Thirteen soldiers were acquitted and twenty-three convicted of various charges, including murder and rioting, for which they received prison terms.

From a Letter Published in the *Pittsburgh Courier,* August 21, 1944:

> Last night I went to one of my Army Post theatres, No. 4, Fort Knox, Kentucky, and because of my color, I was forced to sit on the right of the theatre. The Italian internees are free to sit any place they please. Gee! How do they think we Colored soldiers feel about things like that? Is this what they call democracy? . . .
>
> *Pfc. Harold Lawrence*

Two French colonial African sol-diers, probably from Morocco or Algeria, fill the hands of Ameri-can soldiers with candy, in Rouffach, France, after defeating German forces at Colmar.

BLACK NURSES IN ENGLAND

In August 1944, sixty-three African-American nurses arrived at the 168th Station Hospital in England. Amid protests by segregationists that black nurses treating white soldiers would not be appropriate, the War Department relented and the black nurses were assigned to treat German POWs.

Newly arrived African-American army nurses line the rail of their ship as it pulls into port at Greenock, Scotland. They await the lowering of the gangplank to disembark.

22

CAPTIVES OF WAR

[1945]

By January 1945, Japan's vast empire was vanishing rapidly. Next to fall was the Philippines—and the gates of its internment camps. Conditions at the Santo Tomas Internment Camp in Manila worsened steadily from January 1942 to January 1945. From the beginning the Japanese absolved themselves of responsibility for feeding the internees, claiming that they were simply civilians held in protective custody and not prisoners of war. The internees were ordered to set up their own administration for the camp's day-to-day affairs. The Japanese gave the administration, or executive committee, the equivalent of thirty-five cents per person, per day, to operate the camp. The allotment had to pay not only for food, but for medical, sanitation, and maintenance supplies.

For several months individuals were able to buy extra food and other items from Filipino vendors or friends who sold or passed approved items through the fence near the front gate of the compound. With an array of professions among the internee population, including bankers, engineers, dentists, doctors, teachers, clergymen, bakers, shoemakers, carpenters, welders, cosmeticians, hairdressers, dancers, musicians, prostitutes, and golf pros, it was, for a time, possible to get almost any service or amenity at the camp. But as the war's progress started to look less and less favorable for the Japanese, camp conditions worsened.

Living virtually "back to belly," some 700 men slept in a former college gymnasium, each man allotted a space measuring about six-feet long by forty inches wide, about the size of the average front door on a house. Beneath their cots they kept their possessions. Commonly internees waited on long lines for everything—to eat, bathe, get a drink of water, or go to the toilets, where guards doled out toilet paper in measured lengths. A sign in one toilet read: IF YOU WANT PRIVACY, CLOSE YOUR EYES.

All were deprived, yet racial tension existed nearly everywhere, at least early on in their incarceration. On one occasion a fight broke out between a black soldier and the white soldier standing in line behind him at the camp medical dispensary.

"I don't see why I have to wait for a 'shine,' " complained the white soldier, a moment before the black soldier slugged him. Former shipmates from the USS *President Grant,* the two tussled wildly. Their friends broke up the scuffle and quieted them down before the Japanese guards arrived. Some worried that the Japanese would use the fight to inflame Filipino hatred of whites.

A camp trial was held and both men were judged guilty of "breach of the peace" and sentenced to sixty days' probation. If they violated probation, they would have to cut grass for ten days. The decision was publicized over the camp loudspeaker.

"A strange kind of madness swept the camp," remembered nurse Francis Nash. Food became the number-one topic of conversation. A philosophy of positive visualization—"see the food in my mind"—was the mantra introduced to the camp by fellow internee Robert Browne. Browne, who had come to the Philippines as a U.S. Army purchaser, had had an extraordinary and nearly secret life as an accomplished mathematician and philosopher. Of all the courses and lectures taught by the teachers among the internees, none seems to have had more impact on the camp's population than Browne's on mind-power techniques.

"See the orange and taste it," advised Browne. "Feel its nutrients going into your body and making you feel stronger." He encouraged his students to devise as many psychological techniques as possible to overcome their fixation on hunger. Collecting recipes and paying acute attention to each ingredient, said Browne, would aid in overcoming the nutritional deficits that were eating away at both the body and the mind.

Browne's philosophy spread throughout the camp and may have actually helped defer or at least delay some of the intense psychological pain associated with malnutrition and starvation. The visualization technique became a camp phenomenon. Individuals carried menus and read recipes like novels. With simply the fist of one hand, creative practitioners made turkey legs or hamburgers, carrots and corn from their fingers, curled leaves became ice cream cones, and they drank imaginary milk, juices, tea, coffee, and other beverages—some ice cold.

After a period at Santo Tomas, Browne was transferred to Los Baños, where he and 800 "able-bodied" men were moved in December 1943. At both camps, Browne taught courses on Asian and "Esoteric Christian" philosophy, including his own visualization techniques. As the war progressed, internees were challenged to survive on less than 700 calories per day. Most men and women had lost between forty and sixty pounds. Browne himself, who gave away much of his own food allotment to others, dropped from 212 pounds to 120. Many prisoners were convinced that the Japanese were trying to kill them systematically through starvation.

By October 1944, two people per month were dying from malnutrition-related illnesses. By February 1945, the death rate had climbed to three a day. A Japanese doctor associated with the camps demanded that the words "malnutrition" and "starvation" not be written on internee death certificates.

On February 3, 1945, American planes swooped overhead and American tanks rolled into the Santo Tomas camp, freeing over 3,000 internees. (Six American soldiers were killed in the takeover.) On February 23, 1945, the Marines raised the flag on Mt. Suribachi, on the island of Iwo Jima. On that same Friday morning, about twenty-five miles south of Manila in the Philippine Islands, the 11th Airborne Division began the rescue operation at Los Baños. American paratroopers, Filipino guerrillas, and an army reconnaissance platoon surprised the Japanese troops in the middle of their morning calisthenics.

"At about six forty-five A.M., much to our surprise and unbounded joy, we saw the paratroopers in the skies," recalled Browne in an August

1945 interview. "They were quickly joined on the north of the camp by the guerrilla forces. A terrific battle ensued between the paratroopers and the Japanese guards, while an American plane flew overhead bearing in large letters 'RESCUE,' thereby informing us what the battle was all about."

In about thirty minutes the raiding party killed more than 180 enemy soldiers. (American and Filipino casualties included two dead and three wounded.) Military intelligence had learned that the 2,130 internees were to have been executed later that day. Within four hours, all were taken safely from the camp. "No wonder General MacArthur said, 'God was certainly with us today,' " said Browne.

Seventy-four-year-old Isaac Lloyd survived all but the last day of his internment in a Japanese camp. Badly injured when a liberators' artillery shell hit the prisoners' quarters, he died shortly afterward. (Army Chief of Staff Colin Powell later proclaimed, "I doubt that any airborne unit in the world will be able to rival the Los Baños prison raid. It is the textbook airborne operation for all ages and all armies.")

Due to Walter Loving's health and political influence, he and his wife were released from Santo Tomas two years earlier. However, in February 1945, they were forced to flee Manila. Separated from his wife, Loving was on a line of some 900 men being led through the streets by Japanese soldiers, when he reportedly met his end. Ordered to run to the beach, many of the men were shot by the guards, when Loving turned to the soldiers and shouted, "I am an American. If I must die, I'll die like an American." He was then beheaded by an enemy guard.

Robert T. Browne

In 1920, *The Mystery of Space,* a book about religious philosophy and science, by mathematician and philosopher Robert T. Tecumtha Browne, received much critical praise and acclaim, certainly more than any such book ever before written by an African American. But those who raved about his work were not aware of its author's race. Even Browne's editor and publisher (Dutton) did not know that they had entered into a book contract with a black author. Maintaining a racial "cover" throughout the prepublication process, he communicated cautiously with his editor, only by mail and never in person or even by telephone.

The *New York Times*'s eminent reviewer Benjamin De Casseres decreed Browne's 400-page opus the "greatest of all latter-day books on space." In arguably the single most colorblind review by a major newspaper of an African-American author, De

Newspaper photograph of Robert T. Browne following his return to the United States from the Philippines in 1945.

ROBERT T. BROWNE, famous mathematician, philosopher and author, was a prisoner of the Japs for three years. Mr. Browne and others were miraculously rescued by paratroopers and guerilla flhters on the day when the Japanese had planned to massacre the prisoners at Santo Tomas and Los Banos prison camps.

Casseres lauded Browne in a way never before experienced by a black writer: "It is written by a mathematician, a mystic and a thinker, one who, endowed with a tremendous metaphysical imagination, never lets go any point of the threads of reality. Lucid and logical, with a pen that never falters, Mr. Browne advances steadily from page to page upon the fortress of science, laying outpost after outpost in the dust. He knows all the weapons of the astronomers, the mathematicians, the atomists, and the lesser-act mystagogues. He knows them all and laughs at them."

British physicist E. N. Andrade deemed the first-time author's effort to be filled with "profoundly original thoughts," and critic Lilian Whiting described Browne's work as "one of the most fascinating books imaginable." In view of such fully pedigreed acclaim, Browne's race trepidation may have seemed overblown, or even paranoid. Still, he had once confided to his librarian friend Arthur Schomburg his concern for the black author—that "if the world knows he is black, his work will not be given its due."

Yet Browne's greatest fear about the reception he might receive following the unveiling of his race came true. Nothing in the way of book signings, press parties, or interviews greeted his auspicious literary arrival. His blackness did become known to his editor and publisher and, presumably, to the critics who were the early champions of his work. Apart from the placement of his book on a *New York Times* recommended list a few weeks after its review, Browne, and his career, went unrecognized.

Recognition was not wholly lacking among his African-American contemporaries. At the dawning of the "Harlem Renaissance" in 1921 he was elected vice president of the American Negro Academy, for which he and historian Carter G. Woodson revised its constitution; and Schomburg invited him to prepare a talk on Einstein's "Theory of Relativity" for the academy's annual meeting. However, not a single major African-American journal is known to have reviewed his book.

John Edward Bruce, a black historian and scholar, better known for his criticism than compliments, placed Browne on a short list of history's black geniuses. In a 1921 speech at Mother A.M.E. Zion Church in Harlem, Bruce ranked Browne with no less than Terence Afer, Alexander Pushkin, Phyllis Wheatley, Paul Laurence Dunbar, and DuBois:

"Of the later writers who have taken high rank in fields hitherto unexplored by Negro authors, I want to call to your attention the recent work of a young gentleman of color, Mr. Robert T. Browne, called *The Mystery of Space*, declared by the ablest critics of the daily press and literary reviews to be the most

Children aboard the SS Jean Lafitte, *bound for the States with internees freed from a Japanese internment camp in the Philippines, gather around Pendleton "Bumblebee" Thompson in April 1945. Thompson volunteered as cook in the Los Baños camp where they were all interned.*

remarkable book on this subject of the century. It has run through two editions I am informed by its author and a third is being printed. . . . One of the most capable book reviewers of the *New York Sun,* now the *New York Herald,* a few months ago devoted almost two columns to a review [of] Mr. Browne's book, and almost exhausted superlatives in his analysis of its contents, this reviewer, as have dozens of others on journals and magazines here and abroad, placed this young Negro author of a great scientific work on the highest pinnacle ever attained by any Negro writer in America, or Europe. Perhaps all of them did not know that he is a Negro, but the real scholar takes no note of a man's color, if his brain functions properly for the ben-

Chief Specialist John J. Gilmartin gives members of his U.S. Naval Hospital basketball team last-minute instructions before a game. The team was one of the first integrated navy sports teams.

efit of human kind. For in the democracy of brains, there is no color."

Almost eighty years later, judging Browne to be one of America's most "significant unsung African Americans," San Diego State University librarian Robert Fikes, Jr., could find no mention of him in any public records or academic archives beyond 1921—not even a death certificate. In a five-page essay in the 1998 *Negro Educational Review,* Fikes contemplated "the unsettling circumstance that Robert T. Browne, at age 39, seems to have abruptly disappeared from the face of the earth just two years after the publication of his book."

In the course of researching this book, my discovery of an August 1945 interview in the *New York Amsterdam News* with internment camp survivor Robert T. Browne led to the unraveling of the saga. Following his three-year internment, Browne had returned to the United States where he later remarried and adopted a child from the Philippines. In 1950 Browne founded the Hermetic Society, a theosophical religion. He died in 1978.

More than 4,000 of the Bataan prisoners died aboard "Hell Ships." During transfer to Japan and other Pacific ports to slave labor camps, U.S. planes and navy ships, unaware that POWs were aboard, sunk three vessels loaded with American POWs. Of the 1,782 men aboard one prison ship, only eight survived when a U.S. Navy submarine sunk it as it left Manila Harbor on October 11, 1944.

BENNY AND THE GIS

As a boy growing up in the Philippines, Benny Rosell spent most of WWII hiding from the Japanese soldiers encamped near his home in Parang. But in late 1944 American forces retook the island and transformed it into a large military base.

"Every day I watched the black soldiers working. I thought it was strange that the white and black soldiers did not work together. But the black soldiers were more friendly to me." Mostly he watched the soldiers from the 824th Amphibious Truck Company and other black units loading and unloading war materials from the ships docked offshore.

Benny was "adopted" by the soldiers who were camped nearby. He visited them almost every day. He regularly attended evening church services conducted in a tent beneath tall coconut trees. "I loved to sing, and the black soldiers let me sing at their service one night.

"I sang 'I Love to Tell the Story'—afterward they said, 'Let's go visit your parents,' and they brought food and clothing for me and my family and for many of the other children. They gave my mother two pairs of pants and asked her if she could make me some clothes—and she did. Those guys were very special to me and my family."

In 1952 Benny arrived with his family in the United States. He settled in Salina, Kansas, where he became a schoolteacher and Christian minister.

WACs Overseas

[1945]

"Bend your butt! Bend your lazy butt!" Every single day, from our first minute in uniform we were trained in military procedure, how to talk, how to walk, when to wake up, when to eat, when to sleep. "Bend your lazy butt! Suck that belly in! Straighten up! Go home, lady! No, sister, this ain't no charm school. You're in the Army now!" And boy, didn't we know it.

PFC. NORMA K. MOORE

By the winter of 1945, a colossal backlog of mail caused the army to reconsider its deployment of black WACs. The relocation of more than 500,000 servicemen onto the European Continent since D-Day had resulted in a vast accumulation of mail in British warehouses and delayed its delivery, for months, to the front lines. Further delays in the delivery of mail had the potential of dampening soldier morale just as American armies thrust into the German homeland, where they expected to meet stiff resistance.

The army first permitted black members of the WACs to serve overseas in the winter of 1945, when it created the 6,888th Central Postal

In Birmingham, England, Maj. Charity Adams and Capt. Abbie N. Campbell inspect the 6,888th Central Postal Directory Battalion, the first contingent of black WACs sent overseas.

Directory Battalion, an all-black unit, and assigned some 850 African-American women to it. The unit, based in Birmingham, England, and later in France (in Rouen and Paris), routed mail to millions of members of the armed forces in Europe. The members of the 6,888th postal unit were the first black women many Britons in Birmingham had ever seen, and they shattered stereotypes.

"These WACs are very different from the colored women portrayed in the films, where they are usually either domestics or the outspoken old-retainer type or sloe-eyed sirens given to gaudiness of costume and eccentricity in dress," the *Birmingham Sunday Mercury* noted. "The WACs have dignity and proper reserve." The 6,888th Postal Battalion was the first and only contingent of black WACs sent overseas. "Our job was to keep up with the addresses of our fighting men who were almost constantly on the move, and see that their mail reached them," wrote Pfc. Lucia Pitts in her diary. An average of 30,000 address changes had to be made every day.

"In Paris, as elsewhere abroad, colored WACs were a surprise. White as well as Negro soldiers looked at us as if they couldn't believe their eyes. They'd yell anywhere, 'American WACs!' and usually follow with the line: 'You're the first American (or colored) girl I've seen in three (or two) years!' It was almost impossible for us to sit at a street café and pay for our own drinks; someone almost invariably came along and insisted on treating."

In Rouen the battalion suffered its only tragedy. Three of the women—Mary Bankston, Mary Barlow, and Dolores Brown—went for a drive in the French countryside and never came back. The army vehicle in which they were riding crashed, killing two of them instantly; the third died a few days later.

"Sergeant Browne was our company drill sergeant and she was tough, but she was generally fair. She whipped us into shape. She was gay and she was open about it and I believe she was quite proud of herself," observed Private First Class Moore.

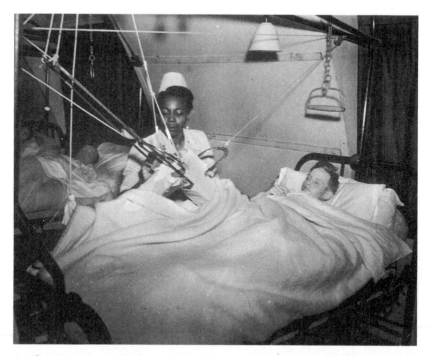

Lt. Florie E. Gant is assigned to care for a German patient at a prisoner-of-war hospital somewhere in England.

For some WACs the presence of lesbians made for an uncomfortable situation. But, as noted by military historian Brenda Moore, homosexuality was a fact of life in the 6,888th, as it was in other organizations, both inside and outside the military. Some interviewees in Moore's comprehensive study of the 6,888th had made unsolicited comments about gay lifestyles within the unit, stating that they would have preferred that such activity had never existed. "They tried to stay in clusters; all of their friends in a little unit in and of itself," said a WAC. "One buddy got in touch with the other buddies and they formed their own little clique."

But the fact that lesbians were in the unit did not pose a problem for everyone. "I imagine some in the army today might be outraged to learn that gay women soldiers are buried at Normandy," said Private First Class Moore. The three women were buried at the Normandy American Cemetery in Bayeux.

ON MARCH 7, 1945, sixty black WACs staged a sit-down strike at Lovell General Hospital at Fort Devens, Massachusetts. Trained to be medical technicians, the black women were assigned to scrub floors and toilets, wash windows, and perform other menial tasks. At a meeting to air their grievances with the hospital's commander, Col. Walter M. Crandell, answered their protests by telling them, "Black girls are fit only to do the dirtiest type of work, because that's what Negro women are used to doing." Taking full credit for their menial assignments, he told them that he would not have black WACs serving as medical technicians. Disgusted with the colonel's response, the women walked out on him.

On March 10, the sixty were formally ordered to return to work or be held in violation for failing to obey a direct order. Four of the WACs refused to return to duty and were arrested. Six of the WACs were ultimately court-martialed; four were convicted and found guilty of disobeying a superior officer. The four convicted WACs were each sentenced to one year at hard labor, ordered to forfeit all pay and allowances, and given dishonorable discharges.

Black organizations protested the army's handling of the situation. Under pressure from the White House and Congress, the War Department reversed the convictions and dismissed all charges. African Americans pushed harder and insisted that Colonel Crandell be investigated and punished. The War Department refused and officially closed the matter.

Somewhere in France, April 23, 1945
From: Sgt. Ralph J. Fowler
My dear friend,

 I must admit I was surprised to hear from you and your letter was appreciated so very much. I should have written some time ago but you know how it is, always putting off until tomorrow.

 Hitler is about cornered now, so I may be seeing you before long.

Ralph

THE HOLOCAUST

[1945]

The most moving moment of my life was the day the Americans arrived [at Buchenwald], a few hours after the SS had fled. It was the morning of April 11. I will always remember with love a big black soldier. He was crying like a child—all the pain in the world and all the rage. Everyone who was there that day will forever feel a sentiment of gratitude to the American soldiers who liberated us.

ELIE WIESEL

One of many concentration camps liberated by the Allies, Buchenwald became the first symbol for America of the horrific experience of millions who suffered and died under the Hitler regime.

"What I saw in Buchenwald was the face of evil," said Sgt. Leon Bass of the 1,834th Engineer Combat Battalion. "It made me know that human life is sacred. Because when I walked through those gates in the spring of April 1945, I was totally unprepared for what I saw."

Precise details about the mission to transport survivors from the Nazi death camp had not been conveyed to the engineer, ambulance, and quartermaster companies that were rushed to the site. But a rumor spread rapidly, up and down the ranks, that all were about to get their first close view of one of Hitler's death camps. Hardened soldiers who thought they had "seen it all"—had not. As General Eisenhower later said, if American soldiers didn't know what they were fighting for, now they knew what they were fighting against.

"I saw what I can refer to now as the walking dead," said Bass.

An electrified barbed-wire fence surrounded the compound where the American convoy found 20,000 prisoners. Nearly one thousand men, women, and children died daily at Buchenwald. To the horror of the American soldiers, thousands of inmates were reduced to skin and bones. More than 500 bodies were piled and rotting in the sun. Some labor units balked at the assignment to transport the badly diseased or to bury the dead. German citizens from nearby villages were ordered to handle the decaying bodies. Hundreds of local citizens were also brought to the camp to bear witness to the atrocities.

Within twenty-four hours, the engineering units repaired the camp's water supply, and ambulances and trucks began the evacuation of the most serious cases to a nearby field hospital. Disease was rampant at the camp, and many bodies were burned to prevent the spread of epidemics.

Letter from Cpl. Lance Johnson to Lawrence Reddick. Johnson gives an account of his experience touring a concentration camp for the Jews.

CLEAN UP

"We were told it was a 'clean up' operation at some place called a concentration camp," remembered one truck driver. To most black soldiers the assignment did not cast them as heroic liberators.

"Nobody said we would see people stacked up like old wood limbs, dead, burned and all of them starved," said a quartermaster sergeant. "It made me pray that this was the closest I would ever get to hell." Like the experience of Wiesel, many of the camp survivors encountered white and black Americans.

On April 15, 1945, CBS radio newsman Edward R. Murrow broadcast from the camp: "There surged around me an evil-smelling stink, men and boys reached out to touch me. . . . In another part of the camp they showed me the children, hundreds of them. Some were only six years old. One rolled up his sleeves, showed me his number. It was tattooed on his arm. B-6030 it was. The others showed me their numbers. They will carry them till they die."

The children with tattoos were Jewish children who had been transferred to Buchenwald from the death camp at Auschwitz in Poland when it closed in January 1945.

"I had never seen a black person before," said Simon Rozenkier about the black soldiers he encountered in the first days of liberation at Buchenwald. "But these black soldiers looked very good to me because they were taking me to freedom."

A survivor of Auschwitz and Buchenwald, Rozenkier, a native of Poland, was sterilized when he was fourteen years old in the Nazi program to destroy the capacity of "inferior races" to reproduce. "They told me they were injecting me with vitamins." His parents and four siblings were killed at the camps.

"One black soldier I will never forget because he offered me candy, but I had to tell him no, which must have surprised him and maybe offended him," said Rozenkier. "But I could not explain very well that I had dysentery, and because I had dysentery, we were told not to eat candy or we could die from the effects. I don't know if he understood my rejection of the candy, but I would have wanted him to know that I appreciated his kindness."

"We carried people twenty-one hours a day for eight weeks," said Melvin Darden of the 567th Ambulance Company, who arrived at Dachau, near Salzburg, Austria, on April 30, six hours after U.S. troops liberated the camp and its nearly 20,000 survivors.

Many African Americans were imprisoned in German concentration camps during the war. Some, like jazz musician Valaida Snow, were caught in German-occupied Europe and were imprisoned in Axis internment camps. According to holocaust researchers, African, Euro-African, and American blacks were also held in the Nazi concentration-camp system. Many were worked to death on labor projects or died as a result of mistreatment. Others were never imprisoned but were instead immediately killed by the SS or the Gestapo.

Artist Josef Nassy, who was living in Belgium, was arrested as an enemy alien and held for seven months in the Beverloo transit camp in Belgium before he was transferred to Germany, where he spent the rest of the war in internment camps at Laufen and Tittmoning. Jean Voste, an Afro-Belgian, was imprisoned at Dachau. Jean Marcel Nicolas, a Haitian, was incarcerated at Buchenwald and Dora-Mittelbau concentration camps in Germany. Bayume Mohamed Hussein from Tanganyika (now Tanzania) died at the Sachsenhausen camp, near Berlin.

In Germany, about 200 black American soldiers were held in German POW camps, including pilot Lt. Darwin Nicholas, who was kept at a Gestapo prison in Butzbach, and Lionel Romney, a sailor in the U.S. Merchant Marine, who was incarcerated at Mauthausen.

BLACK POWs IN GERMAN CAMPS

The Statue of Liberty was hidden by fog as four troopships entered New York harbor on June 6, 1945. Aboard were 1,065 former American prisoners of war, including 46 black ex-POWS. Upon their arrival many spoke of the cruelty encountered, including beatings and shortages of food and water.

"[I have] to give the devil his due," said Sgt. Mulford Brown, a twenty-five-year-old sergeant from Washington, D.C. Black American soldiers were treated "no worse" than other American troops, Sergeant Brown told a white reporter upon his return to the United States. But for virtually all American POWs, the experience was tough with much suffering.

Black British pilot Cy Grant from British Guyana gave the Germans credit too for treating him exactly like the white prisoners. Grant was held at a POW camp for two years after being shot down in 1943: "The only racism that I encountered [there] was from an American . . . a corporal or something who happened to be in this holding camp. And he called me a nigger one or two times, but I got nothing from the Germans. They didn't single me out for any special treatment." But some black Americans were mistreated and killed in the camps.

"IT WAS ROUGH there, really rough. We marched through snow up to our knees, some of the fellows without their shoes which the Germans had taken from them," said SSgt. Albert DeByers, who with other POWs was "herded out" early one morning in subzero weather to march through the snow to a railroad car to the infamous Stalag IX-B, known as Bad Orb, located near Orb, Germany.

On December 18, 1944, a black American soldier was singled out and killed during a march to Stalag IV-B near Muehlberg, Germany. At Stalag 7A, on April 1, 1945, in Moosburg, Germany, an SS guard executed a black American. But the worst treatment of enemy soldiers by the Nazis was applied to colonial African soldiers. In March 1945, more African soldiers were held in German POW camps than American soldiers. Among the more than one million Allied POWs were 754,600 French soldiers of whom more than 100,000 were black colonial soldiers. The remainder were 199,500 British and 75,850 Americans. Algerian, Moroccan, Senegalese, and other French black soldiers were customarily treated badly and murderously by the Nazis.

On July 16, 1945, four surviving inmates testified that SS member Alfred Moreta had carried out the execution of more than one thousand black Senegalese soldiers who were held at a slave labor camp in Frizlar, Germany, for allegedly stealing potatoes.

Alberta Hunter gives a concert for soldiers in Burma illuminated by truck headlights.

THE WERETH 11

The German onslaught into Belgium killed thousands of Allied troops, and many black and white soldiers wre captured. On December 17, 1994, eleven men of the 333rd Artillery Battalion eluded the enemy, and they made their way through the dense forest and fog to a house in Wereth, a tiny hamlet in eastern Belgium. There, Mathias Langer gave the black soldiers refuge in his home. Langer gave them food and shelter, but a neighbor woman had spotted them and reported their presence to the SS.

"My father told the Germans that we only had wanted to help the men get warm," remembered Langer's daughter, Tina. "They said, 'When we are finished with them, they won't be cold anymore.' "

The eleven men were held at gunpoint and then dragged out of the house where they were forced to lie on the frozen ground. The SS taunted the men for more than an hour, then made them march to a field in front of a German tracked vehicle. In a field about 500 meters from Langer's house, the men were further tortured before being bayoneted to death.

The bodies lay in the field for more than a month before another army unit found and buried them. An army investigation found "all evidence indicates a ruthless mass butchery" of the black soldiers. A conclusion that

On the back of this photograph, Alberta Hunter inscribed "a few of untouchable children and myself in Rangoon."

was "obvious by the multiple hideous wounds on the victims." Some had their finger severed to remove gold rings, others were bayoneted in their eyes, and vehicle track marks were found across their bodies.

Despite the willingness of Langer and other eyewitnesses to identify and testify against the the SS guards, whose unit was known, the case was not pursued. According to some military historians, the case was dropped because the victims were black. Seven of the men were buried in Europe and four were returned to the United States for burial. (In 2004 a memorial for Wereth 11 was established in Belgium at the site of the massacre.)

Alberta Hunter

Bob Hope became the symbol of the traveling entertainer performing for American servicemen overseas, but the model for dedicated globe-trotting artists began with Alberta Hunter. Singing jazz, blues, and popular music, she had performed in Europe, Africa, and Asia for more than twenty years before the war, an experience that she considered a warm-up to WWII.

In 1944, Hunter and her unit of five entertainers were the first USO company to complete the China-Burma-India (CBI) tour—a winding journey that took the troupe through jungles and monsoon-flooded trails, including the famed Ledo Road. Regarded as the most dangerous tour among the war theaters, other troupes had started the harrowing journey but they found the going too tough.

"Sweltering heat, fever, jungles, wild tigers, Jap snipers, leeches and other insects that latch onto the skin so tight that the only way they can be removed is by burning them off," was said by a Burma traveler who vowed never to return. But after completing the seven-month tour, Hunter said she was ready to go back.

"I am getting ready to tour again," she said at a stop in southeast Asia.

"I tell you the pleasant smiles that came over the faces of the boys is enough for me," Hunter said. "It means so much to them."

"CBI is swamped with bugs," she added. "If you open your mouth, they will fill it up. Many times I had to go to the army hospital to have bugs removed from my mouth and ears. The boys would shut off the jeep lights and flashlights to dispel the insects. So I found myself singing many times in the dark."

In June 1945, Hunter performed at the biggest postwar diplomatic party in Europe, at the special invitation of General Eisenhower. Hunter's personal scrapbook is filled with news clippings of the event:

"The wine, the liquers, the filet-mignon, the petits fours and everything else which General Dwight D. Eisenhower served at his headquarters here today for Soviet Marshall Georgi K. Zhukov went over well, but it took a Negro sextet from the United States to put the party in the groove," reported the *International Herald Tribune.*

"Alberta burst in and started to sing. It was 'Some of These Days.' Ike Eisenhower looked up, smiled, put down his fork, and beat time on the table. General Zhukov looked sternly at the entertainer, turned his head a bit to hear her clearly, then suddenly smiled the biggest smile I ever saw," said Chicago radio correspondent George Grim-Cowles. Hunter "sang exactly seven of Gen. 'Ike' Eisenhower's favorite tunes with the genial general joining in."

One newspaper reported that General Eisenhower "apparently well hep himself, passed up a list of great theatrical names now on the conti-nent to select the sextet headed by Alberta Hunter."

Immediately after the war, Hunter and her troupe then traveled back to Tokyo, where they gave performances for members of the occupation army in Japan. When the USO program ended in December 1945, she began filling engagements with the Veterans Hospital Camp show.

"I regard entertainment of these poor souls in these hospitals one of the greatest services that can be rendered," she asserted. "It is amazing to what extent many of these men, broken in bodies, mentally affected by the shocks of the war, still maintain such high spirit. All of us needs to visit these hospitals at times just to see how well we are doing."

Alberta dropped out of show business in 1954 to attend nursing school and began working as a licensed practical nurse at a hospital in New York City. She retired from nursing in 1977 at age eighty-one to resume her singing career.

A Tale of Two Soldiers

Former Pfc. Norma Moore: On Easter Sunday 1944, at Fort Jackson, South Carolina, all of us WACs were sitting out in front of the colored womens' barracks. Some of the girls were dolled-up in their uniforms, as young men were coming by all day to meet women or to make dates. I think I was the only one who wasn't waiting for a guy to stop by—because I did not join the army to meet a man—but I knew a lot of girls did. I was just sitting on the grass alone, reading a book of poetry.

Former S. Sgt. Willard Moore: All I could see then was the prettiest girl in the world sitting by herself.

NM: So the rest of the story is there was one soldier named Sgt. Bill Moore who all the girls thought was so handsome. They were all whis-pering his name that Sunday when he came strutting up the walk, be-cause, you see, he had a date with one of the girls in my barracks. All of them were giggling and acting silly, but I did not do any of that.

WM: I don't remember anyone else.

Sgt. Willard Moore, ca. 1943.

NM: I kept my eyes in my book. But I looked up just one time, and he was looking straight at me.

WM: Something told me straight away that she was for me.

NM: He stopped to talk to me and he asked me for a date. I told him it just did not seem right to be on his way to take one girl out and then ask another for a date. I said yes, but I do not know why. Ordinarily I would have scolded him.

Pfc. Norma Kay DeFreese Moore, ca. 1944.

WM: She said yes because the good Lord can make you do lots of good things if you listen. Two weeks later I asked this very lovely, very smart young lady to marry me.

NM: It was a pretty quick engagement. And probably the craziest thing I ever did, looking back. We got married and he shipped out to England, and then to France and Germany, and I shipped out to England. I really didn't know if I would ever see him again.

WM: I couldn't see God leading me to the person who would become my wife—and then blowing me up.

NM: But, sadly, death happened to a lot of soldiers, unmarried and married.

WM: It happened to a lot of guys. I always carried the thought that it would not happen to me. But I would have died knowing I had found the woman I loved.

NM: On our first wedding anniversary, on June 12, 1945, my husband and I were reunited for one day in Rouen, France.

WM: I got word that my wife was on the same continent and that was all I needed to hear. After all the war and ugliness I had seen, I had to see the person I loved most.

NM: He somehow got a message to my captain, and she was the only one who knew he was coming. A girlfriend took me to a little café and there he was—my husband who I had not seen for twelve whole months. Well, we just hugged and kissed. He bought me a tin of the best-tasting semisweet Swiss chocolate I ever had—then or since. He could not stay long and I was scared for him because he was as close to being AWOL as you could possibly get. But he wanted to stay with me a while longer. I know he believed he could talk his way out of being AWOL, and somehow he did. I was just thrilled to see him. Up until then, I think that was the best day of my life.

WM: The war was almost over and we had stopped at a river on the Russian border. I was fishing and I didn't see it when a German captain came walking up to me. Lord, I thought, how am I going to keep from getting shot by this man? But he handed me his gun, a Luger. I saved it, but somebody stole it from my duffle on the way home.

THE FREEMAN FIELD MUTINY

On March 10, 1945, fourteen black officers of the 477th Bomb Group entered the white officers' club at Freeman Field, Indiana. They sat down and ordered drinks and cigarettes, but were refused service. The black officers left without incident. Though army regulations prohibited racial segregation in recreational facilities, officers' clubs routinely excluded black officers. To get around the order the base commander devised a scheme effectively designating all white officers as permanent "base officers" and black officers as temporary. The club was, of course, open only to permanent officers.

The base's commanding officer, Maj. Gen. Frank "Monk" Hunter, made his position clear:

> The War Department is not ready to recognize blacks on the level of social equal to white men. This is not the time for blacks to fight for equal rights or personal advantages. They should prove themselves in combat first. There will be no race problem here, for I will not tolerate any mixing of the races. This is my base and, as long as I am in command, there will be no social mixing of the white and colored officers. The single Officers Club on base will be used solely by white officers. You colored officers will have to wait until an Officers Club is built for your use. Are there any questions? If there are, I will deal with them personally.

A few weeks later, on April 3, 1945, Lt. Coleman A. Young, a former union organizer from Detroit, called a meeting among black officers at Freeman Field. After a discussion of the situation, the plan was that black officers would enter the "whites-only" officers' club in small groups of three to five. Their tactic was designed to be nonviolent and nonconfrontational, the objective being merely to heighten attention on the policy. On April 5, a crop of new black members of the 477th arrived at Freeman Field. At about 7:00 P.M., nineteen of them went to the officers' club to request service. All doors to the club were ordered locked, except for the front door. All were ordered to leave and were told they were "placed under arrest in quarters." They left and the club returned to normal—until another fourteen black officers entered the club. They, too, were told to leave, their names were taken, and they were arrested in the same manner.

An hour later, 1st Lt. Oliver Goodall, a dark-skinned officer, and 2nd Lt. Roger C. Terry and 2nd Lt. James V. Kennedy, two fair-skinned black officers, were sent in to test the guard's perception of race. The guard stopped only the darker officer, grabbing him. All argued their right to enter the club, and all were arrested and the club was closed for the night. The next day, waves of black officers entered and were arrested.

A total of 162 black officers were arrested for entering the whites only officers' club and for refusing to sign a statement agreeing to stay out of the club. The action spread to the 619th Bombardment Squadron. The War Department directed charges be dropped against 159 of the officers, all but three involved in the jostling incident. Facing a possible death sentence for disobeying military orders, Goodall and Kennedy were found not guilty by a court-martial panel, but Lieutenant Terry was convicted and fined $150.

The 477th Bomb Group (Medium) never got into combat as a result of its white commander's bigoted personnel policies. (On August 12, 1995, the Air Force vindicated all of the black officers and set aside the conviction of Lieutenant Terry, returning his $150.)

On March 24, 1945, the Red Tails flew cover for B-17s on a major bombing mission on the Daimler-Benz tank factory in Berlin. The 1,600-mile-round-trip attack was the longest in the history of the Fifteenth Air Force. On this run, Charles Brantly, Roscoe C. Brown, Jr., and Earl Lane, each shot down a German Me-262 jet fighter aircraft. The jets were among the first seen in the war. For their achievements that day, the group received a Distinguished Unit Citation.

A TALE OF TWO PILOTS

As a fighter pilot, 1st Lt. John Leahr always flew a few thousand feet above or below the bombers he escorted over enemy territory. The all-black 332nd Fighter Group protected its bombers better than any other escort squadron in the U.S. Army, but because of segregation, the black and white pilots rarely, if ever, knew each other.

"Because of segregation, we never knew one another, but for fifty years I had wanted to meet just one to say thank you," said Herb Heilbrun, a former bomber pilot.

In 1995, Heilbrun read about a reunion of the Tuskegee Airmen at a hotel in Cincinnati. He walked into a reception and asked to meet a pilot. "If there is a flier here, I'd like to give him a hug for saving my behind." He was introduced to John Leahr. Heilbrun embraced Leahr and said, "I've waited fifty years to meet one of you guys. You saved my tail on many a day."

The two men assumed they had never crossed paths before, but after trading stories they discovered they had flown together on at least two bombing raids, first on a December 16, 1944, mission over Czechoslovakia to strike a major oil refinery; and then, on the following day, Leahr and his squadron escorted Heilbrun and a squad of B-17s to bomb an oil refinery in Germany.

Lt. John Leahr

Capt. Herbert Heilbrun

In fact, they had more in common. Both grew up in Cincinnati. They had even attended the same elementary school. "John couldn't remember me and I didn't remember him, even though I remembered there were only two colored children—that's what we called black children then. I could remember the little girl because she had the same first name as my mother, Mary Louise. But I could not remember John." Leahr had no recollection of Heilbrun.

Heilbrun went home and opened an old photo album. In it was a 1928 photo of his second-grade class.

"I sent a copy of our class photo to John, and I said, "If that black guy in the picture is you, well, that kid behind you is me!" In the photograph of forty children, the two eight-year-olds stand very close to one another. "I am almost touching him," said Heilbrun.

"I'm not in some nameless grave in Germany or at the bottom of the Adriatic Sea because of John and the Tuskegee Airmen."

MOROTAI

On Morotai, the job of the 93rd Infantry was to mop up the 600 Japanese soldiers who remained on the island and to capture their commander, Col. Muisu Ouchi. The Japanese colonel was considered dangerous and a top priority of the 93rd's mission. The cagey colonel was attempt-

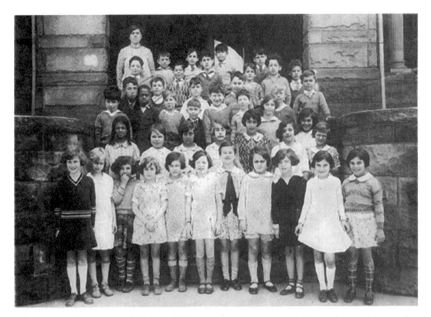

Classmates John Leahr and Herbert Heilbrun stand next to each other in their 1928 second-grade class photo.

ing to make contact with the nearby island of Halmahera, where there were 40,000 Japanese soldiers.

After Ouchi eluded the division's patrols for several weeks, the 93rd's motto became "Cherchez Ouchi." On July 30, a twelve-man patrol from the 25th Infantry stalked Ouchi to his headquarters on the Tijoe River, where they found Japanese soldiers resting in the hot afternoon sun. After more than an hour of maneuvering to get into the best positions around the camp, one American soldier shouted in Japanese: "Surrender and we won't hurt you."

The enemy soldiers ran and the Americans opened fire. According to an American war correspondent, one black soldier grabbed a Japanese officer who lay wounded on the ground.

"Where's Colonel Ouchi?" he asked hurriedly.

"I am Colonel Ouchi," replied the muddy-faced Japanese soldier.

"Well, Colonel, I got orders to bring you in alive," the soldier answered.

The quick fight netted the then-highest-ranking Japanese officer captured in the war by American soldiers. The encounter left nine enemy dead and without any injuries to the American soldiers.

BLACK TROOPS RECEIVE FIRST FORMAL SURRENDER OF JAPANESE

On the afternoon of August 22, several "duck (Dukw) loads" of black soldiers landed at Aka Island, twenty miles west of Okinawa, to accept the first formal surrender of a Japanese possession. Standing behind their white commanding officer, Col. Julian Hearne, Jr., the 24th Infantry oversaw the surrender by Japanese major Yoshihiko Noda. Two infantrymen planted the American flag on Aka, while the rest of the 24th Infantry rounded up the Japanese soldiers into a prison camp.

Nicholas Kramer, a twenty-one-year-old Dutchman, recorded one of the most important dates in his life: "13 Apr. 1945—Bevrijding Franse Troepen [liberation by French troops]." Walking on a road from Gaggenau, Germany, where he had been conscripted as a forced laborer at a Daimler-Benz factory that manufactured truck parts, he saw an approaching tank "with a big, black soldier [French Moroccan] sitting in the turret.
"That's when I knew I was free," said Kramer.

. . . The white fellows treated us like brothers. We did everything together. Went out hunting for German frauleins together. There were a southern colored boy from South Carolina and a southern white boy from Georgia. The two of them used to go out to see two sisters. We all managed to fraternize despite warnings to the contrary.

Then I ran across some loot when we met the Russian soldiers. We went to a town almost demolished. There was a building almost a palace and I saw whole lot of loot. Got a . . . couple of Leica cameras. Also picked up an ermine fur coat. It was about $2,000 worth of merchandise and I sent this stuff home in a big package. The next morning when I'm in a fox-hole, a jeep comes my way and the driver asks me my name which I tell him. He *drops the big package in my fox-hole with the statement, "That's loot, you can't send it home!" So here I am in a fox-hole with this package. Then we got orders to move on, to take a town and while the others were running with their guns, here I was struggling with this package. I finally got a friend of mine to help me with it. I tried to give away the stuff but nobody wanted it. I kept the fur coat. I even lined my fox-hole with it. (Luxury, huh?) After marching about 10 mi. with my ermine, it was so hot and heavy I finally had to trade it in for a couple of dozens of eggs. (not a bad trade-in). By this time the War was over with Germany and I wanted to come home.*

Cpl. S. E. Martin

Soldiers in Burma stop to read President Truman's Proclamation of Victory in Europe, May 9, 1945.

A GI and a WAC get married in Rouen, France, August 19, 1945. Chaplain William T. Green reads the benediction at the marriage ceremony of Pfc. Florence A. Collins, a WAC of the 6,888th Postal Directory Battalion, to Cpl. William A. Johnson of the 1,696th Labor Supervision Co.

AN AMERICAN GI AND A GERMAN WOMAN

Sgt. Edward Saunders of Pennsylvania was forced to resign from the U.S. Army in order to marry his fiancée, a twenty-three-year-old German woman. The two met as a result of Saunders's decision not to make a trip with his buddies to see Berlin. For some reason, he said, he wanted to see Munich instead. "He was handsome and intelligent," said Maria Saunders. "All of my family and friends liked Edward very much."

"It was the Americans who had the problem," said Saunders. "The army was dead set against it." To marry Maria, he was forced to resign from the military. "I was not allowed to marry her while in uniform."

"Here I was fighting the Germans, being readily accepted by her family, with no reservations," said Saunders, a former member of the 442nd Quartermaster Truck Battalion. "Our marriage did not phase the people who were supposed to be our enemy, but back home, it made a difference."

In September 1945, they were married and returned together to the United States. In April 2003, Maria died after a long bout with cancer. They were married fifty-seven years.

VICTORY

[1945]

WAR'S END

Three months after the defeat of the Germans, black troops from the European and Mediterranean theaters of operation began arriving in the Philippines. When the Pacific war started, in 1941, the United States had only a few hundred airplanes in the Pacific region. By 1945, nearly 20,000 war and transport planes were in the Pacific, including the B-29 Superfortress, considered the ultimate air weapon of the war. Black soldiers built many of the runways for the Superfortresses.

In the Iwo Jima landings in February 1945, the all-black 442nd and 592 Port companies and the 471st, 473rd, and 476th Amphibious Truck (aka DUKW or *duck*) companies were attached to the Marine assault. Three DUKWs ferried ammunition and equipment from supply ships in transport areas offshore to the beach. They also evacuated casualties from the beaches. They constructed and repaired airfields even before the fighting ended as the island bases nearest Japan were the final stepping-stones to the heart of Japan.

Assignments for black soldiers on the islands ran the gamut of combat and labor, including maintaining Japanese POW and civilian refugee camps. At a Saipan airfield in July 1945, one white B-29 crewmen had a surprising but life-saving encounter with black soldiers. Sgt. Roger Erickson's plane, bound for a Japanese target, experienced serious trouble on take-off and was sliding fast toward the ocean:

> We skidded in the rain and mud, which came from new drainage ditches which were being installed, but not completed . . . We as a crew did not know that the command had designated African-American troops to line the sides of the runways, just in case of any accidents. Before I knew what was happening a very large black man reached in through the cockpit window and jerked me from the plane.

From Iwo Jima, Guam, Okinawa, Saipan, and Tinian, B-29s struck relentlessly at the Japanese mainland. Black ordnance and depot workers handled most of the bombs that went into the enormous stockpiles on each island. Many also loaded the bombs aboard the planes, including a new weapon, napalm.

India, June 10, 1945
From: Lucia Straham
To: Dear Mother

. . . Your daughter almost has no place to lay her nappy head . . . the place is filthy. I guess the ants will really eat me up. My tent will be nice when it is finished—but I can't think of going over there with no lights—no water—no food.

Listen, it is ok to send a fruit cake with nuts, and to send a can of salted nuts. They do not spoil.

For a small box of odds and ends, please send the following: sponge powder puff Good talcum (Shocking or Chanel)

Cream O-do-ro-no—2 or 3 jars

Quest (2 or 3 cans)

Modess (I don't like the Kotex we get here)

Socks—size 10½ and kinda high

June 24

We're still roughing it somewhat in our tents. Mine leaked last night. I have no rugs down yet and I'm anxious to get them because the floor is concrete & snakes do very well on a smooth surface.

India, August 30, 1945
From: Lucia Straham
To: Dear Mother

. . . Well, did I tell you I looked out my back door the other morning and there was a huge elephant staring me in the face. . . . Then night before last, someone tried to come into our area. He peeped into the M.P. tent & when they called, he ran. They tried to shoot him, but missed. I have sent another box home—the one containing housecoat; a ring; bracelet (from China); a silk scarf from China; 2 cigarette cases & a package for Lois Hunt from Rodney. The other is a box containing my brown and the black and pink dress, before it molds away. Have shoes gone over & dress cleaned. Well, this is about all I can think of—except for Christmas concentrate on—cotton pants, brassieres (size 36 B), talcum; Quest; Montail lipstick; colognes; Chanel, Shocking, Matchabelli—Foods. . . .

For a small box of odds + ends, please send the following: Sponge powder puffs Box talcum (Shocking) Cream O-do-ro-no-2or3 jars (Chanel) Quest (2 or 3 cans) Modess (I don't like the Kotex we get here) Socks - any 10½ + kinda high

Letter from Lucia Straham in India to her mother in August 1945, requesting items from home.

In 1945, tons of napalm, an incendiary weapon made of jellied gasoline and magnesium, began to whistle down on Tokyo, Kobe, and Nagoya. On March 9, 334 B-29s took off from the Marianas, roared over Tokyo, and rained down napalm containers on the city. One-quarter of all buildings were consumed by fire, and 84,000 people were killed. On August 2, 855 Superfortresses wiped out six Japanese cities in one day. In August 1945, B-29s flew 6,000 sorties over Japan. At the time more than 200,000 black soldiers were scattered throughout the Pacific and Far East, including New Caledonia, Calcutta, India, and China.

On August 6, 1945, "Little Boy" (the first of the two atom bombs used against Japan in the war) exploded about 1,800 feet above the city of Hiroshima. About a dozen black scientists had worked on the Manhattan Project, which developed the world's most destructive weapon. Dr. Lloyd Quarterman of Columbia University and Dr. Moddie Taylor of Howard University both received merit certificates for their work on the project.

In *War Without Mercy: Race and Power in the Pacific War,* historian John

A U.S. Marine gives candy to a child at a refugee camp in Tinian.

Enlisted men aboard the USS Ticonderoga *hear the news of Japan's surrender, August 14, 1945.*

Dower argues that the Pearl Harbor attack provoked a genocidal-like rage among Americans. Adm. William Halsey, Commander of the South Pacific Force, adopted the slogan "Kill Japs, kill Japs, kill more Japs," and public-opinion polls in the United States consistently showed that 10 to 13 percent of all Americans supported the "annihilation" or "extermination" of the Japanese as a people.

> When they announced the war was over, we were shooting off guns and having a good old time—until the white officers saw us shooting and took the guns away from us—from just the black soldiers.
>
> *Sgt. James Yancey, 369th Infantry,*
> *93rd Division*

COMING HOME

With news of Japan's surrender came spontaneous celebrations. At military posts around the world, sirens that once warned of danger wailed the good news across the land, while at sea, thousands of ships whistled joyously for hours. In the United States, Times Square got most of the press coverage, but in cities and small towns "from Harlem to Honolulu," school was out, traffic halted, and factories shut down for a single day of merriment and relief. Across America, police and fire horns sounded, churchbells chimed, and in backyards shotguns were blasted by younger brothers, fathers, and family members whose longing for their returning soldiers was nearing an end.

"We thanked God for every letter, every telephone call that we got from my brothers in those days right after the war," said Marcus Moore, then a fifteen-year-old high school student who awaited the return of six older brothers to their Alabama farm. "I think my father held in his heart throughout the war that each son would come home alive. I know my mother did."

Still, the news "sort of numbed us" said one returning soldier of the all-black 399th Port Battalion, which had been overseas for thirty-eight months. "We are not sure what we are going to do next." His only certainty, he told a reporter, was that "I am going home."

The uncertainty that confronted millions of returning veterans was eased by the GI Bill of Rights, a law that President Roosevelt and the Congress had had the foresight to enact more than a year before the war ended. Signed by FDR on June 22, 1944, the GI Bill provided benefits for veterans that included: education and training; a loan guarantee for a home, farm, or business; job training assistance; and unemployment pay of $20 per week for up to fifty-two weeks.

To be eligible for educational benefits, a veteran had to have served ninety days or more after September 16, 1940, and have an honorable discharge. Veterans were entitled to full-time training for one year plus a period equal to their time in service, up to a maximum of forty-eight months. The Veterans Administration paid the educational institution up to a maximum of $500 a year for tuition, books, fees, and other training costs, plus a subsistence allowance of up to $50 a month. This was increased to $65 a month in 1946 and to $75 a month in 1948. Allowances for veterans with dependents were higher.

The total cost of the World War II education program was $14.5 billion. In the peak year of 1947, veterans comprised 49 percent of college enrollment. Millions of veterans who would have flooded the job market instead opted for education, thus minimizing unemployment during the demobilization period. When they did enter the job market, many were better prepared to contribute to the support of their families and society.

A veteran of the 6,888th Postal Battalion, Pvt. Allie Love Davis used the GI Bill to earn both her B.A. and M.A. degrees in elementary education. Cpl. Virginia Lane Frazier of Minneapolis earned a degree in business; and Pfc. Willie Whiting of Chicago used the GI Bill to attend law school.

Thousands of black veterans took advantage of the benefits immediately after they left the military. But many veterans were unable to access the education benefits. The few black colleges were flooded with applicants, and most other colleges accepted white students only. Job-training programs were segregated in the South and under local white supervision. Black veterans were one-third of the WWII vets in the South but got one-twelfth of the job-training slots. Home buying was skewed against black veterans, too. Many black veterans bought new homes with the help of a Veterans Administration mortgage, but they were limited as to where they could buy homes.

Harry Belafonte served in the navy as a munitions loader, and just missed being sent to Port Chicago. "The Navy came as a place of relief for me. It gave me the chance to learn to read and write and to get off

OCTOBER 23, 1945 Branch Rickey announces the signing of Jackie Robinson as a player for the Montreal Royals, the Brooklyn Dodgers minor-league affiliate. On October 7, 1945, Rickey wrote to sportswriter Arthur Mann: "The greatest untapped reservoir of raw material in the history of the game is the black race! The Negroes will make us winners for years to come."

the streets of Harlem and the kind of degradation that surrounded me as I grew up. But I was also driven by the belief that Hitler had to be defeated. Although we had a lot of villainy here at home, he was certainly the most visible illustration of what would happen if fascism went unchallenged."

At the end of the war, Belafonte felt that black Americans had made good on their end of the bargain. "Our expectations were high."

Victories over discrimination in the military and on the home front during the war heightened black expectations and renewed the commitment of African Americans to dismantle America's system of racial segregation. The NAACP Legal Defense and Educational Fund took the lead, prosecuting cases that challenged racial segregation in education, public accommodations, housing, and employment.

The Congress of Racial Equality (CORE) organized the first "freedom ride" to integrate public transportation facilities in 1947. But perhaps the greatest symbol of black postwar progress took place at Ebbets Field on April 10, 1947, when Jackie Robinson played in his first game for the Brooklyn Dodgers, breaking the major league color barrier.

"It wasn't that Jack Robinson was playing baseball," said former Negro League star Leon Day. "It was that a black person was being treated equal, and simply being given a chance. Jackie Robinson marked D-Day on American soil."

The war's end did not stop the librarian Reddick from keeping up his one-man campaign to hold politicians and military commanders accountable for racism in the armed forces. In 1947 he challenged General Eisenhower to state for the record his opinion on discrimination in the military. Particularly galling to Reddick was America's continuing inability to recognize and celebrate the contributions of black soldiers, most of whom, now nearly two years after the war, were still thankless:

War Department
The Chief of Staff
Washington
12 February 1947
Dear Mr. Reddick,
    Both as Chief of Staff and as an American citizen I oppose any discrimination in the rights and privileges awarded American soldiers

based upon color or race. A soldier's worth to the service and the country can be measured only by his ability and his will to give the best within him. Service of Negroes in the United States Army has not always received the public recognition or realistic appreciation it merited. . . . I look forward to its appearance in print.

Sincerely,
Dwight D. Eisenhower

The end of the war also marked the end of the Fair Employment Practices Commission, which President Roosevelt had established back in 1941 to stop job discrimination in defense hiring. President Truman put up no fight when Congress killed the wartime agency, but he did form a President's Commission on Civil Rights, which investigated strategies to end the nation's legacy of pervasive and perpetual racial segregation. In a politically courageous act, Truman defied a threatened filibuster by segregationists, and on July 26, 1948, he issued an executive order abolishing segregation in the armed forces and ordered full integration of all the services. The segregated era of the American military was finally coming to an end.

EPILOGUE

I was six years old in 1958 when my paternal grandfather died and I saw tears in my father's eyes for the first time in my life. I remember being fascinated at his pain, and a bit shaken to see that, like me, he, too, could find reason to cry. But the next morning the sadness that had overcome him the night before seemed gone. Our family piled into our '57 Chevrolet Biscayne with enough fruit, sandwiches, cold fried chicken, cookies, books, and comic books to last four kids for our two-day, 1,200-mile journey from New York to Alabama.

Driving along the old U.S. Highway 1, my father talked about how he and his fellow soldiers had had to navigate the dusty and dangerous road from Saint-Lô to Paris. The story he told was very different from the version I would later see in television replays of the 1952 movie *Red Ball Express,* starring Jeffrey Hunter (with black soldiers playing only a secondary part in the adventure). In the evening he and my mother talked about where we would stop for the night. I could not fully understand why we were passing by countless well-advertised motels with the VACANCY sign lit up. At about midnight we reached a colored boardinghouse near the Virginia–North Carolina border, unadvertised—except to those black families who could afford the *Negro Traveler's Green Book,* which listed colored "tourist homes" like the four on Holbrook Street in the border town of Danville, Virginia.

The boardinghouse was run by a hospitable old black man who had two small rooms available. My mother and sisters stayed in one room, and my father, brother, and I slept together in another room, all of us in a single bed. Early the next morning, my father woke us and we washed up in the sink. We then rejoined my mother and sisters at the old man's kitchen table for a breakfast of bacon, eggs, toast, milk, and a cup of hot chocolate. Then we continued on to Alabama and my grandfather's funeral.

It was the first time I could remember hearing my father talk about the Red Ball Express and World War II. In the 1950s most all boys, black and white, were proud of their fathers' war experience. So was Emmett Louis Till, who never knew his father; he knew only that Louis Till had died during the war. When Emmett was found dead in a Mississippi river, bloated beyond recognition, in July 1955, it was his late father's initialed signet ring on his swollen finger that identified him. At the trial, prosecutor Robert Smith handed Mamie Bradley the ring. He asked if it was the one she had given to her son when he was a young boy.

"Yes, but his hand was too small to wear it at the time," testified Mrs. Bradley at the trial of the four men charged with killing her son. "However, since he was twelve years old, he has worn the ring on occasions, using Scotch tape or a string to keep it from coming off. When he left Chicago he was looking for some cuff links in his jewelry box and found the ring and put it on his finger to show me that it fit and he didn't have to wear a tape anymore." Like Emmett Till, my earliest idol was my father.

As a kid in the 1950s, our favorite sport was baseball, but our favorite game was war. We called it playing war. Technically, only one side could be American, but it was common for both sides to claim the U.S. flag at the start. Officially, only the winning side—that is, the team with the captured flag, the most prisoners, or the fewest kids crying—could declare itself American (the champions).

Our war games were stocked with weapons. Toy pistols, rifles, and machine guns were plentiful. If we needed heavy artillery, we made it. Logs became cannons, and tricycles, bikes, and wagons were transformed into jeeps, tanks, trucks, or ambulances. Clumps of dirt, with rocks removed, served as grenades and mortar shells. We also had real war artifacts.

We used real helmets, but only if they were battered and not a prized possession of our fathers. The real helmets were reserved for the older kids, who held the "military commander post." Us smaller kids wore our shiny olive-green, but crackable, plastic helmets.

Most of the authentic stuff we kept in a clubhouse museum. We had great respect for these items, especially the battered helmets, a rusty Japanese sword, about one dozen empty shell casings, and a grenade (defused). High-ranking captured enemies were required to wear a German helmet, which my older brother found buried in a cousin's backyard. No one wanted to wear the dread helmet because an actual German soldier had worn it. Worse, he probably died wearing it.

Nor were we strangers to death in war. Three cousins had died in WWII, but the body of only one had been returned to the States. One cousin who served would not attend July Fourth celebrations, or any other fireworks event, because it "brought back the war." A normally jovial and fun-loving man, he would wimper at the sound of a hunting rifle. He jumped even at distant thunder.

One of my favorite uncles lost an eye in the war. Like my father, he was a mechanic during and after the fighting. At six feet two inches tall, he was a strong, proud, no-nonsense sort of man who would tell any man, or even a smart-alecky kid, that he did not take shit from anybody. He meant it, and his glass eye, even when he smiled, made him look a little more fierce than he actually was. He had lost his eye not in combat but in a baseball game between two GI teams—one white, one black.

One day while he and my father were alone in our garage, I was playing nearby and overheard him tell a story about playing in that game while stationed in France. It turned out that a white player was pitching against him and threw the baseball at his head—intentionally—hitting him in the eye. I did not know until researching this book that he had never told the story of how he lost his eye to his children.

In that respect, my uncle was very much like my folks, and many other black parents of the 1950s who lived in the North. He would not pass racial fear on to his children. At a time when vicious racial hatred was featured on the front page of newspapers and on television, they felt the need to create a safe haven of equality for their children, even if it was not entirely real.

Witnessing a new era of lucid nightly images of black American children, women, and men being set upon by attack dogs, knocked down by fire hoses, and beaten by police, perhaps they were trying to spare their own children from a lifelong psychology of defeat. They rejected all negative and problematic predictions about blacks, particularly as it pertained to the aspirations of their own children. Poverty and crime were not permissible options in our future. They knew that we needed to believe we were Americans, too.

Theirs was not a government-as-savior mentality. Neither needing nor seeking public assistance, they worked nine-to-five jobs, plus overtime, plus double shifts. They wanted a good economy for America, advancement for themselves, and progress for all black Americans. They were about as likely to vote Democrat as Republican—Eisenhower grabbed 40 percent of the black vote in 1956.

Like all Americans, they wanted the best for their children, and to achieve it they taught us a hybrid philosophy of Booker T. and DuBois. They asserted, they demanded, and they voted. But they gave their children a strong work ethic and marching orders for life, which, expressed simply, came down to: do "twice as good" as white children so that we could become whatever we hoped to be, and never be denied our full rights as Americans. We were shielded from bold racial hatred. If race did become an obstacle, we would simply do our best to get around it. We would never cry about it.

American racism had instilled in them an essential resilience and patience, but they were not timid in their everyday dealings with white folks. More armchair activists than marchers, they embraced the philosophy and supported the political tactics and legal maneuvering of the NAACP, were cautious in their acceptance of Martin Luther King, Jr., and never gave Malcolm X a chance.

Like many American kids, I watched television nearly every day of my life. I knew then that there were two Americas, but I didn't really care. All of the characters in my favorite shows were white. Lassie and Timmy didn't need colored friends to make me watch. The only colored kids on television were Buckwheat and Stymie, and they were nothing like me. Such a personal embarrassment were they that it never crossed my mind to ask for more colored characters on the *Little Rascals* or any other show. And as much as I wished to be Beaver's pal, he did have a friend whom he called Whitey. I dreaded to think what Beaver and his buddies might have called me.

IN 1960 OUR family moved to a new house in a new town. My father had become the first black member of the New York State chapter of the International Union of Operation Engineers. The union boss thought my father was part Italian, and so he was sent out on jobs. My father didn't tell him otherwise. And he was known popularly among his coworkers as "Alabam"—for his southern accent. He was blue-collar, but as a union mechanic he earned more than most white-collar workers, about $20,000 a year. I can remember the white real estate agent telling my father when each prospective house would "sell to colored." The house I liked best was in a town called Pine Bush. A three-bedroom white wood-frame house on ten acres of land with a brook running along the property.

The owner, a French woman, walked us through the house. In the living room she showed my parents a prized possession. From a small wooden writing desk, which was set up like a shrine in the sparsely decorated room, she very carefully produced a personal letter to her, signed by Adolf Hitler. How it came into her possession neither I nor my mother can remember. Perhaps she had been connected to the Vichy regime that governed France during the German occupation. We do recall that she was very proud of her memento. I was fascinated to see Hitler's signature. Apart from my birth certificate, this was the first real historic document I had ever seen. My father bought the house and property for $16,000. When we moved in, my biggest disappointment was that the letter was gone. I had assumed it would come with the house.

The former owner did leave a complete forty-year collection of *Life* magazines in the attic. During summer vacations I read every one. Most interesting to me were those from WWII. *Life*'s coverage of the war was more extensive than any other American magazine. For four years there were weekly pictures of soldiers and civilians, on the home front and in the battlefield. *Life* photographers covered nearly every aspect of the war, and conveyed images of enormous impact. The photos of naked women inmates at a Nazi concentration camp took my adolescent mind in a direction far away from arousal.

OUR NEW TOWN was a rural community of about 2,000 people, with only one other black family. On my first day of school in the fourth grade, I had a tough start. When I got off the bus that morning, a smiling blond-hair boy called me "nigger." My brother was called names, too, but he was much stronger and tougher than I, and he fought back. Morris beat up bigger and older white kids every day for about a week. Then the name-calling stopped. Because of his fierce reputation as one who would beat the hell out of any kid who dared call us names, I was given a sort of unwritten kid's ticket of acceptance. After that first week, I was pretty much set, racially speaking, for the rest of my grade-school life. One of my best friends was Alan, a small Jewish boy who caught hell almost every day. A few kids, some who acted friendly to me, seemed to delight in making his life miserable. I thought the only difference between Alan and myself was that he didn't have a big brother.

The subject of my race rarely came up during my first year at Pine Bush. Perhaps in a discussion of slavery the subject of "Negroes" was introduced in social studies, but neither my teacher, Mr. Doty, nor anyone in my class ever noted that there was at least one Negro, me, in our class—at least not to me personally. By the end of my fourth-grade year, I was happy with my new friends, all of whom were white.

Our fifth-grade teacher, Mr. Roger Golden, was something of a "character." New to the school, he was young and played folk songs on the guitar and sang for us at least once a week—once "if you are good," twice if we were bad. Mr. Golden was also unashamedly Jewish. Of all our subjects, he valued social studies and current events most highly, and by the end of the week he had pronounced all of us idiots for not knowing or caring enough about current events worldwide. He appointed me "class historian," and I kept a log of all of our special activities throughout the school year.

In November 1961, our class discussed Adolf Eichmann, the Nazi officer who was tried and convicted of supervising the extermination of many Jews. Both Mr. Golden and my friend Alan had lost family members in the Holocaust. I brought to class a 1945 *Life* magazine, an issue featuring a Nazi concentration camp. We saw pictures of soap and lampshades made from human flesh. We each wrote an essay about the horrible treatment of humans by Hitler's government. I thought it made a powerful impact on all of us. But a boy sitting near me drew a picture that he said was Alan in an oven. He laughed and told me to pass it on. I gave it back to him, without comment.

The Cold War was the biggest issue of our era. I had more bad dreams about the atomic bomb than I ever had about civil rights. On February 20, 1962, we took a class trip to Mr. Golden's home to watch the Cape Canaveral launch of astronaut John Glenn on his small black-and-white television set. Settling in as *almost* a regular white kid did have its psychological costs, and I didn't need a shrink to tell me.

I think Mr. Golden noticed it first. When the subject of the Civil War and slavery came up, I offered no personal testimony about the plight or contributions of the slaves. In fact, I can remember arguing that the Negro slaves (presumably my own ancestors) should not have been freed immediately from slavery. I said that the Emancipation Proclamation should have been delayed a decade or so, so that blacks could have gotten a firmer economic foothold in society. I can also remember classroom discussions about slavery when I felt like crawling under the table. Who wanted to be related to slaves? My father told me a lot about the pride he had in his ancestors, but he couldn't tell me enough about slaves to make me proud enough to tell my classmates about my own great-grandfather.

Perhaps seeing a need to boost my racial pride, my father constantly made me read books about black historical figures like Frederick Douglass, Harriet Tubman, and Ralph Bunche. Mostly the information I could find about notable black Americans were entries in encyclopedias because there were no books on black heroes in my school library. As if he were getting nervous about my sense of self, he would tell me his story about cutting George Washington Carver's hair for the umpteenth time.

By the sixth grade, something quite apart from any obvious racial or family issue occurred, changing my academic life dramatically. One Sunday evening just before the end of the school year, after studying for a few hours for a final science exam, I became upset by the possibility that my straight-A average might suffer from a B if I didn't do well. So distraught was I that for the next hour or so I seriously considered and planned my suicide. Thankfully, the thought of killing myself never progressed to an actual attempt.

I went to talk to my mother. She was in the living room reading a book, and I quietly explained to her that I might get a B in science. Her response absolutely stunned me. She smiled and said that a B would be okay—as long as I had tried my best. From that peculiar day in my childhood, my intense academic-achievement impulse disconnected in a way that I am certain saved my life.

I did well scholastically, though not super-well. I was a good athlete, though not great, and I was a popular guy. My classmates elected me president every year from the seventh through the eleventh grade. My senior year I ran for student body president and won. No, I was not twice as good as any one of them, but I was clearly not intimidated by race. In fact, in sports, I could feel the increasing intimidation of my white teammates anytime we played a school with black players.

"These are colored boys we're playing," our Pine Bush football coach would tell us. To my coach, the boys on opposing teams from predominantly Irish or Italian communities had enviable attributes, which he termed "aggressive and hard-nosed," but "these colored boys" from city schools like Newburgh or Kingston "could be dangerous." I was a fairly solid fullback and linebacker (MVP in my senior year), but even I was beginning to fear colored boys!

MY ACADEMIC AND social life in my six years of junior high and high school could have reflected the life and aspirations of any normal American student, black or white. My main academic goal was to be able to read as fast as President Kennedy, but I never did. I did make it to 1,000 words per minute—not as fast as the president's 1,200 wpm, but quick enough to help me to do research or preread a book before buying it.

I thought of myself as being just like my classmates. Psychologically, my classmates were *my people. Other people* were battered and hosed on the television news; and they really were not a part of my world. For me in my protected world in rural upstate New York, the images of burning cities, looting, and riots in Detroit, Watts, and Harlem were far far away from my reality.

To keep my own sense of compatibility with my classmates, I likely distanced myself from any events with a racial theme. Maybe it was to preserve my own dignity or simply to keep my friends. Like most Americans, I remember where I was when President Kennedy got shot. The night Dr. King was shot I went to a high school dance with my friends.

THE ROAD TO BAGHDAD

By the time of my transition from high school to college, in 1969, patriotism was definitely not cool. Nor was being an American. My brother enlisted in the air force and served (and survived) in Vietnam. But I let my prospects of military service ride entirely on luck—the draft lottery. My birth date (the basis for the lottery) drew a very high number, 360, so I never had to make the choice—to fight for my country or let someone else do the fighting.

In 1969, I graduated from high school and made plans to attend Northeastern University in Boston, as a liberal arts major, in the fall. That summer I worked as a construction laborer at nearby West Point Military Academy. My contact with the army was watching the cadets march on my lunch hour. My friends and I looked forward to attending a big music concert that was being planned just a few miles from our town, the Woodstock Music and Arts Festival. The event was like nothing we or America had ever seen before, 400,000 young people of all races, backgrounds, religions, and musical interests—there was something for everyone at Woodstock—and everyone appeared seriously to desire peace and equality. For one three-day weekend it seemed that the earth had changed its course, that a new generation had arrived.

In Boston that fall, I demonstrated against the war, and I wrote often to my brother, an air force staff sergeant stationed at Da Nang. Hearing from him that one day he had walked out of his barracks only seconds before a North Vietnamese rocket hit it, killing six airmen, squelched any lingering interest I had in fighting for my country.

My Woodstock generation became quickly known for its pacifism, but beneath its hippie façade was the foundation of the yuppie generation. By Woodstock's first anniversary, the kids who had found pleasure in old clothes and making their own music were discovered by Madison Avenue, and we were being sold brand-name blue jeans and stereo component sets. Many of my friends were social liberals—but becoming curiously conservative in their career plans. It was almost epidemic, only months removed from the peace and socialism of Woodstock, they were making plans, certainly more developed than my own plans to graduate and make a lot of money. One generation removed from World War II, we had come to revere both peace and profit.

Even counter-cultural students like my best friend, Steve, who was one of Boston's biggest marijuana-dealers, wanted to get rich. Rock bands were constantly at our Mission Hill apartment to purchase marijuana. A delivery of 150 kilos, each wrapped in brown paper, stacked against our living room wall, attracted nearly every reggae, R&B, and rock-and-roll band that played in Boston—including some very hip but nervous white guys from a local group called Aerosmith. The possibility of the Boston police showing up at our door was more frightening to me than the Vietcong. My closest brush with war came in the Middle East. And it was there that I met the one person, a nonblack and non-American, who triggered most my zealous interest in my family, as well as in American and world history.

In 1973 I took a year off from my studies at Northeastern University in Boston to see the world. My intent was to spend a year in Spain, but once in Europe, I wanted to go everywhere, especially to Egypt. From Spain, I went by boat, bus, and car (hitchhiked) through Morocco, Algeria, and Tunisia. Unable to enter Libya because its anti-American leader Khadafy would not admit anyone with a U.S. passport, I detoured to Italy, Greece, and Turkey.

After seven countries my money dried up. I needed to find a job to sustain my travels, and so I took the advice of a seasoned fellow trekker from Lebanon, who recommended that I go south to Israel, where I could find work on a kibbutz. But he warned me: do not tell border officials in Syria or Jordan of my plans to go to Israel.

His name was Mohammad Ali—not the boxer (his was a very popular name in the region)—and he gave me my first lesson in Middle East politics. I was to tell customs officers at each Arab nation in my path to Israel that my destination was Baghdad. Otherwise, he predicted, I would be denied entry or delayed for so long that I would never get to Israel over land. At the Turkish-Syrian border I followed his advice. I told Syrian border officials, I am on my way to Iraq.

My personal fortune reduced to two ten-dollar American Express travelers' checks, I traded my last pack of American cigarettes for a late-night bus ride to Aleppo.

When I arrived, it was after midnight, and I waited outside a closed coffee shop for the next bus to Damascus. From dusk to late morning I watched a convoy of tanks, antiaircraft vehicles, missile launchers, and more than 2,000 or 3,000 Syrian soldiers march by. They hoisted their rifles to a cadence of "One, two, three, Arabi" (in Arabic, of course).

An English-speaking Syrian man seated next to me laughed and told me that some of the soldiers were chanting a bouncing cadence of "Kill-one-Jew, Arabi!" (it rhymed in Arabic). The man told me that war would come soon, that the Arab nations should shut off oil to the United States for its friendship with Israel, and Israel itself must be eliminated "from the face of the earth." Because, he said, there is no God in Israel. His hatred for Jews was unlike any expression of hate I had ever heard before—though it did remind me of the vicious statements made by white supremacists in the 1950s. Before departing on another bus, he bid that God be with me in my travels.

From Damascus, I bargained an incredibly cheap ride to Amman, Jordan. Sharing a taxi with three other passengers, I paid $3 for the 150-mile ride through the desert. With now only $17 in my pocket, I was pleased to have made such a good deal for myself. But I was surprised when we passed through a small town and a rock hit my side of the car. A fellow passenger told me to expect more rocks because we were riding in a Palestinian-owned cab. Angry Syrians pelted our car with stones in nearly every town we passed.

At the Syrian-Jordan border, with my driver and traveling partners all within earshot, I claimed Baghdad as my final destination. But once in Amman, I finally had to fess up about my next stop: Israel.

My entry to Jordan required me to report to a local police station after twenty-four hours. But with so little money, I didn't waste any time. I went directly from the taxi depot to the station. At the station the policemen and soldiers were very friendly. One or two asked if I could help them emigrate to the United States. I was very nervous when it came time to make my travel intentions clear. In the company of the other men, I just about whispered my request to the senior officer. I wanted a visa to enter Israel.

The friendliness I had felt from the soldiers evaporated instantly. I was ordered into a room in which about one dozen men armed with rifles and machine guns trained their weapons on me as I was interrogated for four hours about why I wanted to go to Israel.

Only for a few days, I said, just long enough to get a plane ticket back to the United States I avoided being jailed as a vagabond only because of the hospitality of a Jordanian family. After my interrogation I wandered through the streets of Amman and stopped at a closed church, where a young minister and his family gave me room and board. After a week I was given approval to go to Israel. I paid for a ticket and I traveled with a busload of Palestinian migrant workers across the Jordan River, via the Allenby Bridge, into Israel. About twenty yards south of the narrow wooden bridge, a Soviet-made jet fighter lay crashed, nose down, in the riverbank, a remnant of the 1967 Six-Day War.

An Israeli official boarded the bus, and upon learning I was an American, apologized for the inconvenience of traveling with the migrant workers and directed me off the bus, to join a line of white American Christian pilgrims at a more pleasant border checkpoint. In the company of the pilgrims I was asked to declare how much money I was bringing into the country. I told him ten dollars—which brought gasps and laughter from the surrounding pilgrims. The officer said I would not be allowed to enter Israel with so little money, and he brusquely directed me to wait for the return bus to Amman.

When he walked away from me, I recalled a sometimes valuable lesson of bigotry—that we "all look alike"—and I took off my eyeglasses, walked around the corner, and joined the long Palestinian waiting line to enter Israel. No problem. I went from the border to a kibbutz placement office in Tel Aviv, where I found work as a volunteer at Kibbutz Ein Hamifratz in northern Israel.

Upon my arrival at Ein Hamifratz, the kibbutz manager greeted me cheerfully. She examined my passport, scrutinized its pages, then abruptly apologized to me for having traveled so far on misinformation from the placement office. No positions available, she said coldly, but I could stay for a day or two before leaving.

She then asked, "Is your mother Arab?" The question actually did not surprise me. I had been asked if I was Arab many other times on my journey. I knew fairly well the feeling of being mistaken for someone other than good-old American Negro. No, I said. I am just black. I did not even specify American. Just black.

She confided to me a few months later that she had reported me to Israeli authorities. Not because I was a black American, she said. She had reported me because she could see from my passport that I had visited five Arab nations, including two of Israel's worst enemies in the past four weeks. With terrorism a constant problem in Israel even in 1973, concern about suspicious persons was simply routine. Within a few weeks I was pretty well accepted into the kibbutz community.

Many members of the kibbutz were Holocaust survivors—in fact, most of the people there were over thirty years old. Everyone had lost family members, including my closest friend on the kibbutz, Rachel. Most were from Germany, though they no longer spoke German, because it reminded them of the horrific era. Even speaking German in their presence was considered poor taste.

One woman, Hannah, whom I noticed almost every day, was the first person I had ever seen with a series of tattooed numbers on her forearm. I was stunned to see those marks of the Holocaust, and from that moment I felt the need to talk to her. But either I was too shy, or

Bill and Kay Moore at home in Warrenton, N.C. in 1999.

simply afraid that I would say something totally stupid, and I could not bring myself to approach her during most of my stay on the kibbutz. I was friends with many of the men and women on the kibbutz, but I had only one conversation with Hannah.

It was near the end of my six-month visit, only a few days before the Yom Kippur War began (October 1973). I had just returned from a week's vacation away from the kibbutz and had visited lots of sites in Israel, including Yad Vashem, the Holocaust museum in Jerusalem. Hannah sat next to me at dinner in the large kibbutz dining room. She said nothing for several minutes, then, in fair English, she asked me where I was from.

I told her: America.

My answer didn't seem sufficient to her. She asked me again. I told her the name of my state. New York. She shook her head, then she added a few more words. "Your family, your family—your people," she said insistently.

She motioned with her hand, in a rowing motion, insisting that I think my answer again, as deeply and thoroughly as I could. Otherwise she would never be able to understand me, nor I her. Like my mother and father, who had tried to instill a sense of history and pride in me, Hannah had sent me on the longest research project of my life, to discover my American family.

In the circuitous nature of my life—and of everyone's life—Hannah is truly a member of my family. Since I met her, more than thirty years ago, I have felt a kinship and presence in my mind that I can express only as ancestral or angelic, like a human Sankofa, the African symbol that tells us to look to the past to understand the future. Hannah, like my mother and father, knew that freedom is precious—and long-lasting—only if we are willing to defend it.

FIGHTING FOR AMERICA

Like most Americans, September 11 affected me profoundly and gave me a real connection to World War II. That morning I watched from a few blocks away as the second plane, United Airlines Flight 175, crashed into the World Trade Center. Thousands of people in the street and millions watched on television as the billowing red fireball rose up the south tower, and we knew from that instant that the nation was under attack. The assault was so awful and so sudden that even my six-year-old son wanted to get his licks in on the enemy. The next day he asked for an American flag.

A world war of a new and vastly different sort was already under way by that horrific Tuesday morning. Not coherent nor influential enough in its philosophy to create a nation or army, international terrorism, with its arsenal of fear, shock, chaos, and destruction, has affected every nation of the world with its perverse superpower. Not since World War II have we Americans seen our lives so altered for reasons of defense and day-to-day safety. Yet a monumental lesson was in the works for this generation in the events of that one day, perhaps to go along with the rarely considered lessons from the dozen or so generations that preceded 9/11.

At the time when I was traveling in the Middle East, Prime Minister Golda Meir made a profound remark about the constant tension between Israel and its neighbors. She believed she knew the reason for the hatred between the Arabs and the Israelis. She said that when the Arabs loved their children more than they hated the Jews, there would be peace. As a parent I know that only the most unthinkable circumstances could make me hate anyone more than I could love my own children, and certainly an Arab might make the same statement about an Israeli and his love for his children. Anyone living anywhere on our planet might say the same thing, whether their family has lived in America for 40 days or 400 years; or in Europe, Asia, or Africa for the last 4,000.

How America chooses to fight this world war will leave a lasting legacy upon us and the rest of the world. No American plan for fighting a war will ever be more eloquent or more simple than the goal outlined by President Roosevelt with his "Four Freedoms," which included: freedom of speech and expression—everywhere in the world; freedom of worship—everywhere in the world; freedom from want—everywhere in the world; and freedom from fear—everywhere in the world. Emphatic about the need for freedom everywhere, FDR may well have advised, sixty years later, that when America, and every nation of the world, lives up to its great promise, the wicked and cowardly terrorists of the world will disintegrate.

I believe that a poem written by American poet Langston Hughes is the leit motif of the twenty-first century's world war against terrorism. "A Dream Deferred" supposes that everyone has a dream. Girls and boys, men and women, in America and throughout the world—everyone has a dream:

> What happens to a dream deferred?
> Does it dry up
> like a raisin in the sun?
> Or fester like a sore—
> and then run? . . .
> Maybe it just sags
> like a heavy load.
> Or does it explode?

On January 18, 2000, my father joined the WWII veterans who passed from this life. Most of them have died without their children or grandchildren knowing even one story about their heroism, their bravery. They have died without ever being called heroic, but history shows that they were heroes. They have kept our dreams alive.

PASSING THE FLAG ON

I did give Terence our nation's flag, and some patriotic advice that I hope he will both follow and perfect upon:

Give allegiance to your country, not because any generation of Americans was greater than yours, but because you want your generation to be the greatest of all. Carry the flag, because freedom, democracy, and fairness are together the essence of America. Raise up the flag—for it is the symbol of the world's best chance for peace and hope.

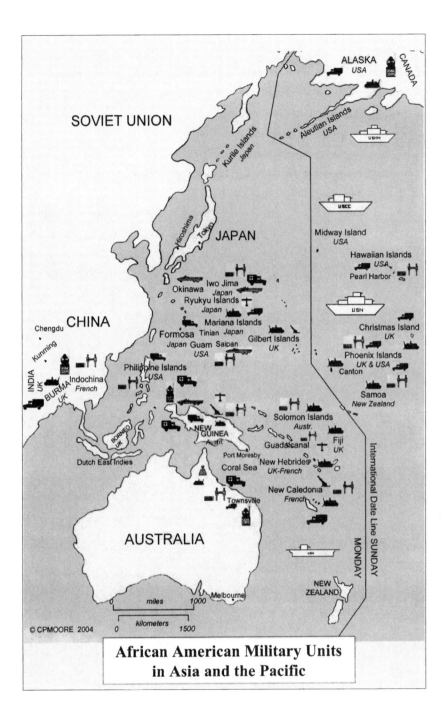

**African American Military Units
in Asia and the Pacific**

© CPMOORE 2004

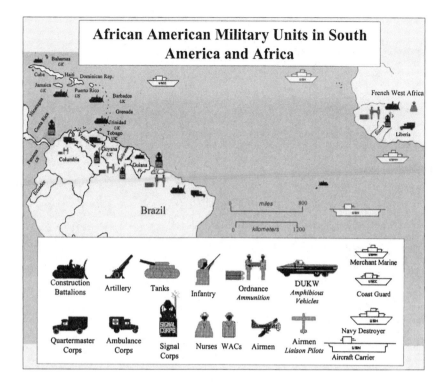

African American Military Units in South America and Africa

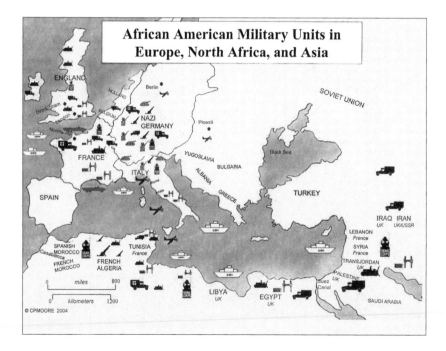

African American Military Units in Europe, North Africa, and Asia

© CPMOORE 2004

Appendix

AFRICAN-AMERICAN ARMY/AIR CORPS UNITS STATIONED IN EUROPE, AFRICA & ASIA

AMPHIBIAN

463 Amph Truck Co
467 Amph Truck Co
819 Amph Truck Co
821 Amph Truck Co
822 Amph Truck Co
469 Amph Truck Co

BAND

92 Infantry Div, Band
428 Army Service Force Band

CHEMICAL

32 Chem Decon Co
81 Chem Co
82 Chem Co
84 Chem Co
85 Chem Co
86 Chem Co
87 Chem Co
165 Chem Co
171 Chem Co
755 Chem Depot Co
759 Chem Depot Co
761 Chem Depot Co
762 Chem Depot Co

ENGINEER

95 Engineer Gen Services Rgt
95 Eng GS Rgt, Med Det
320 Eng Combat Bn
354 Eng GS Rgt
354 Eng GS Rgt Band
354 Eng GS Rgt, Med Det
356 Eng GS Rgt
356 Eng GS Rgt, Med Det
364 Eng GS Rgt
364 Eng GS Rgt, Med Det
365 Eng GS Rgt
365 Eng GS Rgt, Med Det
366 Eng GS Rgt
366 Eng GS Rgt, Med Det
374 Eng GS Rgt
374 Eng GS Rgt, Med Det
375 Eng GS Rgt
375 Eng GS Rgt, Med Det
377 Eng GS Rgt
377 Eng GS Rgt, Med Det
383 Eng GS Bn
383 Eng GS Bn, Med Det
388 Eng GS Rgt
389 Eng GS Rgt
389 Eng GS Rgt, Med Det

390 Eng GS Rgt
390 Eng GS Rgt, Med Det
392 Eng GS Rgt
392 Eng GS Rgt, Med Det
403 Eng Water Supply Bn
412 Eng Dump Truck Co
413 Eng Dump Truck Co
415 Eng Dump Truck Co
416 Eng Dump Truck Co
417 Eng Dump Truck Co
433 Eng Dump Truck Co
434 Eng Dump Truck Co
438 Eng Dump Truck Co
549 Eng Co (Light Pontoon)
569 Eng Dump Truck Co
577 Eng Dump Truck Co
580 Eng Dump Truck Co
581 Eng Dump Truck Co
582 Eng Dump Truck Co
764 Eng Dump Truck Co
827 Eng Aviation Bn (EAB)
827 EAB, Med Det
829 EAB
829 EAB, Med Det
847 EAB
847 EAB, Med Det

859 EAB
859 EAB, Med Det
923 Eng Aviation Rgt
923 Eng Aviation Rgt, Med Det
1130 Eng Combat Group
1221 Eng Fire Fight Det
1222 Eng Fire Fight Det
1223 Eng Fire Fight Det
1226 Eng Fire Fight Det
1227 Eng Fire Fight Det
1228 Eng Fire Fight Det
1229 Eng Fire Fight Det
1230 Eng Fire Fight Det
1231 Eng Fire Fight Det
1232 Eng Fire Fight Det
1233 Eng Fire Fight Det
1234 Eng Fire Fight Det
1235 Eng Fire Fight Det
1236 Eng Fire Fight Det
1237 Eng Fire Fight Det
1238 Eng Fire Fight Det
1239 Eng Fire Fight Det
1240 Eng Fire Fight Det
1310 Eng GS Rgt
1310 Eng GS Rgt, Med Det
1313 Eng GS Rgt
1313 Eng GS Rgt, Med Det
1314 Eng GS Rgt
1314 Eng GS Rgt, Med Det
1317 Eng GS Rgt
1318 Eng GS Rgt
1323 Eng GS Rgt
1325 Eng GS Rgt
1328 Eng Construction Bn
1329 Eng GS Rgt
1332 Eng GS Rgt
1349 Eng GS Rgt
1371 Eng Dump Truck Co
1372 Eng Dump Truck Co
1373 Eng Dump Truck Co
1451 Eng Dump Truck Co
1510 Eng Water Supply Co
1511 Eng Water Supply Co
1512 Eng Water Supply Co
1645 Eng Utilities Co
1695 Eng Combat Bn
1696 Eng Combat Bn
1697 Eng Combat Bn
1698 Eng Combat Bn

1699 Eng Combat Bn
1700 Eng Combat Bn
2141 Eng Fire Fight Det
2142 Eng Fire Fight Det

ORDNANCE

57 Ordn Ammo Co
64 Ordn Ammo Bn
64 Ordn Ammo Bn, Med Det
65 Ordn Ammo Bn
65 Ordn Ammo Bn, Med Det
70 Ordn, Ammo Bn
70 Ordn Bn, Ammo Med Det
100 Ordn Ammo Bn
100 Ordn Ammo Bn, Med Det
101 Ordn Ammo Bn
101 Ordn Ammo Bn, Med Det
169 Ordn Depot Co
489 Ordn Evacuation Co
538 Ordn Hvy Maint Co
569 Ordn Ammo Co
570 Ordn Ammo Co
571 Ordn Ammo Co
572 Ordn Ammo Co
573 Ordn Ammo Co
574 Ordn Ammo Co
581 Ordn Ammo Co
582 Ordn Ammo Co
583 Ordn Ammo Co
584 Ordn Ammo Co
586 Ordn Ammo Co
587 Ordn Ammo Co
588 Ordn Ammo Co
589 Ordn Ammo Co
592 Ordn Ammo Co
593 Ordn Ammo Co
596 Ordn Ammo Co
597 Ordn Ammo Co
598 Ordn Ammo Co
599 Ordn Ammo Co
600 Ordn Ammo Co
606 Ordn Ammo Co
607 Ordn Ammo Co
619 Ordn Ammo Co
624 Ordn Ammo Co
626 Ordn Ammo Co

637 Ordn Ammo Co
638 Ordn Ammo Co
639 Ordn Ammo Co
641 Ordn Ammo Co
646 Ordn Ammo Co
646 Ordn Ammo Co
647 Ordn Ammo Co
648 Ordn Ammo Co
651 Ordn Ammo Co
654 Ordn Ammo Co
655 Ordn Ammo Co
657 Ordn Ammo Co
668 Ordn Ammo Co
672 Ordn Ammo Co
675 Ordn Ammo Co
676 Ordn Ammo Co
679 Ordn Ammo Co
694 Ordn Ammo Co
695 Ordn Ammo Co
855 Ordn Hvy Auto Mnt Co
1459 Ordn MM Co
1708 Ordn MM Co
1717 Ordn MM Co
1720 Ordn MM Co
1727 Ordn MM Co
1736 Ordn MM Co
1839 Ordn MM Co
1840 Ordn MM Co
1912 Ordn Ammo Co
1912 Ordn Ammo Co
1929 Ordn Ammo Co
1930 Ordn Ammo Co
1954 Ordn Depot Co
1961 Ordn Depot Co
1962 Ordn Depot Co
3001 Ordn Base Depot Co
3002 Ordn Base Depot Co
3005 Ordn Base Depot Co
3008 Ordn Base Depot Co
3076 Ordn MVD Co
3077 Ordn MV Assem Co
3078 Ordn MV Assem Co
3254 Ordn Base Depot Co
3257 Ordn Base Depot Co
3258 Ordn Base Depot Co
3259 Ordn Base Depot Co
3260 Ordn Base Depot Co
3261 Ordn Base Depot Co
3262 Ordn Base Depot Co
3264 Ordn Base Depot Co
3265 Ordn Base Depot Co
3289 Ordn Base Depot Co

3418 Ordn Auto Mnt Co
3550 Ordn Auto Mnt Co

HOSPITAL

25 Station Hospital
317 Medical Bn
428 Medical Bn
429 Medical Bn
558 Ambulance Co
567 Ambulance Co
587 Ambulance Co
588 Ambulance Co
589 Ambulance Co
590 Ambulance Co
591 Ambulance Co
592 Ambulance Co
701 Med Sanit Co
703 Med Sanit Co
705 Medical Sanit Co
724 Med Sanit Co
736 Med Sanit Co
740 Med Sanit Co
749 Med Sanit Co
754 Med Sanit Co

INFANTRY & ARTILLERY

92 Infantry Div
317 Engineer Combat Bn
320 Barr Balloon Bn
320 Barr Balloon Bn,
    Medical Det
333 Field Art Bn
333 Field Art Bn, Medical
    Det
350 Field Art Bn
351 Field Art Bn
365 Infantry Rgt
370 Infantry Rgt
371 Infantry Rgt
452 Anti-air Art
452 Anti-air Art, Medical
    Det
578 Field Art Bn
597 Field Art Bn
598 Field Art Bn
599 Field Art Bn
600 Field Art Bn
614 Tank Destroyer Bn
758 Tank Bn
761 Tank Bn
777 Field Art Bn

827 Tank Destroyer Bn
969 Field Art Bn
999 Field Art Bn

AIR FIGHTER

99 Fighter Sq
99 Fighter Sq, Maint
322 Fighter Group
322 Fighter Group, Maint

PORT

95 Port Co
214 Port Co
215 Port Co
216 Port Co
216 Port Co
217 Port Co
222 Port Co
223 Port Co
224 Port Co
225 Port Co
226 Port Co
226 Port Co
227 Port Co
228 Port Co
229 Port Co
238 Port Co
239 Port Co
240 Port Co
241 Port Co
254 Port Co
255 Port Co
256 Port Co
257 Port Co
258 Port Co
259 Port Co
260 Port Co
261 Port Co
262 Port Co
263 Port Co
264 Port Co
265 Port Co
270 Port Co
271 Port Co
272 Port Co
273 Port Co
306 Port Co
307 Port Co
308 Port Co
309 Port Co
319 Port Co
320 Port Co
321 Port Co

322 Port Co
323 Port Co
324 Port Co
325 Port Co
362 Port Bn
386 Port Bn
386 Port Bn, Medical Det
433 Port Co
434 Port Co
435 Port Co
436 Port Co
437 Port Co
477 Port Bn
485 Port Bn
485 Port Bn, Medical Det
490 Port Bn
490 Port Bn, Medical Det
494 Port Bn
494 Port Bn, Medical Det
498 Port Bn
498 Port Bn, Medical Det
499 Port Bn
500 Port Bn
502 Port Bn
509 Port Bn
511 Port Bn
512 Port Bn
513 Port Bn
514 Port Bn
515 Port Bn
520 Port Bn
521 Port Bn
526 Port Co
527 Port Co
528 Port Co
529 Port Co
530 Port Co
531 Port Co
532 Port Co
533 Port Co
542 Port Co
543 Port Co
544 Port Co
545 Port Co
546 Port Co
552 Port Co
554 Port Co
556 Port Co
559 Port Co
560 Port Co
561 Port Co
575 Port Co
580 Port Co

581 Port Co
582 Port Co
583 Port Co
584 Port Co
585 Port Co
586 Port Co
587 Port Co
588 Port Co
589 Port Co
594 Port Co
596 Port Co
597 Port Co
598 Port Co
599 Port Co
600 Port Co
601 Port Co
602 Port Co
625 Port Co
628 Port Co
629 Port Co
630 Port Co
631 Port Co
640 Port Co
641 Port Co
642 Port Co
643 Port Co
644 Port Co
645 Port Co
646 Port Co
647 Port Co
648 Port Co

POSTAL & POLICE

112 Army Postal Unit
115 Army Postal Unit
122 Army Postal Unit
136 Army Postal Unit
152 Army Postal Unit
511 Army Postal Unit
6888 Central Postal Bn
92 Military Police Platoon
780 Military Police Bn

QUARTERMASTER

26 QM Bn
27 QM Group,
   Headquarters
49 QM Bn
80 QM Bn
89 QM Bn
89 QM Bn, Med Det
91 QM Bn
91 QM Bn, Med Det
101 QM Service Co

102 QM Bn
102 QM Bn, Medical Det
103 QM Bn
104 QM Bn
104 QM Bn, Medical Det
105 QM Bn
106 QM Bn
122 QM Bn
157 QM Bn
157 QM Bn, Med Det
174 QM Bn
174 QM Bn, Med Det
176 QM Bn
176 QM Bn, Med Det
180 QM Bn
181 QM Bn
182 QM Bn
183 QM Bn
206 QM Bn
206 QM Bn, Medical Det
210 QM Bn
210 QM Bn, Med Det
211 QM Bn
211 QM Bn, Med Det
236 QM Bn
238 QM Bn
239 QM Bn
244 QM Bn
244 QM Bn, Med Det
245 QM Bn
248 QM Service Bn
249 QM Service Bn
260 QM Bn
260 QM Bn, Med Det
262 QM Bn
262 QM Bn, Med Det
269 QM Bn
269 QM Bn, Med Det
271 QM Bn
271 QM Bn, Med Det
272 QM Bn
272 QM Bn, Med Det
273 QM Bn
274 QM Bn
274 QM Bn, Med Det
274 QM Service Bn
274 QM Service Bn, Med
   Det
279 QM Service Bn
303 QM Bn
304 QM Bn
308 QM Bn
308 QM Bn, Med Det
310 QM Bn

312 QM Bn
312 QM Bn, Med Det
395 QM Trk Co
396 QM Trk Co
397 QM Trk Co
398 QM Trk Co
402 QM Trk Co
512 QM Bn
512 QM Bn, Med Det
514 QM Bn
519 QM Bn
520 QM Bn
520 QM Bn, Med Det
521 QM Bn
522 QM Bn
529 QM Bn
529 QM Service Bn, Med
   Det
532 QM Bn
534 QM Bn
534 QM Bn, Med Det
535 QM Bn
535 QM Bn, Med Det
535 QM Bn, Med Det
537 QM Bn
537 QM Bn
537 QM Bn Med Det
541 QM Bn
544 QM Bn
544 QM Bn, Med Det
548 QM Bn
553 QM Bn
554 QM Bn
554 QM Bn, Med Det
555 QM Bn
556 QM Bn
556 QM Bn, Med Det
558 QM Bn
559 QM Bn
559 QM Bn, Med Det
560 QM Bn
560 QM Bn, Med Det
561 QM Bn
561 QM Bn, Med Det
562 QM Bn
563 QM Bn
565 QM Bn
565 QM Bn, Med Det
567 QM Bn
567 QM Bn, Med Det
569 QM Bn
571 QM Bn
572 QM Bn
611 QM Bn

613 QM Depot Co	3128 QM Service Co	3248 QM Service Co
628 QM Bn	3130 QM Service Co	3249 QM Service Co
628 QM Bn, Med Det	3131 QM Service Co	3263 QM Service Co
629 QM Bn	3133 QM Service Co	3264 QM Service Co
687 QM Bn	3134 QM Service Co	3267 QM Service Co
687 QM Bn, Med Det	3136 QM Service Co	3275 QM Service Co
688 QM Bn	3137 QM Service Co	3276 QM Service Co
762 Chem Depot Co	3143 QM Service Co	3279 QM Service Co
951 QM Service Co	3168 QM Service Co	4054 QM Service Co
952 QM Service Co	3169 QM Service Co	4055 QM Service Co
953 QM Service Co	3170 QM Service Co	4056 QM Service Co
954 QM Service Co	3171 QM Service Co	4057 QM Service Co
955 QM Service Co	3172 QM Service Co	4058 QM Service Co
956 QM Service Co	3173 QM Service Co	4059 QM Service Co
957 QM Service Co	3174 QM Service Co	4061 QM Service Co
958 QM Service Co	3175 QM Service Co	4082 QM Service Co
959 QM Service Co	3186 QM Service Co	4083 QM Service Co
960 QM Service Co	3187 QM Service Co	4084 QM Service Co
961 QM Service Co	3188 QM Service Co	4085 QM Service Co
962 QM Service Co	3189 QM Service Co	4086 QM Service Co
963 QM Service Co	3190 QM Service Co	4087 QM Service Co
964 QM Service Co	3191 QM Service Co	4089 QM Service Co
965 QM Service Co	3194 QM Service Co	4090 QM Service Co
966 QM Service Co	3196 QM Service Co	4091 QM Service Co
972 QM Service Co	3197 QM Service Co	4092 QM Service Co
973 QM Service Co	3198 QM Service Co	4093 QM Service Co
974 QM Service Co	3199 QM Service Co	4129 QM Service Co
978 QM Service Co	3201 QM Service Co	4130 QM Service Co
979 QM Service Co	3203 QM Service Co	4131 QM Service Co
980 QM Service Co	3208 QM Service Co	4132 QM Service Co
987 QM Service Co	3209 QM Service Co	4145 QM Service Co
988 QM Service Co	3210 QM Service Co	4146 QM Service Co
989 QM Service Co	3212 QM Service Co	4147 QM Service Co
990 QM Service Co	3213 QM Service Co	4148 QM Service Co
1513 QM Bn	3214 QM Service Co	4149 QM Service Co
1514 QM Bn	3215 QM Service Co	4150 QM Service Co
1516 QM Bn	3216 QM Service Co	4176 QM Service Co
1517 QM Bn	3217 QM Service Co	4177 QM Service Co
1519 QM Bn	3218 QM Service Co	4182 QM Service Co
1576 QM Bn	3219 QM Service Co	4183 QM Service Co
1586 QM Bn	3220 QM Service Co	4184 QM Service Co
1962 Ordnance Depot Co	3222 QM Service Co	4185 QM Service Co
3102 QM Service Co	3223 QM Service Co	4190 QM Service Co
3103 QM Service Co	3224 QM Service Co	4191 QM Service Co
3104 QM Service Co	3225 QM Service Co	4192 QM Service Co
3105 QM Service Co	3226 QM Service Co	4193 QM Service Co
3110 QM Service Co	3227 QM Service Co	4194 QM Service Co
3111 QM Service Co	3229 QM Service Co	4195 QM Service Co
3112 QM Service Co	3230 QM Service Co	4196 QM Service Co
3117 QM Service Co	3235 QM Service Co	4197 QM Service Co
3123 QM Service Co	3237 QM Service Co	4201 QM Service Co
3124 QM Service Co	3238 QM Service Co	4204 QM Service Co
3125 QM Service Co	3241 QM Service Co	4211 QM Service Co
3126 QM Service Co	3247 QM Service Co	4212 QM Service Co

4401 QM Service Co
4402 QM Service Co
4403 QM Service Co
4404 QM Service Co
4405 QM Service Co
4406 QM Service Co

QM BAKERY

155 QM Bakery Co
269 QM Bakery Co
270 QM Bakery Co
271 QM Bakery Co
416 QM Bakery Co
417 QM Bakery Co
419 QM Bakery Co
611 QM Bakery Bn
615 QM Bakery Bn
3002 QM Bakery Co
3010 QM Bakery Co
3016 QM Bakery Co
3017 QM Bakery Co
3026 QM Bakery Co
3033 QM Bakery Co
4351 QM Bakery Co
4355 QM Bakery Co
4357 QM Bakery Co
4358 QM Bakery Co
4359 QM Bakery Co
4363 QM Bakery Co
4364 QM Bakery Co
4369 QM Bakery Co
4371 QM Bakery Co
4373 QM Bakery Co

QM GASOLINE SUPPLY

208 QM Gas Supply Bn
433 QM Gas Supply Co
434 QM Gas Supply Co
449 QM Gas Supply Co
450 QM Gas Supply Co
656 QM Gas Supply Co
657 QM Gas Supply Co
847 QM Gas Supply Co
3858 QM Gas Supply Co
3859 QM Gas Supply Co
3877 QM Gas Supply Co
3878 QM Gas Supply Co
3896 QM Gas Supply Co
3897 QM Gas Supply Co
3898 QM Gas Supply Co
3899 QM Gas Supply Co
3900 QM Gas Supply Co
3913 QM Gas Supply Co

3914 QM Gas Supply Co
3915 QM Gas Supply Co
3916 QM Gas Supply Co
3918 QM Gas Supply Co
3919 QM Gas Supply Co
3920 QM Gas Supply Co
3933 QM Gas Supply Co
3934 QM Gas Supply Co
3936 QM Gas Supply Co

QM LAUNDRY

154 QM Laundry Platoon
248 QM Laundry Section
249 QM Laundry Section
422 QM Laundry Co
457 QM Laundry Co
459 QM Laundry Co
461 QM Laundry Co
463 QM Laundry Co
465 QM Laundry Co
595 QM Laundry Co
597 QM Laundry Co
598 QM Laundry Co
599 QM Laundry Co
600 QM Laundry Co
900 QM Laundry Co

QM TRUCKS

47 QM Trk Rgt
49 QM Trk Rgt
380 QM Trk Co
381 QM Trk Co
382 QM Trk Co
385 QM Trk Co
403 QM Trk Co
427 QM Troop T Co
428 QM Trp T Co
429 QM Trp T Co
430 QM Trp T Co
431 QM Trp T Co
432 QM Trp T Co
439 QM Trp T Co
440 QM Trp T Co
441 QM Trp T Co
442 QM Trp T Co
443 QM Trp T Co
444 QM Trp T Co
445 QM Trp T Co
446 QM Trp T Co
447 QM Trp T Co
448 QM Trp T Co
519 QM Trk Rgt
641 QM Trp T Co
642 QM Trp T Co

643 QM Trp T Co
644 QM Trp T Co
645 QM Trp T Co
646 QM Trk Co
647 QM Trp T Co
650 QM Trk Co
658 QM Trk Co
659 QM Trk Co
660 QM Trp T Co
661 QM Trp T Co
666 QM Trk Co
667 QM Trk Co
668 QM Trk Co
669 QM Trk Co
669 QM Trk Co
670 QM Trk Co
670 QM Trk Co
751 QM Trk Co
1511 QM Trk Rgt
1512 QM Trk Bn
1512 QM Trk Bn, Med Det
1515 QM Trk Bn Avn
1517 QM Trk Bn, Med Det
1520 QM Trk Bn
1520 QM Trk Bn, Med Det
1907 QM Trk Co
1908 QM Trk Co
1929 QM Co Trk
1933 QM Trk Co
1938 QM Trk Co
1944 QM Trk Co
1945 QM Trk Co
1946 QM Trk Co
1947 QM Trk Co
1949 QM Trk Co
1950 QM Trk Co
1957 QM Trk Co
1958 QM Trk Co
1965 QM Trk Co
1966 QM Trk Co
1968 QM Trk Co
1969 QM Trk Co
1970 QM Trk Co
1994 QM Trk Co
1997 QM Trk Co
2004 QM Trk Co
2005 QM Trk Co
2014 QM Trk Co
2016 QM Trk Co
2019 QM Trk Co
2022 QM Trk Co
2023 QM Trk Co
2024 QM Trk Co
2028 QM Trk Co

2030 QM Trk Co
2032 QM Trk Co
2034 QM Trk Co
2044 QM Trk Co
2045 QM Trk Co
2047 QM Trk Co
2049 QM Trk Co
2054 QM Trk Co
2055 QM Trk Co
2056 QM Trk Co
2057 QM Trk Co
2077 QM Co Trk
2085 QM Trk Co
2091 QM Trk Co
2093 QM Co Trk
2103 QM Trk Co
2104 QM Trk Co
3313 QM Trk Co
3314 QM Trk Co
3325 QM Trk Co
3326 QM Trk Co
3327 QM Trk Co
3345 QM Trk Co
3383 QM Trk Co
3384 QM Trk Co
3395 QM Trk Co
3397 QM Trk Co
3399 QM Trk Co
3400 QM Trk Co
3403 QM Trk Co
3409 QM Trk Co
3412 QM Trk Co
3413 QM Trk Co
3414 QM Trk Co
3417 QM Trk Co
3418 QM Trk Co
3419 QM Trk Co
3420 QM Trk Co
3433 QM Trk Co
3434 QM Trk Co
3435 QM Trk Co
3436 QM Trk Co
3437 QM Trk Co
3438 QM Trk Co
3439 QM Trk Co
3440 QM Trk Co
3457 QM Trk Co
3458 QM Trk Co
3459 QM Trk Co
3493 QM Trk Co
3497 QM Trk Co
3510 QM Trk Co
3511 QM Trk Co
3512 QM Trk Co

3533 QM Trk Co
3543 QM Trk Co
3544 QM Trk Co
3549 QM Trk Co
3552 QM Trk Co
3682 QM Trk Co
3683 QM Trk Co
3684 QM Trk Co
3685 QM Trk Co
3686 QM Trk Co
3687 QM Trk Co
3688 QM Trk Co
3689 QM Trk Co
3690 QM Trk Co
3691 QM Trk Co
3692 QM Trk Co
3861 QM Trk Co
3862 QM Trk Co
3863 QM Trk Co
3864 QM Trk Co
3865 QM Trk Co
3866 QM Trk Co
3867 QM Trk Co
3868 QM Trk Co
3869 QM Trk Co
3870 QM Trk Co
3871 QM Trk Co
3872 QM Trk Co
388 QM Trk Co
3901 QM Trk Co
3902 QM Trk Co
3903 QM Trk Co
3904 QM Trk Co
3905 QM Trk Co
3906 QM Trk Co
3907 QM Trk Co
3908 QM Trk Co
3909 QM Trk Co
3910 QM Trk Co
3911 QM Trk Co
3912 QM Trk Co
3965 QM Trk Co
3966 QM Trk Co
3967 QM Trk Co
3968 QM Trk Co
3981 QM Trk Co
3982 QM Trk Co
3983 QM Trk Co
3984 QM Trk Co
3985 QM Trk Co
3986 QM Trk Co
3987 QM Trk Co
3988 QM Trk Co
3989 QM Trk Co

3990 QM Trk Co
3991 QM Trk Co
3992 QM Trk Co
4001 QM Trk Co
4002 QM Trk Co
4003 QM Trk Co
4004 QM Trk Co
4005 QM Trk Co
4006 QM Trk Co
4007 QM Trk Co
4008 QM Trk Co
4009 QM Trk Co
4010 QM Trk Co
4011 QM Trk Co
4012 QM Trk Co
4029 QM Trk Co
4030 QM Trk Co
4031 QM Trk Co
4032 QM Trk Co
4041 QM Trk Co
4042 QM Trk Co
4043 QM Trk Co
4044 QM Trk Co
4046 QM Trk Co
4047 QM Trk Co
4049 QM Trk Co
4050 QM Trk Co
4051 QM Trk Co
4251 QM Trk Co
4252 QM Trk Co
4253 QM Trk Co
4254 QM Trk Co
4255 QM Trk Co
4262 QM Trk Co
4263 QM Trk Co
4264 QM Trk Co
4265 QM Trk Co
4266 QM Trk Co
4267 QM Trk Co
4268 QM Trk Co
4269 QM Trk Co
4270 QM Trk Co
4271 QM Trk Co

QUARTERMASTER SERVICES

212 QM Maintenance
   Bn
229 QM Salv Collecting
   Co
237 QM Salv Collecting
   Co
238 QM Salv Co
244 QM Salv Bn

303 QM Railhead Co
304 QM Steriliz & Bath
  Bn
304 QM Steriliz & Bath
  Bn, Med Det
306 QM Railhead Co
307 QM Railhead Co
308 QM Railhead Co
309 QM Railhead Co
310 QM Railhead Co
470 QM Maint Bn
512 QM Maint Bn
512 QM Maint Bn, Med
  Det
514 QM Maint Bn, Med
  Det
514 QM Maint Bn
519 QM Maint Bn
520 QM Maint Bn
522 QM Maint Bn
524 QM Car Co
532 QM Salv Repair Co
540 QM Salv Repair Co
551 QM Railhead Co
560 QM Maint Bn
560 QM Maint Bn, Med
  Det
573 QM Railhead Co
574 QM Railhead Co
575 QM Railhead Co
577 QM Railhead Co
592 QM Salv Repair Co

593 QM Salv Repair
  Co
823 QM Fumiga & Bath
  Co
824 QM Fumiga & Bath
  Co
851 QM Fumiga & Bath
  Co
854 QM Fumiga & Bath
  Co
855 QM Fumiga & Bath
  Co
856 QM Fumiga & Bath
  Co
857 QM Fumiga & Bath
  Co
858 QM Fumiga & Bath
  Co
863 QM Fumiga & Bath
  Co
867 QM Fumiga & Bath
  Co
998 QM Salv Co
999 QM Salv Co
4193 QM Steriliz Co
4222 QM Car Co
4223 QM Car Co
4224 QM Car Co
4226 QM Steriliz Co
4227 QM Steriliza Co
4228 QM Steriliza Co
4229 QM Steriliza Co

SIGNAL CORPS

29 Signal Co
37 Signal Co
40 Signal Co
40 Signal Co, Med Det
41 Signal Co
41 Signal Co, Med Det
42 Signal Co
42 Signal Co, Med Det
92 Signal Co
257 Signal Co
258 Signal Co
259 Signal Co
261 Signal Co
267 Signal Co
268 Signal Co
269 Signal Co
270 Signal Co
3254 Signal Co
447 Sig Co
447 Signal Co, Med Det
448 Signal Co
448 Signal Co, Med Det
459 Signal Co
459 Signal Co, Med Det
460 Signal Co
460 Signal Co, Med Det
461 Signal Co
461 Signal Co, Med Det
534 Signal Co
535 Signal Co

AFRICAN-AMERICAN ARMY AND AIR UNITS
IN THE PACIFIC AND ASIA

AIR BASE SECURITY

901 Air Base Sec Bn
903 Air Base Sec Bn
922 Air Base Sec Bn
924 Air Base Sec Bn

AIR CARGO

4 Air Cargo Resupply Sqd
5 Air Cargo Resupply Sqd

AMPHIBIAN

471 Amph Truck Co
472 Amph Truck Co
474 Amph Truck Co
475 Amph Truck Co
476 Amph Truck Co
477 Amph Truck Co

488 Amph Truck Co
490 Amph Truck Co
491 Amph Truck Co
493 Amph Truck Co
494 Amph Truck Co
495 Amph Truck Co
496 Amph Truck Co
811 Amph Truck Co
812 Amph Truck Co
813 Amph Truck Co
814 Amph Truck Co
820 Amph Truck Co
824 Amph Truck Co
825 Amph Truck Co
826 Amph Truck Co
827 Amph Truck Co
828 Amph Truck Co

ARTILLERY & INFANTRY

Americal Division, Co C
25 Infantry Reg
93 Infantry Division
103 Infantry Reg
368 Infantry Reg
49 Coast Artillery Bn
93 Division Artillery
593 Field Artillery Bn
594 Field Artillery Bn
595 Field Artillery Bn
596 Field Artillery Bn
7 Cavalry Weapons Troop
  Div
8 Cavalry Headquarters
  Troop

77 AA Gun Bn
207 AA Artillery Bn
234 AA Gun Bn
466 AA Artillery Bn
477 AA Artillery Bn
503 AA Gun Bn
726 AA Signal Battery
741 AA Artillery Gun Bn
742 AA Artillery Gun Bn
870 AA Artillery Bn
933 AA Gun Bn

AVIATION

345 Aviation Sqd
383 Aviation Sqd
384 Aviation Sqd
385 Aviation Sqd
386 Aviation Sqd
387 Aviation Sqd
388 Aviation Sqd
389 Aviation Sqd
391 Aviation Sqd
435 Aviation Sqd
436 Aviation Sqd
437 Aviation Sqd
455 Aviation Sqd
457 Aviation Sqd
458 Aviation Sqd
459 Aviation Sqd
460 Aviation Sqd
461 Aviation Sqd
462 Aviation Sqd
463 Aviation Sqd
464 Aviation Sqd
465 Aviation Sqd
466 Aviation Sqd
467 Aviation Sqd
468 Aviation Sqd
469 Aviation Sqd
470 Aviation Sqd
471 Aviation Sqd
473 Aviation Sqd

BAND

93 Infantry Division Band
289 Army Ground Forces
  Band
291 Army Ground Forces
  Band
299 Army Ground Forces
  Band
415 Army Service Forces
  Band

CHEMICAL

28 Chem Decontam Co
29 Chem Decontam Co
702 Chem Co
704 Chem Maint Co
891 Chem Co

ENGINEER

45 Eng General Service Rgt
91 Eng Gen Serv Rgt
96 Eng Gen Serv Rgt
97 Eng Gen Serv Rgt
318 Eng Combat Bn
567 Eng Dump Truck Co
568 Eng Dump Truck Co
575 Eng Dump Truck Co
570 Eng Dump Truck Co
571 Eng Dump Truck Co
573 Eng Dump Truck Co
576 Eng Dump Truck Co
585 Eng Dump Truck Co
738 Eng Base Depot Co
765 Eng Dump Truck Co
766 Eng Dump Truck Co
768 Eng Dump Truck Co
769 Eng Dump Truck Co
771 Eng Dump Truck Co
772 Eng Dump Truck
773 Eng Dump Truck Co
774 Eng Dump Truck Co
795 Eng Dump Truck Co
810 Eng Aviation Bn (EAB)
811 EAB
822 EAB
823 EAB
828 EAB
839 EAB
848 EAB
849 EAB
855 EAB
856 EAB
857 EAB
858 EAB
867 EAB
868 EAB
869 EAB
870 EAB
890 Eng Aviation Co
891 Eng Aviation Co
892 Eng Aviation Co
893 Eng Aviation Co
927 Eng Aviation Rgt
1188 Eng Base Depot Co

1224 Eng Fire Fight Det
1225 Eng Fire Fight Det
1311 Eng Gen Ser Rgt
1312 Eng Gen Ser Rgt
1315 Eng Construction Bn
1322 Eng Gen Ser Rgt
1351 Eng Dump Truck Co
1356 Eng Dump Truck Co
1357 Eng Dump Truck Co
1361 Eng Dump Truck Co
1395 Eng Construction Bn
1462 Eng Maintenance Co
1517 Eng Water Supply Co
1518 Eng Water Supply Co
1519 Eng Water Supply Co
1534 Eng Dump Truck Co
1862 EAB
1863 EAB
1864 EAB
1868 EAB
1869 EAB
1882 EAB
1883 EAB
1887 EAB
1889 EAB
1894 EAB
1895 EAB
1908 EAB
1909 EAB
1918 Eng Truck Co
1919 Eng Aviation Co
1970 EAB
2700 Eng Dump Truck Co
2701 Eng Dump Truck Co
2801 Eng Service Co
2803 Eng Gen Serv Bn
2804 Eng Gen Serv Bn
2805 Eng Gen Serv Bn
2806 Eng Gen Serv Bn
2807 Eng Gen Serv Bn
2917 Eng Dump Truck Co
2918 Eng Dump Truck Co
2919 Eng Dump Truck Co
3064 Eng Dump Truck Co
3067 Eng Dump Truck Co
3068 Eng Dump Truck Co
3069 Eng Dump Truck Co
3070 Eng Dump Truck Co
3071 Eng Dump Truck Co
3119 Eng Fire Fight Det
3125 Eng Fire Fight Det
3126 Eng Fire Fight Det
3127 Eng Fire Fight Det
3128 Eng Fire Fight Det

GAS SUPPLY

325 Gas Supply Co

MEDICAL

318 Medical Bn
569 Motor Ambulance Co
579 Motor Ambulance Co
888 Motor Ambulance Co

MILITARY POLICE

93 Division Military Police
    Platoon
212 Military Police Co
224 Military Police Co
260 Military Police Co
1387 Military Police Co

ORDNANCE

169 Ordn Bn
240 Ordn Ammo Co
242 Ordn Ammo Co
245 Ordn Ammo Co
247 Ordn Ammo Co
248 Ordn Ammo Co
482 Bomb Squadron
577 Ordn Ammo Co
578 Ordn Ammo Co
579 Ordn Ammo Co
580 Ordn Ammo Co
590 Ordn Ammo Co
594 Ordn Ammo Co
595 Ordn Ammo Co
622 Ordn Ammo Co
628 Ordn Ammo Co
629 Ordn Ammo Co
630 Ordn Ammo Co
632 Ordn Ammo Co
636 Ordn Ammo Co
642 Ordn Ammo Co
643 Ordn Ammo Co
644 Ordn Ammo Co
645 Ordn Ammo Co
650 Ordn Ammo Co
667 Ordn Ammo Co
669 Ordn Ammo Co
669 Ordn Ammo Co
793 Ordn Light Maint Co
1943 Ordn Ammo Co
3610 Ordn Maint Co

PORT

131 Port Co
133 Port Co
135 Port Co
136 Port Co
137 Port Co
138 Port Co
139 Port Co
142 Port Co
145 Port Co
146 Port Co
147 Port Co
148 Port Co
160 Port Co
161 Port Co
162 Port Co
164 Port Co
167 Port Co
179 Port Co
180 Port Co
181 Port Co
197 Port Co
198 Port Co
210 Port Co
218 Port Co
234 Port Co
235 Port Co
236 Port Co
290 Port Co
291 Port Co
292 Port Co
293 Port Co
310 Port Co
311 Port Co
312 Port Co
364 Port Co
372 Port Bn
376 Port Bn
438 Port Co
439 Port Co
440 Port Co
441 Port Co
442 Port Co
443 Port Co
444 Port Co
486 Port Bn
493 Port Bn
504 Port Bn
506 Port Bn
510 Port Bn
538 Port Co
539 Port Co
576 Port Co
578 Port Co
579 Port Co
590 Port Co
591 Port Co
592 Port Co
593 Port Co
603 Port Co
609 Port Co
610 Port Co
611 Port Co
635 Port Co
637 Port Co
638 Port Co
639 Port Co
650 Port Co
851 Port Co
852 Port Co
855 Port Co
856 Port Co
857 Port Co
865 Port Co
867 Port Co
868 Port Co
872 Port Co

QUARTERMASTER

14 QM Car Platoon
28 QM Group
29 QM Group
29 QM Bn
57 QM Bn
71 QM Bn
91 QM Railhead Co
92 QM Railhead Co
93 QM Co
119 QM Bn
119 QM Bakery Co
129 QM Bakery Co
130 QM Bakery Co
151 QM Bakery Co
233 QM Laundry Det
234 QM Laundry Det
235 QM Laundry Det
236 QM Laundry Det
237 QM Laundry Det
238 QM Laundry Det
239 QM Laundry Det
240 QM Laundry Det
241 QM Laundry Det
244 QM Laundry Det
245 QM Laundry Det
246 QM Laundry Det
247 QM Laundry Det
248 QM Depot Co
255 QM Laundry Det

256 QM Bn	627 QM Bn	2284 QM Truck Co
257 QM Bn	630 QM Bn	2301 QM Truck Co
264 QM Bakery Co	848 QM Gas Supply Co	3065 QM Service Co
268 QM Bn	849 QM Gas Supply Co	3077 QM Gas Supply Co
269 QM Laundry Det	893 QM Truck Co	3098 QM Laundry Co
271 QM Laundry Det	894 QM Truck Co	3108 QM Service Co
272 QM Laundry Det	895 QM Truck Co	3239 QM Service Co
275 QM Bn	897 QM Laundry Co	3240 QM Service Co
276 QM Bn	975 QM Service Co	3243 QM Service Co
277 QM Laundry Det	976 QM Service Co	3258 QM Service Co
277 QM Laundry Det	977 QM Service Co	3259 QM Service Co
278 QM Laundry Det	981 QM Service Co	3260 QM Service Co
302 QM Railhead Co	982 QM Service Co	3261 QM Service Co
311 QM Bn	983 QM Service Co	3274 QM Service Co
321 QM Truck Co	984 QM Service Co	3290 QM Service Co
322 QM Truck Co	985 QM Service Co	3291 QM Service Co
323 QM Truck Co	986 QM Service Co	3292 QM Service Co
324 QM Truck Co	991 QM Service Co	3293 QM Service Co
339 QM Laundry Det	992 QM Service Co	3294 QM Service Co
340 QM Laundry Det	993 QM Service Co	3295 QM Service Co
341 QM Laundry Det	994 QM Service Co	3296 QM Service Co
342 QM Laundry Det	1906 QM Truck Co	3297 QM Service Co
343 QM Laundry Det	1916 QM Truck Co	3388 QM Truck Co
344 QM Laundry Det	1918 QM Truck Co	3665 QM Truck Co
361 QM Laundry Det	1932 QM Truck Co	3697 QM Truck Co
369 QM Laundry Co	1943 QM Truck Co	3753 QM Truck Co
372 QM Bn	1954 QM Truck Co	3754 QM Truck Co
372 QM Laundry Det	1963 QM Truck Co	3829 QM Truck Co
373 QM Laundry Det	1998 QM Truck Co	4013 QM Truck Co
374 QM Laundry Det	2007 QM Truck Co	4039 QM Truck Co
384 QM Truck Co	2011 QM Truck Co	4070 QM Service Co
390 QM Truck Co	2012 QM Truck Co	4071 QM Service Co
393 QM Truck Co	2013 QM Truck Co.	4102 QM Truck Co
420 QM Bakery Co	2015 QM Truck Co	4103 QM Truck Co
466 QM Truck Co	2017 QM Truck Co	4104 QM Truck Co
467 QM Truck Co	2020 QM Truck Co	4105 QM Truck Co
469 QM Truck C	2021 QM Truck Co	4106 QM Truck Co
490 QM Bn	2025 QM Truck Co	4107 QM Truck Co
491 QM Bn	2026 QM Truck Co	4109 QM Truck Co
492 QM Bn	2027 QM Truck Co	4110 QM Truck Co
493 QM Bn	2031 QM Truck Co	4111 QM Truck Co
494 QM Bn	2039 QM Truck Co	4112 QM Truck Co
521 QM Group	2045 QM Truck Co	4113 QM Truck Co
531 QM Bn	2046 QM Truck Co	4116 QM Truck Co
539 QM Bn	2052 QM Truck Co	4117 QM Truck Co
540 QM Bn	2053 QM Truck Co	4121 QM Truck Co
557 QM Bn	2058 QM Truck Co	4122 QM Truck Co
569 QM Railhead Co	2059 QM Truck Co	4123 QM Truck Co
570 QM Bn	2278 QM Truck Co	4124 QM Truck Co
572 QM Railhead Co	2280 QM Truck Co	4125 QM Truck Co
589 QM Laundry Co	2281 QM Truck Co	4126 QM Truck Co
591 QM Salvage Repair Co	2282 QM Truck Co	4161 QM Fumigation &
594 QM Laundry Co	2283 QM Truck Co	Bath Co

4207 QM Service Co.
4208 QM Service Co
4209 QM Service Co
4210 QM Service Co
4216 QM Service Co
4217 QM Service Co
4342 QM Service Co
4344 QM Service Co
4345 QM Service Co
4464 QM Service Co
4481 QM Salvage Repair
   Co
4482 QM Salvage Repair
   Co
4513 QM Service Co
4514 QM Service Co
4515 QM Service Co
4516 QM Service Co

4517 QM Service Co
4524 QM Service Co

RECONNAISSANCE

93 Reconnaissance Troop

SALVAGE

536 Salvage Repair Co

SANITARY

721 Sanitary Co
722 Sanitary Co
725 Sanitary Co
728 Sanitary Co
735 Sanitary Co
739 Sanitary Co
742 Sanitary Co
745 Sanitary Co

747 Sanitary Co
759 Sanitary Co

SIGNAL CORPS

93 Signal Co
539 Signal Hvy Construct
   Co
702 Signal Co
704 Signal Co
715 Signal Co
716 Signal Co
717 Signal Co
719 Signal Co
743 Signal Co
760 Signal Co

STATION HOSPITAL

268 Station Hospital

ILLUSTRATION CREDITS

MOORE FAMILY COLLECTION: xxi, xxii, both images xxviii, xxx, 192, both images 303, 334

NARA (U.S. NATIONAL ARCHIVES AND RECORDS ADMINISTRATION): 22, 24, 32, 63, 80, 86, 89, 92, 109, 113, 114, 122, 123, 127, 128, 129, 132, 136, 138, 159, 164, 179, 188, 200, 208, 218, 226, 229, 233, 236, 237, 239, 240, 243, 244, 245, 250, 251, 255, 257, 260, 262, both images 277, 285, 290, 291, 311, 312, 316

SCHOMBURG CENTER FOR RESEARCH IN BLACK CULTURE: 4, 6, 15, 16, 64, 69, 99, 100, 101, 130, 131, letter 140, 207, 225, 234, 246, 253, 258, 263, 283, 286, 296, 298, 299

COURTESY OF JOHN LEAHR: 307, 309

COURTESY OF HERBERT HEILBRUN: 308

COURTESY OF BRIAN VINCENT DAVIS: 65

COURTESY OF MANILA AMERICAN CEMETARY: 35

COURTESY OF THE LIBRARY OF CONGRESS: 14

U.S. MARINE CORPS PHOTO ARCHIVES: 315

U.S. ARMY CENTER OF MILITARY HISTORY, ARMY ART COLLECTION: 39, 59, 61, 74, 78, 83, 133, 140, 173, 180, 181, 219, 242, 261

U.S. NAVY PHOTO ARCHIVES: 82

AIR FORCE HISTORICAL RESEARCH AGENCY: 25

INDEX

ABOUT THE AUTHOR

CHRISTOPHER PAUL MOORE is a teacher, a historian, and a specialist in African-American history. Research coordinator for the New York Public Library's world-renowned Schomburg Center for Research in Black Culture, he has put together several major exhibitions about African Americans. Moore is a contributor to *The New York Times* and *USA Today*. He has participated in the creation of a number of books connected to the Schomburg Center, including *Jubilee: The Emergence of African-American Culture.*